Forty Whacks

Forty Whacks

NEW EVIDENCE IN THE LIFE AND LEGEND OF
LIZZIE BORDEN

DAVID KENT

WITH FOREWORD BY ROBERT A. FLYNN

Emmaus, Pennsylvania

Printed in the United States of America

Unless otherwise noted, photographs and documents courtesy of the Fall River Historical Society

Packager: Nan K. Smith
Cover Designer: Stan Green
Text Designer: Amy Fischer

Library of Congress-in-Publication Data

Kent, David, 1923–1992
  Forty whacks: new evidence in the life and legend of Lizzie Borden/ David Kent; foreword by Robert A. Flynn.
      p. cm.
  Includes bibliographical references.
  ISBN 0–89909–351–5 hardcover
  1. Murder—Massachusetts—Fall River—Case studies. 2. Borden, Lizzie, 1860–1927. I. Title. II. Title: 40 whacks.
HV6534.F2K46   1992
364.1'523'0974485–dc20   92–9799
                                                                         CIP

Distributed in the book trade by St. Martin's Press

2 4 6 8 10 9 7 5 3 1   hardcover

To ROBERT A. FLYNN, not so much to repay
but to acknowledge a very large debt.

And . . . perforce, to LIZZIE.

Contents

Foreword

In the two years that David Kent and I knew each other, we became fast friends.

It all started when my wife, Anita, received a phone call in my absence from "a fascinating man in Louisiana" who wanted to buy anything we had in our bookstore related to the Lizzie Borden case. He told Anita he was "a Borden aficionado" and that he was writing a book and a play. After we sent him the volumes he had requested, David wrote to me asking my opinion of his early writings. We began to correspond—and that was the beginning of an increasingly close friendship.

David, I found out, was a Virginia-born writer and businessman, transplanted to Shreveport, Louisiana. He had first learned of Lizzie during World War II when he was stationed at the U.S. Army base at Camp Edwards on Cape Cod, not far from Fall River, Massachusetts. The story fascinated him—as it has so many—and his curiosity about the case only intensified during the intervening years. Following an illustrious record of combat action (two Purple Hearts, two Bronze Stars, and a Silver Star), David pursued careers that combined his interests in writing, advertising, government, radio, and show business. But he was certain that, some day, he would explore the details—and, if possible, discover the truth—of the infamous "Fall River Tragedy" that had fascinated him as a young man.

What drew us together, of course, was our common interest in the deep mysteries of the Borden affair. As we began to delve more deeply, we kept up a voluminous correspondence, and our telephone calls were numerous. David made several visits to my home in Portland, Maine, and together we made research journeys to Fall River, New Bedford, and Boston.

On our first visit to Fall River, David was introduced to Neilson Caplain, past president of the Fall River Historical Society and a great Borden scholar. It was Neilson who made it possible to have complete access to Borden material—in particular, the newly acquired Knowlton-Hilliard papers and never-before-published photographs that appear in this book.

Though in failing health, David hoped to see his book published in time for the 100th Anniversary Symposium on Lizzie Borden at Bristol Community College in Fall River, and he looked forward to seeing his play premiered by the Fall River Little Theatre for the same occasion. His death in early January 1992, at the age of sixty-eight, seemed tragically premature.

"He was an intense man with a tremendous sense of humor—and a memory to be envied," said a Shreveport friend who had known him for years. "His interests were such that he would delve into something right to the very core."

That, indeed, was the person I knew. In the all-too-brief time that I worked with him, he had somehow assimilated the myths, distortions, innuendoes, biases, and prejudices of the Lizzie Borden case, digested it all, and emerged from his intense research with what I believe to be the essence of historical truth.

"I have tried to be the only writer who has simply laid out the intriguing facts and let the reader come to his own conclusion," David wrote.

A generous goal indeed—and his accomplishment is on the pages that follow. But the final conclusion, as he promised, is yours.

Robert A. Flynn
Portland, Maine
June 1992

Preface

William F. Buckley, Jr., once said that if one had absolutely incontrovertible proof that Columbus discovered America in 1482 rather than 1492, the information would be of no worth; you could not change "history."

Unfortunately, such may also be the case with Lizzie Borden.

To the certain knowledge of all who have even a passing familiarity with the infamous Borden murders of 1892, Lizzie Borden took an axe and gave her mother 40 whacks. And when she saw what she had done, she gave her father 41. For a hundred years, children have innocently skipped rope chanting that jingle to the tune of "Ta-Ra-Ra-Boom-De-Ay," and they are on their way to a second hundred years.

This bit of doggerel is at least as familiar as the one saying that in 1492, Columbus sailed the ocean blue. It even recently appeared in a Japanese children's book with an illustration of a slant-eyed Lizzie brandishing an axe and the jingle credited to "Mother Goose."

Whimsically, it should be noted that a jury of her peers voted unanimously that Lizzie had *not* killed her father and mother, and whoever did, used a hatchet, *not* an axe. The unfortunate lady was not her mother but her *step*mother, and it was not 40 whacks that did her in, only 18. And finally, Lizzie's father died of just 10 whacks, far short of 41.

The savage slaying of Abby and Andrew Borden by, as they say, person or persons unknown, has fascinated and tormented psychologists, psychiatrists, and devotees of mayhem for a century. It has been called an insoluble mystery, turning on a missing weapon, a bloodstained dress that may never have existed, perjured testimony, and a lady's impeccable character. The world's fascination with the Borden enigma has been sustained for a hundred years by the truism that, in all the annals of American crime, it remains *the* perfect one—pristine in all its elements, made crystalline clear by a century of exhaustive research, yet still defying solution.

At the centennial of the mystery the pro-innocent and the pro-guilty camps are about evenly divided. On the fringe of the bivouac are those sensation writers who hold out for the guilt of other minor players in the drama.

In 1893, when Lizzie's trial was over, Edwin H. Porter, crime reporter for the Fall River, Massachusetts, *Globe,* published a 312-page book based largely on the stories he had written covering the murder, investigation, and trial. He called it *The Fall River Tragedy,* with the subtitle *A History of the Borden Murders.* It purported to cover the story from the first cry of "Murder!" to the end of Lizzie's trial. For more than 30 years, scholars of the mystery assumed it to be "The Bible" on all that had taken place.

In 1924, Edmund Pearson undertook the first comprehensive retelling of the story. Early on it became obvious to him "The Bible" was a flawed document. He compared the minutes of the inquest, the preliminary hearing, and the trial transcript with what Porter had written. He also had access to a 150-page scrapbook containing exhaustive newspaper coverage that had been assembled by William M. Emery, a reporter for the New Bedford, Massachusetts, *Evening Journal.* This treasure is still intact and now owned by Robert A. Flynn of Portland, Maine. It was obvious to Pearson that Porter's dedication to Lizzie's guilt had clouded his capacity to judge and colored his account of the events. While his book *was* a compilation of many facts, it was not a "history"; it was more a literary hoax.

Porter, literally from the first day, had decided Lizzie was guilty of the murders. To sustain his belief, he had systematically abridged the testimony and evidence favorable to her and had underlined with a dark pencil all those things supportive of his theory. Witnesses who had testified favorably toward Lizzie were often missing from his account or, at best, appeared only as one who had "testified," but with no word of what had been said. Pernicious testimony, on the other hand, was carried in lurid detail.

Knowledge of what Porter had done was unwittingly obscured when Lizzie, learning of the publication, was rumored to have bought up all but about 25 subscription copies and had them destroyed. Thus, only a few ever saw what Porter had written and were unaware of his distortions. But scholars ferreted out the half-dozen copies held in public libraries and other institutions and these became the sourcebooks for all research. Fortunately for historians, Porter's book was rescued from limbo in 1985 and reprinted by King Philip Publishing Company of Portland, Maine.

Regrettably, Pearson, too, believed Lizzie was guilty, and he, too, was unimpressed by the verdict of innocence rendered by the 12 good men and true who had listened to the evidence and judged her. Like Porter, he was determined to carry his point, and he liberally adopted Porter's tactic of tilting the evidence. For every deviation he corrected in Porter's book, he added one of his own. He was, for instance, aware of the Harvard cover-up detailed in Chapter 12 of this book, but he made no mention of it—perhaps because it weakened his case against Lizzie. The truth was now obscured under *two* layers of myth.

A third was added when a crime writer, Edmund Radin, wrote a best-seller in 1961. In it he pointed out examples of both Porter's and Pearson's loose-playing with the facts, but in his zeal to establish himself as *the* authority on the Borden case, he concocted the bizarre theory that it was not Lizzie who was guilty but the hapless servant girl, Bridget Sullivan, a possibility unsupported by any evidence or even serious consideration at the time.

What had actually been done or said was now a hodgepodge of legends and fantasies, but this was only the beginning. One book by Victoria Lincoln, who traded on the fact she had lived in Fall River as a child, claimed that Lizzie was a victim of epilepsy and had murdered in a raging fit. Not a scintilla of medical evidence exists to support this arcane conclusion, save that Lizzie occasionally suffered from headaches during her menstrual periods!

Another author of sensations, Evan Hunter, theorized that Lizzie was a lesbian and had slain Mrs. Borden when she had been caught *in flagrante delicto* with her lover—again, Bridget.

In his book, *Lizzie,* Frank Spiering devoted an entire chapter to perpetuating the hoary legend that Lizzie had once signed a confession of her guilt. The scene of the writing and signing is described in painful detail, including the exact words and gestures of everyone supposedly in the room at the time. One has to dig deep into the bibliography at the end of the book to find a one-paragraph admission that the "confession" is known to be a fake, the signature a forgery.

There was a Broadway play in which Lillian Gish, a thinly disguised Lizzie, killed her stepmother with a flatiron and did her father in with a walking stick. It was so inferior, it was told, that one critic berated the theater manager because his seat faced the stage!

So fascinating is the Lizzie legend, Agnes de Mille composed a ballet on the subject, *Fall River Legend,* and Jack Beeson composed an opera.

In 1975, Elizabeth Montgomery appeared in a grotesque movie depicting Lizzie as a delusionary zombie, stalking nude from room to room toting a hatchet dripping blood, which she disposed of in the earthen toilet in the basement. Undoubtedly millions have seen it. (It still runs on late-night TV.)

The truth may never catch up.

All and none of which has anything to do with Lizzie's guilt or innocence, but illustrates how fantasies have become facts and to what extent writers have maneuvered simple truths to set into type their private versions of what took place. When an appalling crime was committed in a pious and repressed society such as that of Fall River in 1892, a scapegoat had to be found. That it had to be Lizzie was as irrational and unjust as the witch mania that swept both England and America in the seventeenth century.

The challenge to understand the facts is still here a century later, because the theory persists that no one can commit so complicated a thing as double murder without leaving some clue. The best to be hoped for is to render clues inaccessible except to a patience stronger than the murderer's or an ingenuity more inspired.

The Borden murders have taken their place in the annals of crime as being among the most mystifying of all time. The true story is so baffling, so eternally intriguing, there is no need to flesh it out or alter the facts. As Pearson himself acknowledged, "The Borden case is without parallel, in resolution, in audacity, in intellectual power and in everything that goes to make up the perfect murder. . . . "

If you are meeting Lizzie for the first time here, welcome to the enigma! There will be no attempt in this book to persuade you of either her innocence or her guilt, nor will you be distracted by innuendo or profitless chases after phantoms. When the *outré* is encountered and partiality is obvious, they will be pointed out. Where words are quoted, they are as they were spoken, as far as solid research can establish them.

If I achieve a true and unalloyed telling of the drama, you will be an intrigued student of the murders and an intent juror at the trial.

Justice. Exclamation point. Question mark.

David Kent
Shreveport, Louisiana, 1991

1

An Atrocious Deed

WHAT JACK THE RIPPER is to England, the Borden murders are to America, coming as they did in 1892, just four years after the Ripper first terrorized London's East End.

Whereas the Ripper dealt in quantity, the Borden murders dealt in quality. The Ripper's victims were penny-farthing prostitutes from the darkest of London's slums. The Borden murders, on the other hand, wracked the best of Victorian Society in prosperous Fall River, Massachusetts.

Andrew Jackson Borden, 72, was the president of one of Fall River's major banks; he sat on the board of directors of three others. He was owner of substantial properties, including a new three-story building in the downtown center. He was a director of three of the major cloth mills that supported the economy and the work force of the city. He was halfway to becoming a millionaire, at a time when a million dollars was an astonishing sum.

Moreover, his was a name that conjured if not awe, then certainly respect. The Borden name and power went back 250 years, to the day when Charles I sat on the English throne. Legend was that Andrew's grandfather had named the town of Fall River when it was founded. In 1892, more than 125 families of the Borden name lived in Fall River.

Until the Civil War, Fall River was a prospering but relatively unassuming city. The Rebellion was its making; it developed great cloth mills and a major cotton industry so that, by day, there was a persistent hum of spindles, and by night, a teeming of millhands.

Andrew was the eighth generation of his branch. The progenitor, John, was one of the original landowners of Portsmouth, Rhode Island, when it was incorporated in 1638. Like his scion, Andrew, his driving tendency was the accumulation of real estate.

Today a city of more than 75,000, Fall River owes its existence to a quirk of nature and a wildcat stream the Indians called Quequechan. The stream began as the outflow of two substantial lakes, North and South Watuppa Ponds, on a plateau in the east, and fell 125 feet in less than a mile before going underground. The waterfall created man's waterpower on its way down the raw hills to Mount Hope Bay.

The water wheels and, later, steam engines, built the cotton mills, and they brought the boom that enabled the Bordens to prosper. Andrew's father, however, was one Borden who had *not* prospered. He was a fish peddler, and Andrew had sworn to do better. He began as a carpenter's helper and soon advanced to a career as undertaker in partnership with Frank Almy. They advertised as sole dealers for Crane's Patented Casket Burial Cases—guaranteed to preserve the remains of a loved one longer than any other. How this flamboyant claim could be proved was never said.

His penurious thrift was practiced in 14-hour days of saving this, reselling that, and hoarding the other. How typical it was that on the morning of the day he was murdered, he had picked up a broken, discarded lock, wrapped it carefully in a bit of paper, and taken it home with him.

It was not an unusual sight to see gaunt, Scrooge-like Andrew, in the black, double-breasted Prince Albert and string tie he wore winter or summer, carrying a basket of eggs from his farm to sell on his way to the bank.

Then as now, the Durfee name carried the same connotation as the Borden name in business and social circles in Fall River. It was a name equally as old and respected. From among the daughters of that family, Andrew had married Abby Durfee Gray. It was his second marriage, her first. Now 65, Abby was a retiring, almost reclusive, homebody.

Andrew had fathered, at five-year intervals, three daughters by his first wife, Sarah Morse. Emma was the first. The second, Alice, lived two years. Lizzie was the last, the youngest daughter. Perhaps because he had wanted a son to carry on his name, he gave Lizzie the middle name Andrew. Two years after Sarah died, he married the spinster Abby.

The third day of August, so the newspapers said, had been the hottest day so far in 1892. The issues of the next day, however, made no mention of the weather. Something of far greater interest to the citizens of Fall River crowded out such mundane news; an "atrocious deed" had happened at 92 Second Street.

Two of the town's most prominent residents, the son and daughter of two of the most respected names in Massachusetts, had been "brutally slain" in their home and in broad daylight.

"Brutally slain" was, and still is, newspaper code for a slaying out of the ordinary, not the run-of-the-mill killing rating only a paragraph or two on an inside page. These were names that, in Massachusetts, were equal to the Mellon and Rockefeller names in New York.

The first edition of the *Daily Herald*, prepared, as it undoubtedly was, in a fury of activity, contained a number of errors that would later be corrected, along with extensive and mistaken speculation as to what exactly had taken place, but it captured the essence of the horror and the shock of the crime.

The issue was sold out in a matter of minutes.

SHOCKING CRIME
A VENERABLE CITIZEN AND HIS AGED WIFE
HACKED TO PIECES AT THEIR HOME
MR. AND MRS. ANDREW BORDEN LOSE THEIR LIVES

AT THE HANDS OF A DRUNKEN FARM HAND
POLICE SEARCHING ACTIVELY FOR
THE FIENDISH MURDERER

The community was terribly shocked this morning to hear that an aged man and his wife had fallen victims to the thirst of a murderer, and that an atrocious deed had been committed. The news spread like wildfire and hundreds poured into Second Street. The deed was committed at No. 62 [read 92] Second Street where for years Andrew J. Borden and his wife lived in happiness.

It is supposed that an axe was the instrument used, as the bodies of the victims are hacked almost beyond recognition. Since the discovery of the deed, the street in front of the house has been blocked by an anxious throng, eagerly waiting for the news of the awful tragedy and vowing avengeance on the assassin.

Father Is Stabbed

The first intimation the neighbors had of the awful crime was a groaning followed by a cry of "murder!" Mrs. Adelaide Churchill, who lives next door to the Bordens, ran over and heard Miss Borden cry: "Father is stabbed; run for the police!"

Mrs. Churchill hurried across the way to the livery stable to get the people there to summon the police. John Cunningham, who was passing, learned of the murder and telephoned to police headquarters, and Officer Allen was sent to investigate the case.

Meanwhile, the story spread rapidly and a crowd gathered quickly. A *Herald* reporter entered the house and a terrible sight met his view. On the lounge in the cosy sitting room on the first floor of the building lay Andrew J. Borden, dead. His face presented a sickening sight. Over the left temple, a wound six by four had been made as if the head had been pounded with the dull edge of an axe. The left eye had been dug out and a cut extended the length of the nose. The face was hacked to pieces and the blood covered the man's shirt and soaked into his clothing. Everything about the room was in order and there were no signs of a scuffle of any kind.

Seven Wounds

Upstairs in a neat chamber in the northwest corner of the house, another terrible sight met the view. On the floor between the bed and the dressing case, lay Mrs. Borden, stretched full length, one arm extended and her face resting upon it. Over the left temple the skull was fractured and no less than seven wounds were found about the head. She had died evidently where she had been struck, for her life blood formed a ghastly clot on the carpet.

Dr. Bowen was the first physician to arrive, but life was extinct, and from the nature of the wounds, it is probable that the suffering of both victims was very short. The police were promptly on hand and strangers were kept at a distance. Miss Borden was so overcome by the awful circumstances that she could not be seen, and kind friends led her away and cared for her. A squad of police who had arrived conducted a careful hunt over the premises for trace of the assailant. No weapon was found and there was nothing about the house to indicate who the murderer might have been. A clue was obtained, however. A Portuguese whose name nobody around the house seemed to know, has been employed on one of the Swansey [read *Swansea*] farms owned by Mr. Borden. He had a talk with his employer and asked for the wages due him. Mr. Borden told the man he had no money with him; to call him later. If anything more passed between the men, it cannot be learned. At length the Portuguese departed, and Mr. Borden soon afterward started downtown. His first call was to Peter Leduc's barber shop, where he was shaved about 9:30 o'clock. He then dropped into the Union Bank to transact some business and talked with Mr. Hart, treasurer of the savings bank, of which Mr. Borden was president. As nearly as can be learned after that, he went straight home. He took off his coat and composed himself comfortably on the lounge to sleep. It is presumed, from the easy attitude in which his body lay, that he was asleep when the deadly blow was struck. It is thought that Mrs. Borden was in the room at the time but was so overcome by the assault that she had no strength to make an outcry. In her bewilderment, she rushed upstairs and went into her room. She must have been followed up the stairs by the murderer, and as she was retreating into the furthest corner of the room, she was felled by the deadly axe. Blow after blow must have rained upon her head as she lay unconscious on the floor.

Hurriedly the murderer slipped down the stairs and rushed into the street, leaving a screen door wide open after him in his sudden flight. No sign of blood could be found on the carpet or on the stairs, nor could any weapon be discovered anywhere. Nobody can be found who saw the murderer depart, and it is safe to conclude that he carried so small a weapon that it could be concealed in his clothing. Had he carried a gory axe in his hand, somebody's attention would have been attracted to it.

Then the investigation began. People were at a loss what could have been the motive for such a deed. Mr. Borden's quiet disposition was well known, and, although he was considered wealthy, yet his unpresuming ways were not such as to have invited robbery. In fact, his silver watch was in his pocket and his clothing was not in any way disturbed as to encourage the theory that the foul murder had been committed for gain.

Miss Borden Attracted

The heavy fall and a subdued groaning attracted Miss Borden into the house. There the terrible sight which has been described met her gaze. She rushed to the staircase and called the servant who was washing a window in her room on the third floor. So noiselessly had the deed been done that neither of them was aware of the bloody work going on so near them.

To a police officer, Miss Borden said she was at work in the barn about 10 o'clock. On her return she found her father in the sitting room with a terrible gash in the side of his head. He appeared at the time as though he had been hit while in a sitting posture. Giving the alarm, she rushed upstairs to find her mother, only to be more horrified to find that person lying between the dressing case and the bed, sweltering in a pool of blood. It appeared as though Mrs. Borden had seen the man enter, and the man, knowing that his dastardly crime would be discovered, had followed her upstairs and finished his fiendish work. It is a well known fact that Mrs. Borden always left the room when her husband was talking business with anyone. A person knowing this fact could easily spring upon his victim without giving her a chance to make an outcry. Miss Borden had seen no person enter or leave the place. The man who had charge of her father's farm was held in the highest respect by Mr. Borden. His name was Alfred Johnson, and he trusted his employer so much that he left his bank book at Mr. Borden's house for safe keeping. The young lady had not the slightest suspicion of his being connected with the crime. As far as the Portuguese suspected of the crime was concerned, she knew nothing of him, as he might have been a man who was employed by the day in the busy season. What his motive could have been it is hard to tell, as Mr. Borden had always been kind to his help.

Another statement made by the police, and which though apparently light, would bear investigation, is the following: Some two weeks ago, a man applied to Mr. Borden for the lease of a store on South Main Street that was vacant. After a short time, as Miss Borden was passing the room, loud words were heard, her father making the remark, "I will not let it for that purpose." Quietness was restored in a short while and when the man departed, her father said: "When you come to town next time, I will let you know." That was two weeks ago, but in the meantime the store has been let to another. It was dark at the time of the calling and she did not recognize his features.

Went To Swansey

At 12:45 o'clock, Marshal Hilliard and officers Doherty and Conners presented a carriage and drove over to the farm, hoping that the suspected man would return there in order to prove an alibi. The officers will arrive at the place some time before the man, as the distance is some ten miles, though it is hardly probable that he will return there. What makes it rather improbable that the man suspected is a Portuguese laborer is the statement of Charles Gifford of Swansey. Mr. Gifford says that the only Portuguese employed on the upper farm is Mr. Johnson, and he is confined to his bed by illness. Another man might be employed by Mr. Borden on the lower farm for a few days, but he does not believe it. An attempt was made to reach Swansey by telephone, but no answer was received.

A Significant Incident

Among the significant incidents revealed in the search through the premises was brought to light by John Donnelly, who, with others, searched the barn to see if any trace of the fugitive could be found there. In the hay was seen the perfect outline of a man as if one had slept there over night. Besides this, it was evident the sleeper was either restless or had been there before, because an imprint was found in another part of the hay that corresponded with the outline of the first impression. Somebody may have been in the habit of going there for a nap, but the imprint was that of a person of about five feet six inches tall, and was shorter than Mr. Borden. This has given rise to the suspicion that the murderer may have slept about the place and waited for an opportunity to accomplish his deed.

Another Story

Another sensational story is being told in connection with the murder. It appears that the members of the family have been ill for some days and the symptoms were very similar to those of poison. In the light of subsequent events, this sickness has been recalled. It has been the custom of the family to receive the supply of milk from the Swansey farm every morning and the can was left out of doors until the servant opened the house in the morning. Ample opportunity was afforded, therefore, for anybody who had a foul design to tamper with the milk, and this circumstance will be carefully investigated by the police.

Medical Examiner Dolan, who promptly responded to the call for his presence, made a careful examination of the victims and reached the conclusion that the wounds were inflicted by a heavy, sharp weapon like an axe or hatchet. He found the skull fractured in both instances and concluded that death was instantaneous. As to the blow which killed Mrs. Borden, he thought that it had been delivered by a tall man, who struck the woman from behind.

A Bogus Letter

It is reported that Mrs. Borden received a letter this morning announcing the illness of a very dear friend and was preparing to go to see her. This letter has turned out to be a bogus one, evidently intended to draw her away from the home. In this case it would look as if the assault had been carefully planned. A suspicious character was seen on Second Street this morning who seemed to be on the lookout for somebody, and the police have a description of the man.

Marshal Hilliard, Officers Dowty [read *Doherty*] and Connors went to Swansey this afternoon, but found the men at work on the upper farm who have been employed there of late. The lower farm will be visited at once. William Eddy has charge of this one.

At 2:10 o'clock, a sturdy Portuguese named Antonio Auriel was arrested in a saloon on Columbia Street and brought into the police

station. The man protested his innocence and sent after Joseph
Chaves, clerk for Talbot & Co., who recognized the man, and he was
immediately released.

Sketch Of Mr. Borden

Andrew J. Borden was born in this city 69 years ago. By persever-
ance and industry, he accumulated a fortune. A short time since, he
boasted that he had yet to spend his first foolish dollar. Mr. Borden
was married twice. His second wife was the daughter of Oliver Gray
and was born on Rodman Street. He had two [read *three*] children by
his first wife, Emma and Elizabeth [read *Lizzie*]. The former is out of
town on a visit and has not yet learned of the tragedy.

Mr. Borden was at the time of his death, president of the Union
Saving's Bank and director in the Durfee bank, Globe yarn, Merchants and Troy mill. He was interested in several big real estate
deals, and was a very wealthy man.

Parenthetically, one has to admire the swiftness with which
the small newspaper gathered and published this first story on
the slayings. The first public outcry of "Murder!" had been
given on August 4 at 11:15. The *Herald's* first edition was on the
streets by 2:15 the same day. Except for the speculations by the
police as to how Mrs. Borden met her death, all of which would
subsequently be proved wrong, it is a remarkably thorough and
accurate report.

By midafternoon, hundreds had gathered on Second Street.
Although the water wagons had sprinkled all the downtown
streets to keep down the dust, it was another record hot day,
and there was little to show for their efforts.

The Borden house still stands, now number 240, appearing,
with the exception of a window air conditioner, much as it did
that day in 1892. The barn and backyard are gone and so are the
houses of neighbors Kelly, Churchill, and Chagnon, and in
spite of the encroachment of an abutting print shop and the
bustling bus station across the street, the house still has the
same gaunt, rawboned look it had a century ago.

It is not today a fashionable address for a residence, nor was
it when Andrew Borden bought the property and moved in 21
years before the event. It had been constructed as what was
called a railroad house, built soundly but sparsely for two
families. Separate entrances, one in front that opened onto the
sidewalk, and another on the side, provided access to the upper
and lower apartments. Space-wasting halls were not included

in the design, making it necessary to go from room to room to get to the front or back.

As the reporter noted, Andrew had yet to spend a foolish dollar, and foolishness apparently included such things as electricity, bathrooms, or that newfangled invention, the telephone. His only concession to creature comforts for himself and his family was a furnace in the basement.

Except perhaps by the standards of a miser, 92 Second Street was not befitting the Borden and Durfee names. As in almost every hamlet, village, or city, there is a "right" side of the tracks and a "wrong" side. In Fall River, it was not a railroad track that served as the demarcation line, but the hill that thrust itself up from the rugged shoreline.

In short, society lived up on The Hill; all others, below. That Andrew would not spend a portion of his considerable wealth for a sumptuous home on The Hill may well have been the linchpin of the murders; certainly the prosecution made it one of the core motives in its case against Lizzie.

Meanwhile, the crowd outside continued to grow. It was the day of the police department's annual outing to Rocky Point, a shore resort near Providence, Rhode Island, but if the department was low in manpower, it was not evident as patrolmen and detectives swarmed over the property.

In Massachusetts, the chief of police was called a "marshal," and Fall River's Marshal Rufus B. Hilliard sent his deputy, John Fleet, to the scene.

It must be noted that in 1892, racism was not racism. It was not even recognized as such. After all, didn't everyone know that foreigners were, well, foreign, and not really a part of the social order? Thus, it is not surprising that the first suspect was the first man mentioned who had a foreign name. He happened to be Portuguese, but the same would have occurred if the name had been identifiable with any of the colonies of foreigners who had migrated to America during the industrial boom. Fall River had begrudgingly taken in thousands of laborers from French Canada, China, Portugal, Sweden, Germany, and Ireland as manpower for the burgeoning cloth mills.

Detectives were dispatched to track down the foreigner. Others were sent to interview anyone who had seen *anyone* who did not "fit in." Rumors were plentiful among the onlookers. Detectives were assigned to check out every rumor. The barn was searched, and the 1892 version of an all points bulletin was sent out as fast as carriages could be mustered.

The foreigner was quickly found and just as quickly taken to police headquarters. Fortunately for him, the frightened man had an alibi and a witness. He was released, but not without a shadow following him for the next few days.

At 5 P.M. the *Herald* was on the streets with an extra:

A DEEP MYSTERY
HUNDREDS IN FRONT OF THE BORDEN HOMESTEAD
DISCUSSING THE MURDER
MISS BORDEN HAS NOT THE LEAST SUSPICION
OF THE GUILTY PARTIES
THE STORY OF THE MILK VERIFIED
POLICE SCOURING THE TOWN

The excitement over the Borden murder grows intense. Hundreds block the street in front of the house and are discussing the horrible circumstances. Dr. Dolan, assisted by a half-dozen physicians, has been conducting an autopsy. There are no details to be given to the public.

Further investigation shrouds the affair in deeper mystery. A *Herald* reporter saw an intimate friend of the family who has been with Miss Borden ever since the terrible blow was struck. Miss Borden is anxious that any stories that connect the maid servant, Lizzie Corrigan [read *Bridget Sullivan*], or any of the men at the farms, with the deed be refuted. All of them have been in the family's employ for many years, and Mr. Eddy, the superintendent of one of the farms, is at present so ill that Miss Borden was anxious that the stories should not reach his ears that any of the old help were suspected of the deed. Miss Borden states that she has not the least clue to give the officers. When she went into the house from the barn and saw her father lying with dripping wounds, she was overcome and rushed to the staircase to call the servant and send her for help. Mrs. Churchill, who saw the servant running, enquired the cause, and then went for Dr. Bowen. After Miss Borden had recovered from the first shock, she remembered that Mrs. Borden had not been seen, and asked some of her friends who were with her to go and look for her. John Maude [read *Morse*], a relative of the Bordens, and Mrs. Churchill proceeded through the house and at length found Mrs. Borden where she lay in the chamber upstairs.

The story relative to the suspected milk has been verified, and the doctors will take special pains to look for traces of poison at the autopsy. Even if any are found, it will be difficult to form a clue from this fact, since it has been the custom to leave the can on the doorstep and anybody could have tampered with it.

The police are particularly vigilant and every stranger who excites the least suspicion is stopped and examined. Whether the murderer took advantage of a day when the majority of the police were out of town and could not be called out to hunt for the fugitive can only be conjectured. This is certainly a case that will furnish excellent opportunity for the detective talent of the force, although the clues that are afforded are of the most meager and unsatisfactory character.

As the curious and the morbid milled around outside the Borden house, speculating and wondering, the "detective talent of the force" inside the house was, as the reporter predicted, being sorely tried. The meager and unsatisfactory clues were developing into a far from clear picture of what had taken place that morning. It is doubtful, however, that the *Herald* reporter could have presaged that the mystery would not only baffle the Fall River police but would remain a puzzle a century later.

2

She Is Not My Mother!

DESPITE WHAT HER DETRACTORS would say later, Lizzie was stunned and near fainting. A dozen officers swarmed over the house, each questioning her as to what had happened. The servant girl, Bridget Sullivan, had been the first one up in the household that morning, and her description of what had taken place provided the outline of events.

Bridget was called Bridget by Mr. and Mrs. Borden, but to the daughters Emma and Lizzie she was always "Maggie." A former servant had been named Maggie and was fondly remembered, so her name was perpetuated when the new servant had come three years before.

Bridget was a prototype of the immigrants who journeyed to America during the industrial boom of the late nineteenth century. She was born in Ireland, and for the Irish, Massachusetts had a special lure. Among the immigrant groups in Fall River, the Irish far outnumbered any other nationality.

She had arrived first in Newport, Rhode Island, without family or acquaintances. A year later, she moved to South Bethlehem, Pennsylvania, but Massachusetts had remained her goal; for almost three years she had occupied a small attic room in the third floor rear of the Borden house.

Her duties included washing, ironing, cooking, sweeping, and general household work downstairs. Mrs. Borden, Lizzie, and Emma tended their own rooms.

As she was to testify, Bridget liked her job, the family, and the town. At 26, she was an attractive, full-figured, auburn-haired Irish lass who had many friends among the other servant girls of the town and ample opportunity to go walking out with beaux whenever she chose.

She had risen that morning, she said, with a sick headache, but at her usual time, 6:00 A.M. She, as well as the family members, had all fallen ill the day before with bouts of diarrhea and vomiting.

She had come down the backstairs from her room at 6:15 and, bringing up wood and coal from the cellar, had started her breakfast fire. As she did every morning, she took in the milk can from Mr. Borden's Swansea farm and put out the pan to receive the iceman's morning delivery.

While she was busy with breakfast, John Vinnicum Morse, a guest the previous night, came down, spoke, and sat in the sitting room to wait for the others to appear. Morse was Andrew's brother-in-law, the brother of his first wife, Sarah. He had been a frequent visitor except for the years he had been out West seeking his fortune.

Mrs. Borden came down at 6:30, also using the backstairs from the master bedroom on the second floor, and Mr. Borden followed a few minutes later, carrying his slop pail. There was no bathroom in the Borden house, only an earthen closet in the dirt floor cellar, so the emptying of pails was a morning ritual.

The incredible breakfast set before Abby, John, and Andrew included mutton, appearing for the third day, mutton broth, johnnycakes, cookies, overripe bananas, and coffee. They all ate heartily while Bridget cleaned up the kitchen, waiting for the tinkle of the dining room bell to indicate she could clear away the dishes.

At about 8:30, Morse left by the backdoor, on his way to visit his niece on Weybosset Street. Andrew accompanied him to the door, reminding him that he was expected back for the noon meal. Mrs. Borden took up her duster and puttered in the sitting room; Andrew cleaned his teeth in the kitchen sink.

It was, Bridget said, a typical morning.

At 9:00, Lizzie came down with her slop pail. She, too, had suffered the night with stomach cramps and, understandably, wanted no breakfast of mutton and johnnycakes. She did take a cup of coffee and perhaps a cookie or two.

Barely finishing the breakfast dishes, Bridget fled to the backyard to vomit. When she returned to the kitchen ten minutes later, Lizzie had apparently gone back up to her room. Mrs. Borden, busy with a feather duster in the sitting and dining rooms, told Bridget she would like the windows washed that day, inside and out.

Bridget let the windows down in both rooms, went down to the cellar for a pail and brush, and then outside to draw water in the barn and begin her work.

Andrew, dressed in the same black wool suit he wore winter and summer, left for business downtown and a stop at the post office.

Lizzie appeared at the backdoor and asked Bridget what she was doing. She told Lizzie she would be washing windows outside for a while, and Lizzie could lock the door if she liked, as there was water to be had in the barn. But Lizzie didn't lock the door.

When she finished the outsides of the windows, Bridget began on the insides. She heard someone rattling the front door and went to see who it was. It was Mr. Borden; he had forgotten his key. There were three locks on the door, and as she fumbled to get them all open, she said, "Pshaw!" The expletive may have been stronger, for she heard Lizzie upstairs laugh.

Andrew went into the dining room and then into the sitting room where he composed himself on the sofa and prepared to read the paper and, perhaps, take a morning nap. Lizzie came down to ask if she had received any mail and to tell him that Mrs. Borden had said that she received a note from a sick friend and had gone out.

Lizzie, who had dressed to go downtown when she arose, asked Bridget if she planned to go out that afternoon. Bridget told her she didn't think so; she wasn't feeling well.

"There's a cheap sale of dress goods at Sargents this afternoon for eight cents a yard," Lizzie said. "I'm probably going to pick up some material.

"If you go out," she added, "be sure and lock the door, for Mrs. Borden has gone out on a sick call and I might go out, too." Asked who was sick, Lizzie said she didn't know. "She had a note this morning. It must be in town."

Lizzie took down the ironing board, set it up, and put her irons on the kitchen stove to heat.

It was now 10:55 A.M., and the heat of the kitchen was intense. Bridget said she was tired and queasy again and was going to her room to lie down for a few minutes.

The scene was now set: Mrs. Borden supposedly off on a visit of mercy; Andrew peacefully resting on the sofa; Morse off on business; Lizzie preparing handkerchiefs for ironing; and Bridget resting in her attic room.

Lizzie picked up the narrative of events from this point. Things had been much as Maggie had described, she said, with a few discrepancies as to exactly who was where when, what had been said or done.

Lizzie, who was christened Lizzie, not Elizabeth, was Andrew's youngest daughter and as most would say, his favorite— although there would be those who would say he pandered to her, not out of love, but because of her iron will and her penchant for having her own way.

Her youthful life in Fall River had been, withal, unremarkable. After all, in the 1890s in staid, Victorian New England, what little excitement there was was more likely to take place around the waterfront's roughhouse bars, not in the reserved parlors of the upper class.

She was born on Thursday, July 19, 1860, in the Borden house at 12 Ferry Street. James Buchanan was in the White House but not for long; Abraham Lincoln was debating Mr. Douglas in Illinois.

Her mother died when Lizzie was two years old, and when she was four, Andrew married the spinster, Abby, who, at nearly 40, had undoubtedly given up all hope of wedlock. Whereas Sarah had been young and attractive, Abby was neither. She was a stocky woman of no humor and incapable of displaying either love or affection. But, then, she had those qualities Andrew had looked for: she was steadfast, moral, and undemanding; she was respectful, a good housekeeper, and knew by instinct to leave the room when business was being discussed.

Lizzie was 18 years old when she left Fall River High School and, in that era, little thought was given to her attending college. Young ladies retired to their homes, learned and practiced domesticity, and waited for suitors to call. It has to be noted here that the prospect of courting in the cramped parlor of that mean little house on Second Street, under the glaring eyes of Andrew and the morose Abby, must have been enough to dampen the ardor of any swain. There were some callers, however, because Lizzie was the daughter of one of the town's richest men, but they were not encouraged by either Abby or Andrew.

Her life, traced backward to her babyhood, shows nothing out of the unusual beyond a pronounced reserve of bearing and coolness of demeanor.

Lizzie was only 20 when she was named to the board of the Fall River Hospital, a signal honor for one so young. There she became head of the Fruit and Flower Mission, members of which were counterparts of today's candy-stripers. They visited the sick, the poor, and the homeless with gifts of food, books, and flowers. Her detractors would later say her nomination to the hospital board was in hopes of substantial donations from Andrew, but to say so was to deny the accepted knowledge that Andrew had never been known to give anything to charity.

Her most striking feature was her large, wide-set eyes, alternately pale cerulean if you were her friend, gray and piercing if you were not. The width of her determined jaw kept her from beauty, and her broad shoulders were made more so by the muttonchop sleeves of current fashion.

Now, at 32, she had passed the age of youth and entered the confirmed ways of maidenhood; of even mind with strong religious beliefs and sterner creeds. Her inner shyness was masked by a positive presence and the composure that never left her— even then, as she told Officer Allen about the routine activity of the morning.

Like everyone else in the house, she had spent a restless night but in the morning had felt better, well enough to think of taking some air by walking downtown to one of her favorite stores, Sargents, to choose some calico for a dress or two—a bargain at eight cents per yard.

She had dressed for the outing, she said, in a dress of blue cambrio with a navy blue diamond figure printed on it. She had gone downstairs at about 9:30 and had taken only a cookie (perhaps two) and a cup of coffee for breakfast. She had chatted with Mrs. Borden about inconsequential things and thought of ironing a few of her best handkerchiefs, which she had rinsed out the day before.

Mrs. Borden had told her that she had received a note from a sick friend and was going out for a while to visit her. She would be picking up groceries for the evening meal and was there anything Lizzie would especially like? Lizzie had told her there was nothing particular she craved.

Father had come back from his trip to the post office and had brought her no mail. She had told him of Mrs. Borden's going out and had set up the ironing board and put her irons on to heat.

Had she heard someone bringing the note to Mrs. Borden? No, it had apparently come before she arose or after she came down and had busied herself in the kitchen. She had not heard anyone, nor had she actually seen the note.

While waiting for her irons to heat, she had walked out in the backyard, hoping it was cooler than the kitchen. With no purpose in mind, she had idly picked up a pear or two from under the tree, thinking perhaps the fruit would settle her stomach.

Remembering that she planned to go on a church outing the next Monday to Marion, on Buzzards Bay, the idea of an hour or two of fishing on the cool banks of a stream reminded her that the last time she was at the farm, her fishing lines had no sinkers, and that perhaps she should carry along some small pieces of iron or lead to fashion a few.

She had gone into the barn—once a stable, but now the horses were kept at Swansea—and searched for scraps of metal she remembered being there in a small box. She had found nothing on the ground floor, so she had gone up to the loft. Surprisingly, it felt cooler in the loft, and she had idly searched for the lead pieces, eaten another of the pears, gazed out the window, and stayed, altogether, 30 minutes, or perhaps it was 15 minutes, or somewhere in between.

Coming out of the barn she had heard what sounded like a groan, and she had hastened to the backdoor of the house and, finding it unlocked, had rushed first into the kitchen and then to the doorway of the sitting room.

She opened the door and fell back in horror. Her father was lying on the couch, his face covered with blood. She did not know if he was dead, nor did she examine the gashes about his head or see his eye, gouged out and dangling on his cheek, but she knew his condition was desperate.

She ran to the foot of the backstairs and cried out to Maggie.

"Maggie, come down! Come down quick! Father's dead! Somebody came in and killed him!"

Maggie rushed down and was immediately sent across the street to the duplex home of Dr. Seabury A. Bowen. He was not there, Mrs. Bowen told Maggie, but she assured her he would be right over the moment he returned.

Maggie ran back across the street, this time to be sent to find Miss Alice Russell, a friend of both Emma and Lizzie.

"Go and get her," Lizzie cried. "I can't be alone in the house."

Mrs. Adelaide Churchill, a prim widow who lived next door in what was called the Buffinton House, after Fall River's first mayor, who had resided there, saw the frantic comings and goings and, looking out her kitchen window, saw Lizzie, excited and agitated, leaning against the casing of the back-door. She opened the window and called out, "Lizzie, what's the matter?"

Lizzie responded, "Oh, Mrs. Churchill, do come over! Someone has killed father!"

Mrs. Churchill responded at once and, seeing that no medical help had come, ran off in search of a doctor. On the way, she passed John Cunningham, a news dealer, and asked him to please, quickly, run to the livery stable just down the street and call the police.

There were one or two parts of the two stories that puzzled the police inside the house. First, why had no one seen or heard any intruder? Second, how could anyone have gotten into and out of the house through the multiple-locked doors?

Shorthanded as they were because of the annual outing to Rocky Point, the police department had by now responded in considerable numbers. And so had friends and neighbors. The cramped little house was teeming with activity, and a crowd of hundreds now milled around in the street in front.

Adelaide Churchill and Alice Russell hovered over the ashen-faced Lizzie, alternately wiping her forehead with a cool cloth and fanning her with a straw fan imprinted with the advertisement of the Fall River Ice and Cold Storage Company. They were gathered in the kitchen, out of the way of the policemen who milled around in the entryway, the dining room, and the sitting room.

Patrolman George Allen, new to the force, had been the first officer on the scene. One look at the mangled corpse, and the knowledge that it had one of the town's most prominent names, was all he needed to know. He needed help—the help of superiors. He quickly checked the front door to be sure it was locked, hailed a friend from the crowd, Charles Sawyer, stationed him at the side door to secure the house, and jogged off toward headquarters to report what had happened at 92 Second Street.

Dr. Bowen's carriage pulled up across the street as Officer Allen raced off. Lizzie, pallid and near fainting, motioned him to the sitting room. "Father has been killed."

It took him but a moment to confirm it.

"Have you seen anybody around the place?"

"No. No one."

"Where have you been? Where were you?"

"I was in the barn looking for some iron. Oh, Doctor, I am faint!"

Adelaide and Alice helped her out of the rocker in the suffocatingly hot kitchen and supported her as they moved into the dining room. As Dr. Bowen covered the body of Andrew Borden with a sheet, Lizzie turned in the doorway and and asked if he would send off a telegram to Emma, visiting in Fairhaven, asking her to return home.

As they gathered in the dining room, Bridget suggested that perhaps Mrs. Borden was at the Whitehead's, the home of Abby's half-sister. Lizzie said she didn't think so, but it was possible she had come back; that she had heard a noise.

Maggie, afraid to go upstairs alone, asked Adelaide to go with her to see. They went together, and, in an instant, Adelaide came back into the dining room, white-faced.

"Is there another?" Alice asked.

"Yes! She's up there."

Officer Allen had returned with reinforcements, Officers Mullaly, Doherty, and Wixon. Dr. Bowen also came back, the telegram to Emma having been sent. With him came Medical Examiner William A. Dolan. The news at police headquarters that another victim had been found brought out Officers Harrington and Medley and Assistant City Marshal John Fleet.

Abby Borden's body lay in the guest room at the top of the stairs, wedged between the freshly-made bed and a small dresser. Like Andrew, lying below on the couch, her head had been savagely beaten in. A switch of hair, popularly used to enhance the coiffure or, in Abby's case, to cover advancing baldness, lay nearby on the floor. Dr. Bowen touched the back of her neck to test the body's temperature and, entirely by instinct, felt for the pulse that he knew was not there.

The door to the guest room was then discreetly closed. Sexist as it may sound today, the investigation of Mrs. Borden's death would have to wait; priority went to the man of the house.

Downstairs, Officer Michael Mullaly had checked Andrew's body and found a silver watch and chain, a wallet containing $85.00 in bills, and 65 cents in loose change. He noted that on his little finger was a gold ring. If this had been a murder for money, it had failed.

He tapped on the dining room door and, apologizing, asked Lizzie if there were either hatchets or axes in the house. She unhesitatingly told him there were both and directed Maggie to show him where they were in the basement.

Maggie led him to the cellar and pointed out two axes as well as a claw-headed shingle hatchet. One of the axes was obviously bloodstained, and hairs still clung to the blade. The hatchet was spotted in red, and Mullaly was certain he had found the murder weapon. But Maggie wasn't through yet. From a jog six feet up on the chimney, she lifted down a box of odds and ends and from it took still another hatchet. Surely, Mullaly's cup runneth over.

Upstairs, Lizzie had retired to her room, where Alice and her friend the Reverend E. A. Buck consoled her. She had changed out of the heavy morning dress and donned a pink-and-white striped wrapper with a shirred blouse. Dr. Bowen, concerned, sat with her a few minutes and then gave her a dose of Bromo-Caffeine, a sedative for her nerves.

Assistant Marshal Fleet tapped on the door and Alice admitted him. When had her father returned home, he wanted to know, and what had happened after that?

Lizzie told him of Andrew's fumbling at the door, how he had looked feeble and she had "assisted him to lie down" and gone about the ironing of her handkerchiefs.

"How *long* were you in the barn?" he asked, and her answer was 30 minutes or 15 or 20, she was not sure.

"And *why* were you there?" he wanted to know, and she told him.

"Do you know of *anyone* who might have killed your father and mother?"

"She is *not* my mother, sir. She is my *step*mother. My mother died when I was a child."

It was a statement of fact and simple in itself, but it was a sentence that would echo throughout the investigation, the trial, and the rest of her life.

3

Vinnicum and Other Strange Things

*T*HE ANNALS OF THE BORDEN MURDER case are laced with unexplainable things, the shadowy role played by John Vinnicum Morse being one of the principal ones. One knowledgeable Lizzie buff once remarked that if he had an opportunity to ask Lizzie one question, it would not be about her guilt or innocence, but for an explanation of the behavior of Morse.

His sister, Sarah, had married Andrew 47 years earlier, when Borden was young and struggling. She had borne him Emma, Lizzie, and little Alice, who had not lived. John and Andrew had pioneered a furniture business together but with no particular success. At age 25, John had followed Horace Greeley's advice and gone West, to Hastings Mill, Iowa, where, he said, success had met him at the station. He had come back to Massachusetts, to South Yarmouth, near New Bedford. He was now a horse trader, he said, and had a trainload of horses to prove it. He had come to spend a few days at the Bordens, but strangely, he had not brought a single item of luggage, not a comb, shirt, or toothbrush.

Andrew was his closest friend and had often sought his advice on business matters. It was this close relationship that had brought him to the Borden home the day before.

"Hullo, John," Andrew had exclaimed. "Is that you? Have you had your dinner yet?"

Mrs. Borden had said, "Sit right down. We are just through and everything is hot on the stove. It won't cost us a mite of trouble."

He had eaten and they had talked, he said. He had later gone out on business, returning that night at 8:30. There had been more talk until 10:00, when all had retired.

He was up at six the next day and departed about 9:00 A.M. with the promise that he would return for the noon meal. He had been about buying a pair of oxen and visiting his niece. Amazingly, he could trace his movements minute by minute and street by street, including the number of the trolley he had ridden and the number on the cap of the conductor who had driven it. His remembrances would suit a casebook on alibis.

When he returned at 12:00, he had apparently failed to notice several hundred people massed in front of the Borden house. He walked past the side door where massive Charles Sawyer, in his red plaid shirt, still barred it to entrants. He spoke to no one to inquire about the excitement. Instead, he elbowed his way through the crowd and made his way to the backyard, where he picked up several pears and nonchalantly leaned against a corner of the barn. He showed no curiosity as to why Sawyer was guarding the side door or why policemen were running frantically to and from the house.

Finished with the pears (he would testify later it was one pear, but the officer who had watched him would say it was three), he finally sauntered over, identified himself at the back-door, and went into the house.

"I opened the sitting-room door and found a number of people, including the doctors," he told a reporter. "I entered, but only glanced at the body. No, I did not look closely enough to be able to describe it. Then I went upstairs and took a similar hasty view of the dead woman. I recall very little of what took place."

He had been in the house a total of three minutes. So much for his "closest friend" and "the dead woman."

Dr. Dolan, in his role as police physician, was not unfamiliar with dead bodies, and he did not join in the speculation going around the house as to how Andrew and Abby had met their deaths. Though the science of forensic medicine was not an advanced one in 1892, Dolan could tell by the blackened, thickened blood of Abby's wounds and the fresh, red flow from Andrew's that Abby had already been dead an hour or so when Andrew's time had come.

If Andrew had died at 11:00, Abby had died at 9:30 or 10:00. It made a difference, that span of time when nothing had been seen and nothing heard. This brought the mysterious note back to Dr. Dolan's mind, and he asked Lizzie where it might be; it was important. But she didn't know. They all had searched for it—in Abby's handbag and her sewing box.

"Well, then," Alice offered, "she must have put it in the fire."

Officer Harrington would testify that he had seen Dr. Bowen in the kitchen, reading a scrap of paper. When asked what it was, his reply had been, "Oh, it is nothing. Something about my daughter going somewhere." He had casually dropped it in the stove.

All that day and the next, information flowed into police headquarters from "volunteers" who genuinely wanted to help and from the inevitable seekers of momentary fame. Back now from their annual clambake at Rocky Point, all hands save a few were put to work on the awful tragedy.

The *Herald* of August 5 brought the citizenry up to date on the facts, the rumors, and the speculations:

THURSDAY'S AFFRAY
NO CLUE AS YET TO ITS PERPETRATOR
POLICE WORKING HARD TO REMOVE THE VEIL
OF MYSTERY THAT ENVELOPS THE AWFUL TRAGEDY
A POSTAL CARD THAT WOULD SERVE AS A LINK

Further investigation into the circumstances of the Borden murder shroud it with an impenetrable mystery. Nothing that has ever occurred in Fall River or vicinity has created such intense excitement. From the moment the story of the crime was first told to long after midnight, Second Street was crowded with curious people anxious to hear some particulars that had not been told before. Theories were advanced, some of them plausible enough, but not one could be formed against which some objection could not be offered from the circumstances surrounding the case. Everybody agreed that money was at the bottom of the foul murder, but in what measure and concerning what person could not be conceived. That a bloody deed such as that perpetrated in broad daylight, in a house on one of the busiest streets could have been so quickly and noiselessly accomplished and the murderer escape from the house without attracting attention is wonderful to a degree. Nobody was seen to enter the house by any of the occupants, although all of them except Mr. Borden were busy about the rooms or in the yard.

Was he Concealed?

Could it be that the murderer was concealed inside the dwelling and had awaited a favorable moment to carry out his nefarious plans? The more the circumstances are considered, the more probable becomes this view of the case. People who have carefully examined the ground believe that Mr. Borden was the first victim, and that the killing of Mrs. Borden was by no means unpremeditated. Having accomplished the bloody work downstairs, the murderer slipped stealthily into the rooms above in search of the wife and, finding her in the northwest chamber walking across the floor to the dressing case, had crept up behind her without attracting her attention and delivered the fatal blow.

The plausibility of this view lies in the fact that the fall of Mrs. Borden, who weighed very nearly 200 pounds, would certainly have jarred the building and awakened her husband, who could only have been sleeping lightly on the lounge, as it was but a few moments after his daughter had seen him quietly reading there that the deed was done. Further investigation confirms the belief that Mrs. Borden was not chased upstairs by the murderer because she was so near the end of the room that she would have been forced to turn and face her pursuer, and the cuts on the head would have been a different nature.

Twenty minutes were all the time the murderer had to finish his terrible work; conceal the weapon with which he accomplished his crime, and conceal it in such a way as to leave no traces of blood on the carpet or through the house that would reveal how he escaped; to pass out of the house by the side door within 15 feet of the barn where the daughter was engaged and a like distance from the Buffinton house on the north; pass the length of the house and disappear up or down Second Street. John Cunningham was going down the street about that time, and he saw nobody pass him; and people who live below saw nobody. Had the man run through the orchard and jumped Dr. Chagnon's fence, escaping to Third Street, he would have had to pass the barn door, and would have been seen from the living rooms of the Chagnon abode. How the murderer could have done so much in so short a time and cover his tracks so successfully is not the least mysterious feature in the case.

But The Motive

Certainly nobody who knew Mr. Borden or his wife can furnish any light upon this matter from the relationship with them in business or social circles. Beyond attributing it to money in the abstract, no theory can be advanced that is borne out by the facts thus far revealed. It was not robbery, because things were not overhauled. Mr. Borden was always a close dealer, and his frugality had been the means of amassing a fortune of half a million dollars. Nevertheless he bore himself strictly honest, and if he had expected dollar for dollar and cent for cent he always offered the same to others. Whether he had at some time or other made an enemy in his dealings, one who would have been led by a desire for revenge to stain his hands with life blood, has never been suspected by those outside the family, and may or may not have been true. The only other motive must be laid at the doors of those who would profit by the death of the couple, but people who knew them refuse to accept such a view for a single instant.

Talks with Inmates

There are no new developments in the case to be gathered from the people in the house. Regarding the servant, Bridget Sullivan, a woman of about 25, it is pretty well established that at the time Mr. Borden was assaulted she was in the attic of the house. Her statement to the police is as follows: "I was washing windows most all of the morning and passed in and out of the house continually. At the time Miss Lizzie came downstairs I went to one of the upper rooms to finish the window washing. I remained there until Lizzie's cries attracted my attention; then I came down and went for Dr. Bowen; I never saw any one enter or leave the house."

Miss Borden made the following statement to Officer Harrington as soon as she was sufficiently composed to talk coherently of the affair. It differs in only one particular from the one she told Dr. Bowen, namely, the time in which she was out of the house and in the barn. She said she was about 20 minutes, and, upon being requested to be particular, insisted that it was not more than 20 minutes or less than that time. She said that her father enjoyed the most perfect confidence and friendship of his workmen across the river, and that she was in a position to know this, unless something unusual had happened within a few days. She told the story of the angry tenant, saying that the man came to her father twice about the matter, and he persistently refused to let the store which he wanted for the purpose desired. The only vacant property of Mr. Borden was the room recently vacated by Baker Gadsby and it is thought that this is the place the man wanted to use. Mr. Borden told the man at the first visit to call again and he would let him know about the rental. It is supposed to be an out-of-town man and that he called and found that Johnathon Clegg had occupied the store. It is also thought that the tenant wanted to use the place as a rum shop; this, Mr. Borden would not allow. It may be added that the police attach little importance to this latter matter.

The Medical Examiner

Dr. Dolan was called upon after the autopsy, but he had no further facts to disclose. He described the wounds and said that death must have been almost instantaneous in both cases after the first blow. Acting upon the rumor about the poisoned milk, the doctor took samples of it and saved the soft spots of the body for further analysis. He was of the opinion that the wounds were inflicted by a hatchet or a cleaver, and by a person who could strike a blow heavy enough to crush in the skull. In the autopsy, Drs. Coughlin, Dedrick, Leary, Gunning, Dutra, Tourtellot, Peckham, and Bowen assisted.

Notes

John J. Maher was on a street car on New Boston Road Thursday afternoon rather under the influence of liquor. He was telling that when a reward was offered for the man, he could find him in 15 minutes. When questioned by an officer as to what he really knew, Maher said that a boy had seen a small man with a dark moustache come out of the house at the time of the murder and, going down Second Street, had turned up Pleasant. Maher was locked up on a charge of drunkenness.

Officers Doherty and Harrington have been on continuous duty since the case was reported.

It was rather warm for the officers who were detailed to hunt for the murderer's weapon in the loft of the barn, but they thoroughly examined every corner for the article.

Officers Dyson, Ferguson, Mayall, and Hyde were detailed to watch the house until 1 o'clock, when they were relieved by Officers Doherty, Harrington, McCarthy, and Reagan.

An effort has been made to obtain information relative to the condition of the property left by Abraham B. Borden, father of Andrew. A search at the probate office shows that no will was left by Abraham, and that Andrew J. was appointed administrator of the estate. Andrew J.'s mother left a will, but her property amounted to less than $3,000, and that was all willed to her brothers and nieces.

Officer Medley was one of the busiest men about town Wednesday [read *Thursday*] night, and every remark or idea connected with the tragedy was thoroughly sifted by him.

When the news of the murder reached the people on the excursion,* it seemed too incredible, and a great many would not be convinced until they reached home.

If interest and hard work in the case were to land the perpetrator of the crime into custody, Assistant Marshal Fleet would have the man behind the bars long before now.

Every morning paper in Boston had a representative in this city Thursday night, and as a result, the telegraph operators were kept busy into the small hours of the morning.

The excitement attending the tragedy continued at blood heat throughout the night, and it required a number of officers to keep the street cleared in front of the house up to midnight.

Among the many articles secured on the premises is a crow-bar over three feet long and weighing about nine pounds. It was found in the shed by one of the officers. It appeared at first that there was blood on it, and a hasty investigation by two or three policemen convinced the finder that the substance with which it was spotted was blood. It was consequently brought to the police station where it was found that the spots were nothing else than a few drops of paint and rust.

Morse's Niece

Mrs. Emery, upon whom Mr. Morse called, was disposed to talk freely to Officer Medley, who interviewed her Thursday night. She said in reply to questions that she had several callers during the day, and that one of them was John Morse. "He left here at 11:30 o'clock this morning," she said.

The Oldest Daughter

Miss Emma Borden, who had been visiting in Fairhaven, returned home Thursday evening, having been summoned by the news of the crime. The details of the murder had not been told to her, and she was overcome by the recital. She is the oldest daughter of Andrew Borden by his first wife. All through the early hours of the evening the street was crowded with people, none of whom was admitted to the premises until they had disclosed the nature of their business. A watch surrounded the house, and officers were on guard inside. No further developments were reported. The family retired soon after 10 o'clock and all was in darkness. Undertaker Winward had taken charge of the remains at the request of Miss Borden, and will prepare them for burial.

The Theories Discussed

Today nothing but the murder was talked about on the streets, and the interest continues to be intense. The announcement that the family had offered a reward of $5,000 for the detection of the murderers was the only new item to be discussed.

---

* The police department's excursion to Rocky Point.

The theories which were advanced by those who have been closely connected with the case agree in one thing, and that is that the murderer knew his ground and carried out his blood-thirsty plan with a speed and surety that indicated a well-matured plot.

Detective Seaver and other members of the state police force are assisting the local department in its work and the office of the city marshal is the busiest place in town. New clues are being reported every hour and officers are busy tracking the stories to earth.

Mr. Morse, the guest of the Bordens, is well known in this city where he was born and lived many years. People recall that he went West quite early in life and engaged in raising horses in Iowa. He was said to have had considerable success with his stock and to have gathered together considerable property. Nothing definite about his affairs is known other than that he had told friends that he had brought a train load of horses with him from Iowa to sell, and they were now in Fairhaven.

Significant Disappearance

That letter of which mention was made Thursday as having been sent to Mrs. Borden, announcing that a friend was sick, has since disappeared. The explanation that was given out was that after reading its contents, Mrs. Borden tore it up and threw the pieces in the fire. Bits of charred paper were found in the grate, but not enough to give any idea of the nature of the note. Nobody about the house seems to know where the letter could have come from, and since publicity has been given and considerable importance attached to it, it is considered probable that the writer will inform the family of the circumstances and thus remove suspicions.

Various rumors have been started, one of which was that Miss Borden had assured a friend last winter after a mysterious robbery at the house that her father had an enemy some where. A *Herald* reporter interviewed a lady to whom it was said this story had been told, but she denied any knowledge of it. Another was that the axe had been found in the yard, but the police have not heard of it.

A Tenant Theory

Causes for the murder are arising so fast at the present time that it is nearly impossible to investigate them. Hardly any of them are of sufficient weight to put a person under the ban of suspicion, but all are being thoroughly investigated. The latest story is about a former tenant named Ryan. According to the information, Ryan occupied the upper floor of a house belonging to Mr. Borden, and was so obnoxious that he ordered him to move. While notifying the people, he was compelled to seek the lower floor to escape the torrent of abuse that was heaped on him, and when the family moved, the remark was made that they would like to see him dead. There is nothing more than this in the matter, but as all acts or words in connection with Mr. Borden in the past are being looked into, the affair was looked into and found to amount to nothing.

A Man With A Cleaver

Griffiths Bros., the carpenters on Anawan Street, tell a story which may have an important bearing upon the terrible tragedy. They were driving up Pleasant Street about 11 o'clock Thursday morning, when their attention was drawn to a man who was proceeding rapidly along the sidewalk in front of Flint's building. Under his arm, with the handle down, he carried a cleaver entirely unlike anything they had ever seen. It was the size of the instrument that caused them to take more than a passing glance at it. To them it looked like a tool sometimes used by fish dealers. It had a rusty appearance, as if it had not been used for some time.

The man was dressed very poorly. He had no beard and was short in stature. As the weapon with which the deed was committed has not been found, the carpenters venture the opinion that the cleaver they saw was the means by which Mr. Borden and his wife were killed.

Southard H. Miller,

one of the city's most venerable citizens, and Mr. Borden's intimate friend, was spoken to on the matter. He replied that as far as motive was concerned for the deed he could not answer. He had known Mr. Borden for over a half a century, and his dealings were such that nobody could take offense with him. In all the time he had been acquainted with Mr. Borden, and it was more than an intimate acquaintance, there was never a family quarrel that would, under any circumstances, lead to the perpetration of the act. As far as Mr. Morse was concerned, Mr. Miller had known him for about a year, and in that time he had seen nothing that would prejudice him against the man. Mr. Borden's daughters were ladies who had always conducted themselves so that the breath of scandal could never reach them.

Collected A Chain

The police have followed the case with leads from a dozen standpoints and have collected a chain of circumstantial evidence which points in a certain direction with startling coincidences.

The statement that Miss Lizzie had changed her dress yesterday was denied this afternoon by the servant who stated that the same garment was worn all day.* The story told by Morse of his visit to Flint village has been examined and found to be correct with slight variations in time that are immaterial. There can be no doubt that he was away from the house when the crime was perpetrated.

The police have worked in other directions and have discovered things which bring them face to face with embarrassing difficulties. The poisoned milk theory had been investigated and an unsuccess-

---

* Lizzie *did* change her dress, as both she and Bridget testified. This is either the reporter's error or another of the floating rumors.

ful attempt was found to have been made to purchase a drug at a South Main Street store that may have had something to do with a subsequent development in the case.

The police are guarding these facts and others of an important nature which they possess and a sensation is promised when the time comes to lay all the evidence before the public. The necessity of another search of the premises for the sake of bringing to light the weapon with which the deed was done is being urged. This will furnish an important link in the chain of evidence, and until it has been found it is doubtful whether any definite movement will be made.

A physician who took part in the autopsy told a reporter that if the dead body could speak they would disclose the fact that no mysterious stranger had been around to rob them of life; that the person who committed the foul deed was at that moment not far from the scene and knew just where to lay hands on the weapon. When pressed for a explanation of these mysterious words, the doctor declined further to commit himself, saying that strong suspicions were not trustworthy as evidence.

And so, the unspeakable was almost spoken.

The allusion by the reporter to the possible motive for the murders was the first daring, almost breathtaking hint that, absent any other motive, one had to look to the ones who benefitted from the deaths of Andrew and Abby. An obvious reference to Emma and Lizzie, and since Emma had been away visiting the Brownell's in Fairhaven . . . ?

The remark that the police had "discovered things which bring them face to face with embarrassing difficulties" was another hint, but it was the unnamed physician's prediction as to what the dead bodies might say that came close, for the first time, to accusing Lizzie of the unspeakable.

4

Of Time and
the Murder

*T*HE 30 MINUTES BETWEEN the time Andrew Borden returned
home at 10:45 and the cry of "Murder!" at 11:15 is perhaps
the most studied half-hour in all criminal record, and perhaps
still the most baffling.

At Lizzie's trial, prosecuting Attorney William H. Moody
called attention to the murkiness of that time period in his
opening statement to the jury:

"The time between Bridget's going upstairs and coming
down again must be diminished on the one side by the time
consumed by the washing of a window and a half in the sitting
room and two windows in the dining room and the putting
away of the cloth and the water. On the other side the half hour
between eleven o'clock and half-past eleven must be diminished by the acts of Bridget and the acts of Mrs. Churchill and
the acts of Cunningham."

Close, but no cigar. Right in the first citation; wrong in the second. The time to be examined was not the 45 *minutes* between 10:45 and 11:30, but rather the 30 *minutes* between 10:45 and 11:15, when the first telephone call had been received at the police station. Moody had opened up the question as to what had actually taken place, but instead of following up by giving his version of the events, he opted instead to leave it up to the jury to decide what had happened. It was as if the Commonwealth had rigged up an arc light to shine down the well of the mystery, but instead of being a light in the darkness, it only reflected back the murkiness of what was below. On a second look, objects in the inky spaces vanished like phantoms.

Nobody mentioned the plaguing half-hour again. Someone should have, because a second-by-second examination proves that what was said to have taken place or assumed to have taken place could not have taken place at all.

There are two known checkpoints of time in the sequence of events. Bridget testified at the inquest, and the preliminary hearing, before the grand jury, and at the trial that the city hall bell tolled 11:00 three minutes after she had reached her room to rest. She had verified the time by her bedside clock, which was later checked and found accurate. The police had received Cunningham's call telling of some disturbance on Second Street at 11:15. In addition to the police record, he had dutifully noted the time himself, and his watch had also been checked for accuracy.

During that 15-minute period a number of known events took place; others can only be conjectured.

The distances and times cited hereafter were calculated by the author on the site using a stop watch and following the scenario of those known events. They are *minimum* time allotments for the conversations and responses and the distances hastily covered. They assume almost immediate reactions, which are improbable, but theoretically possible.

10:57:00	Bridget goes to her room to lie down
11:00:00	City hall clock tolls the hour
11:08:00	Lizzie calls out to Bridget to come down
11:08–11:08:45	Bridget rises (puts on shoes?), comes down, is told of murder, questions Lizzie, and is sent to Dr. Bowen's

11:08:45–11:09:30	Gets hat and shawl, crosses street
11:09:30–11:10:00	Knocks (twice?); Mrs. Bowen (perhaps in kitchen?) comes to door, is told of murder, explains that doctor isn't home
11:10:00–11:10:45	Bridget crosses street back to Borden's
11:10:45–11:11:15	Tells Lizzie doctor isn't home, has more conversation, is told to fetch Miss Russell, leaves
11:11:15–11:11:45	Mrs. Churchill, on the street, sees commotion, goes to kitchen, puts down groceries, looks out of window, calls out to Lizzie, and is asked to come over
11:11:45–11:12:30	Mrs. Churchill leaves kitchen, goes out front door, over to Borden's, and to side door
11:12:30–11:13:15	Has lengthy conversation as to what happened and where Lizzie was, goes in sitting room, views body; they decide she should go for another doctor
11:13:15–11:14:00	Mrs. Churchill leaves, hurries to Hall's stable at end of the block
11:14:00–11:14:30	Meets John Cunningham, tells him of murder, and asks him to call police
11:14:30–11:14:45	Cunningham goes to nearest telephone
11:14:45–11:15:00	Calls police

It is doubtful that any of these happenings could have taken place in less than the times allotted. Accepting these times and actions as plausible, there is a *maximum of eight minutes* from the time the city hall bell tolled to the time Lizzie called Bridget to come down—not the 10 or 15 minutes (or longer) testified to by Bridget.

During these eight minutes—even starting the very moment Bridget went to her room—Lizzie could not have gone to wherever the hatchet was hidden (her room, the guest room, the basement?), returned to the sitting room, murdered Andrew, hidden the hatchet, inspected herself, combed her hair and bathed away the inevitable bloodstains, gone back up to her room, changed clothes, hidden the soiled garments somewhere, gone back downstairs, out to the yard, picked up pears, entered the barn, gone up to the loft, eaten the pears, come back down, returned to the house, and, finally, called out to Bridget.

It is manifestly impossible, physically, to do all these things in eight minutes. An eight-minute gap, of course, also leaves no time for a 30-minute, 20-minute, or even 15-minute trip to the barn—with or without allowing time for the murder and all its aftermath.

Because the time the call was received at police headquarters cannot be changed, there is only one other possibility: Bridget did not tell the truth about hearing the city hall bell and this series of events started earlier than eleven o'clock.

But why would Bridget lie? Since she testified that she checked her own clock when she heard the bell toll, her testimony could not have been a simple error; it would have had to be a falsification.

Who gains by altering and constricting the time? Not Lizzie, for if it is left unexplained, it makes the trip to the barn and/or the murder of Andrew a virtual impossibility in so short a span. There simply would not be time for her to do either, let alone both.

The other 15-minute period mentioned by Moody, from 10:45 until 11:00, is equally vague and troublesome.

Downtown, Andrew had stopped by Clegg's store, where carpenters Joseph Shortsleeves and James Mather were doing some repair work. Shortsleeves noted the time when Andrew started home. It was 10:45.

It is reasonable to assume that it took five minutes to walk the three blocks to 92 Second Street. 10:50:00.

Andrew fumbled with the locks on the front door; Bridget quit her work, came to the front door, and admitted him. He went first to the dining room and sat. 10:51:00.

He took a key from the mantle and went up to his room. What for, we cannot know. But a reasonable assumption is that the trip up the backstairs, time for the purpose of his trip, and time to come back down to the sitting room, can be estimated at three minutes. 10:54:00

Lizzie came downstairs, inquired about the mail, told him Abby had received a note and gone out, and walked with him to the sitting room, where he took off his coat, folded it on the couch, and began reading his paper. 10:56:00.

Bridget finished washing two windows in the dining room (at one minute each) and two (at one minute each) in the sitting room, where Andrew was. 11:00:00.

She talked with Lizzie about Abby having gone out and the necessity of locking the doors. She wrung out her cloths, emptied her pail, talked with Lizzie about the probability of her going out, and retired to her room. 11:02:00.

The two quarter-hours have now over-lapped and made it questionable that Bridget could have gone to her room at 10:57. And it is difficult to believe that Andrew could have yet gone to sleep during all this commotion and conversation.

Lizzie is characterized by some theoreticians as a shrewd, calculating executor of an infinitely planned murder. Then how to explain her attempt, as alleged by some, to purchase prussic acid the day before? Failing that, when had there been time to plan an alternative, and how could she have anticipated Morse's surprise visit, when or if he would leave the house in the morning, at what moment he might return, or that Abby would choose that miserably hot day to have the windows cleaned, or in what order Bridget would wash them and be out of view, or that there would be no outcry or struggle from either victim to alert anyone, or at what minute Bridget might enter the house and discover her, bloody hatchet in hand—or a dozen other imponderables.

The alternative is to say that she was impetuous, insane, slaying at random, right and left, with witnesses always within a few feet, virtually doing a clog dance in a minefield. But to say that is to envelop her with an aura of luck, providence, and good fortune such as no murderer ever enjoyed before.

But we cannot have it both ways.

Disorderly conduct, drunkenness, horse theft, and other common breaches of the peace had not stopped while the police of Fall River wrestled with the unprecedented event that had happened on Second Street.

After two days of almost nonstop duty, a major portion of Marshal Hilliard's force was exhausted, bewildered, and wrangling among themselves. His desk at City Hall, a bare stone's throw from the Borden house, was piled high with reports, each, it seemed to him, contradicting the other. A separate stack contained sightings, confessions, abusive letters, letters of advice, threats, and telephone calls from the curious and the cranks. Albert E. Pillsbury, attorney general of Massachusetts, had been on the phone breathing down his neck and asking for a report of the progress being made. Add to all that the routine booking slips, reports to read and sign, and schedules to be made up and, indeed, his lot was not a happy one.

On Saturday morning Marshal Hilliard called together at City Hall the principal officers who had been working on the case. The gritty old building of native white stone was as grim a structure as a prisoner ever entered.

Where are we, he wanted to know? The dozen men systematically reviewed their findings and lack of findings, recited the mysteries that remained unexplained, and gave their speculations as to what the probable answers to them were.

Deputy Marshal Fleet, from the first morning, had maintained that Lizzie was the culprit. He seems to have come to that decision parallel to the moment she had waspishly told him that Mrs. Borden was not her mother, but her stepmother. Officers Harrington and Medley shared his view. The three officers were known to be a tight trio at headquarters, and it is not surprising they would agree one with the other.

The second most popular suspect was the ubiquitous John Vinnicum Morse. Was his unannounced arrival at the Borden house the night before the murders merely a coincidence? He had brought along no sign of luggage, not a toothbrush, comb, or nightshirt, though he had planned, he said, to stay a few days. His disappearance from the house just minutes before Abby was murdered, and his strange behavior when he returned just minutes after Andrew's body was found certainly had a contrived look about them.

The public had their suspicions, too, even if the alibi Morse furnished was apparently airtight. On Friday night, Morse had sneaked out of the house, unseen by the crowd gathered in front, evaded the police guarding the property, and made his way to the post office to, he said, mail a letter. There, he had been recognized emerging, and an angry mob estimated variously at from 400 to 2,000 had surrounded him. Whichever figure is correct, it was clearly a lynch mob, and Officer John

Minnehan rescued him and hustled him back to the house and safety.

The other favorite culprit was Bridget—or more likely, Lizzie and Bridget together. It was hard to make a case against the hapless servant girl alone for there was no apparent motive (other than a pay-off from Lizzie). That theory vanished when, later, after Bridget was arrested, her bail money was put up by the police department, and they secured her a job working for the department until the trial was set.

On Friday, the barn, house, and grounds were searched again and, this time, the proverbial fine-tooth comb was used. A pile of scrap lumber next to the fence in the backyard was examined, board by board. In the barn, hay that filled one corner of the ground floor was turned over, forkful by forkful, into the opposite corner. The floor boards were ripped up. An abandoned well was cleaned out and probed. The ashes in the kitchen stove were sifted in search of a button, a hook, or traces of burned cloth.

Inside the house, five officers spent three hours opening and emptying drawers, boxes, trunks, closets, and cupboards. Mattresses were overturned and dresses turned inside out and inspected for bloodstains.

"We examined everything," Dr. Dolan said, "down to the slightest bump in the wallpaper."

They found nothing.

Two officers had gone to Fairhaven, where Emma had been visiting for the last two weeks. Unquestionably, she had been there and could not have sneaked back to Fall River on Thursday morning. This eliminated her.

Morse's alibi had been checked again. Nothing there.

Public interest in a crime had never been more intense in anyone's memory. The man on the street and the lady in the parlor were, it seemed, less interested in the brutality of the two murders than they were in the intrigue of the puzzle itself. *How* could the murders possibly have been done? *Who* could possibly have committed them? *What* had been the motive? Could a phantom have escaped unnoticed? One enterprising reporter experimented on his own. He walked up Second Street and entered the Borden property, walked beside the grape arbor on the north side, behind the barn, across a fence to the Chagnon property in the rear, across another fence, reentered the Borden property, and this time poked around the unlocked barn and came out to Second Street again, passing the side steps. He was unobserved by Morse, Emma, or Mrs. Churchill, who were all known to be home at the time.

The phantasm of a crazed killer carrying an axe dripping blood and lurching through the streets of Fall River in search of his next victim seemed not at all to be on the minds of the public. They were, instead, preoccupied as amateur detectives and theoreticians, sifting for clues in the gossip whirling around town like leaves before a firestorm. While the twin murders had electrified the nation, they had paralyzed New England.

The principal gossip now dealt with the Eli Bence development. On Wednesday, the day before the murders, Abby and Lizzie were convinced they were being poisoned by someone, perhaps in the baker's bread they had bought or the milk delivered daily from the Borden farm. Andrew, too, had suffered stomach cramps and was retching, but it was Abby who dressed early and knocked on Dr. Bowen's door across the street. He questioned her as to what the family had eaten recently and was undoubtedly appalled to hear their diet had included warmed-over fish and the same leg of mutton served in various guises for three consecutive days. (It would appear again at breakfast and was slated for dinner as well!) There was nothing to be alarmed about, he told her. They were poisoning themselves at their own table.

This was the beginning of the "poison theory" as Lizzie had told the police on Thursday. At the mention of the word, Officers Harrington and Doherty were sent to check all the drugstores in Fall River, New Bedford, and all points in between for recent purchases of poison.

Eli Bence, pharmacist at D. R. Smith's drugstore, on the corner of Columbia and South Main, told them a young lady carrying a fur cape had come into the store on Wednesday, the day before the murders, and sought to purchase 10 cents worth of prussic acid. She wanted it, she said, to kill the moths eating away at her sealskin cape.

Bence had told her the poison could not be purchased without a prescription, and she had left. Though he had never met Miss Borden, she was that young lady, he said.

The debate was heated among the townsfolk and at police headquarters. Wasn't this attempt to purchase a poison *proof*, Harrington wanted to know, that Lizzie had a deadly intent against someone the day before the murders?

The 1890s was the heyday of the newspaper and sober, responsible, factual reporting, before ever there were bylines and "investigative reporters," before radio newscasts "at the top of the hour" or television sound bites and the inevitable "film at eleven."

The *Globe* was the new kid on the newspaper block in Fall River. The *Herald* in the morning and the *News* in the afternoon had been, until a few years before, the two principal papers that had told generations of subscribers what was going on in their town.

The *Globe* set up shop with the avowed purpose of stirring up the market and wooing away the subscribers of both papers. It was the 1892 version of today's supermarket tabloids; its style was called "yellow journalism" in those days and was something theretofore confined to the largest of the major cities, principally New York. If Elvis or a UFO had been sighted in 1892, the *Globe* would have carried it on the front page—above the banner.

On Saturday, the second day after the murders, the *Globe* called immediately for Lizzie's arrest and followed up with a flurry of stories expressing her guilt. It was the tack this paper would follow relentlessly throughout the investigation and trial, and for years after. All of its stories were slanted against Lizzie; many were manufactured. The *Globe*'s police reporter was Edwin H. Porter, who would later use his stories as the basis for his "history," *The Fall River Tragedy*, mentioned in the Preface.

He had a field day with the Bence development. His story said, "The demeanor of Miss Lizzie Borden through the trying ordeal of being confronted with the man who says that she asked about the poison was that of contempt and scorn; in fact, her conduct as seen by the police has been strange."

The fact that no such "confrontation" had ever taken place didn't faze Porter or the *Globe*. It made a helluva story, didn't it?

While the meeting had been going on in Hilliard's office, some 4,000 people, sweating and shoving, had created a gridlock traffic jam on Second Street. It took 20 policemen to maintain a semblance of order. This was the day of the funeral.

At 9:00 A.M., John Morse came out of the Borden house and chatted leisurely with the reporters who had pushed their way up front. He protested his innocence, shaken, perhaps, by his escape from the lynch mob the night before. He pledged his "full cooperation" in the search for the miscreant and invited the "fullest investigation" of his alibi.

The Reverend Thomas Adams, of the First Congregational Church, and City Missionary Edwin A. Buck, a long-time friend of Lizzie's, joined the 75 others who were elbow to elbow inside. In the sitting room, the coffins were displayed side by side. Lizzie, accompanied by Adelaide Churchill, had earlier come down from her room. She stood beside Andrew's bier for a silent minute, wept, and kissed him on the lips.

An ivy wreath was atop his now closed coffin, and a bouquet of white roses tied with a white satin ribbon adorned Abby's. Scriptures were read and hymns sung, but no eulogy was spoken.

At 11:00, Lizzie was the first to emerge from the house, leaning heavily on the arm of undertaker James E. Winward. Those who had already accused her of showing no emotion at the time of the murder or during the days of questioning were later also to profess shock and indignation that she neither showed any emotion nor wore mourning black at the funeral. The truth as to what she wore, however, was recorded by a female reporter in her dispatch to the Boston *Herald*:

"She wore a tight fitting black lace dress with a plain skirt and waist of equally modest cut and finish, while a dark hat, trimmed with similar material, rested upon her head."

As for her emotional state, a *New York Times* reporter wrote:

"Her nerves were completely unstrung as was shown by the trembling of her body and the manner in which she bore down on her supporter. When she reached the carriage she fell back exhausted in the cushions."

Too late. The legend was already set in concrete: Lizzie did not mourn and displayed no human emotion.

Emma, much calmer, followed. She walked quickly and took a seat beside Lizzie, and both fixed their eyes ahead. Neither glanced at the mob in the streets, nor did they seem aware of the raised hats and bowed heads along the route of the cortege as the two hearses and 11 carriages made their way through the downtown section and up The Hill to the Oak Grove Cemetery. The burial service was a private one and only about 40 of the family's closest friends were invited to accompany the remains.

A telegram from the state analyst, stopping the ceremony, had reached the cemetery moments ahead of the burial party. The last rites were halted midway, and the caskets were put into a receiving vault.

The following Thursday, Dr. W. A. Dolan, assisted by Dr. F. W. Draper, with Dr. J. H. Leary and autopsy clerk Dr. D. E. Cone as witnesses, entered the vault, conducted a formal autopsy, and severed the heads of both victims, dispatching them to Harvard University for examination.

Mercifully, the news was kept from the family.

The moment the funeral party left the Borden house, the daily search began again. By now, Andrew Jennings, an attorney who had represented Lizzie once before, had been consulted. Aware there was a possibility that Lizzie might be accused, Jennings was on hand to monitor the search. Again, nothing was unearthed.

The day before the funeral, Marshal Hilliard had called Hosea Knowlton, district attorney for the second district, and asked for a meeting on Saturday that would also include State Police Detective George Seaver, Mayor John Coughlin, and Medical Examiner Dolan. While the funeral cortege moved along its route and while the Borden home was being searched for the third time, the five met in their unannounced session, which lasted until almost 6:00 P.M. The consensus: Lizzie was the probable murderer.

Mayor Coughlin and Marshal Hilliard appeared at the Borden home later that evening and met with Lizzie, Emma, and Morse in the dimly lit parlor.

"I have a request to make of the family," he said, "and that is that you remain in the house for a few days."

Lizzie asked, "Why? Is there anybody in this house suspected? I want to know the truth."

Coughlin hesitated in his answer.

"I want to know the truth," Lizzie repeated.

Marshal Hilliard said nothing, and the Mayor replied, "Well, Miss Borden, I regret to answer, but I must answer yes. You are suspected."

Lizzie stood and calmly faced the two.

"Then I am ready to go right now," she said.

The "Miranda" warning that one has the right to remain silent and have an attorney present during questioning can be recited verbatim by any eight-year-old today who has access to a television set. These rights, however, did not originate with the arrest of Mr. Miranda in the 1970s. They are guaranteed by the Constitution of the United States and were recognized in 1892 in Massachusetts and every other state. But neither Hilliard nor Knowlton mentioned these protections against self-incrimination on that Saturday or at any time to follow. It was a critical error.

On Sunday, the congregation of the Central Congregational Church held a joint service with the First Church, and every pew was filled. Surely, the buzzing before the service began concerned itself more with the murders on Second Street than it did with anyone's immortal soul.

In his prayer, the Reverend W. Walker Jubb invoked divine intercession that the terrible mystery might be cleared away. After the morning sermon, he stepped out of the pulpit to speak directly on the subject that was surely on everyone's mind. His manner was deliberate and his voice impressive and contained. He accurately caught the mood, the perplexity, and frustration of all Fall River residents of all faiths.

"I cannot close my sermon this morning," he said, "without speaking of the horrible crime that has startled our beloved city this week, ruthlessly taking from our church household two respected and esteemed members. I cannot close without referring to my pain and surprise at the atrocity of the outrage. A more brutal, cunning, daring, and fiendish murder I never heard of in all my life.

"What must have been the person who could have been guilty of such a revolting crime? One to commit such a murder must have been without heart, without soul, a fiend incarnate, the very vilest of degraded and depraved humanity, or he must have been a maniac. The circumstances, execution, and all the surroundings cover it with a mystery profound.

"Explanations and evidence as to both perpetrator and motive are shrouded in a mystery that is almost inexplicable. That such a crime could have been committed during the busy hours of the day, right in the heart of a populous city is passing comprehension.

"As we ponder, we exclaim in our perplexity, why was the deed done? What could have induced anybody to engage in such a butchery? Where is the motive? When men resort to crime it is for plunder, for gain, from enmity, in sudden anger, or for revenge. Strangely, nothing of this nature enters into this case, and again I ask—what was the motive? I believe, and am only voicing your feelings fully when I say that I hope the criminal will be speedily brought to justice. . . . "

Without speaking her name, he then directed his remarks to the police rumors, newspaper stories, and back-fence gossip about Lizzie's imminent arrest.

"I trust that the police may do their duty and lose no opportunity which might lead to the capture of the criminal. I would impress upon them that they should not say too much and thus unconsciously assist in defeating the ends of justice. I also trust that the press (and I say this because I recognize its influence and power), I trust that it will use discretion in disseminating its theories and conclusions, and that pens may be guided by consideration and charity. I would wish the papers to remember that by casting a groundless or undeserved insinuation that they may blacken and blast a life forever, like a tree smitten by a bolt of lightning; a life which has always commanded respect, whose acts and motives have always been pure and holy. Let us ourselves curb our tongues and preserve a blameless life from undeserved suspicions. I think I have the right to ask for the prayers of this church and of my own congregation. The murdered husband and wife were members of this church, and a daughter now stands in the same relation to each one of you, as you, as church members, do to each other. God help and comfort her. . . . "

5

The "Inquest"

O N MONDAY MORNING, Marshal Hilliard closeted himself with Second District Court Judge Josiah C. Blaisdell and came away with a warrant for Lizzie's arrest. What he cited as probable cause is not known because no one else was present.

As with all developments in the case, reporters learned of the meeting within minutes and were told, "There will be action soon." They interpreted that assurance to mean an arrest was imminent—that day. But, by 5:00 P.M., nothing had happened.

Hilliard and Knowlton hesitated.

In all probability, with a warrant finally in his hand, Knowlton was struck with the enormity of what they were about to do. There was no reason to believe that any additional evidence would be turned up even though on that day the Borden house was scheduled to receive its fifth search. Every rumor, no matter how absurd, had been investigated; every lead tracked out to thin air. They had no physical evidence; no weapon; no clear-cut motive. Yet, they were about to arrest a young lady of

impeccable character, bearing a name that had been synony-
mous with respectability for 200 years, and to charge her with
committing the most grotesque, heinous crime in anyone's
memory.

Hilliard must have asked himself if his men had left *any* stone
unturned, no matter how insignificant. Was there any *other*
conclusion to be drawn from what little they had?

Knowlton was no novice. He knew he would be the point
man—the man on the firing line. Did the police have a case he
could take with any confidence to a jury—not just the 12 good
men and true who would be sitting in the jury box, but that
other jury massed outside the courtroom?

In the end, he blinked.

Before Knowlton would allow Hilliard to serve the warrant
and thus cast the die, he had to have more. He wanted a further
inquiry of *some* kind, some additional time for questioning,
never mind what it was called.

An inquest, by legal definition, is a judicial inquiry to ascer-
tain what has happened, who has died, and how they died.
This, they already knew. On the other hand, it was not an
accusatory procedure, so attorneys would not be needed to
defend anyone, and this would give Hilliard and Knowlton
great latitude in their quest for more information, more facts,
more evidence, more *anything* to strengthen their case against
Lizzie. They dithered over what to call the meeting and finally
announced they were going to hold an "informal examination"
of various witnesses the following morning at 10:00.

Lizzie's attorney, Andrew Jennings, knew better. She was
already under house arrest and had been told she was suspected of committing the murders. When she was served a
summons ordering her to be present at the meeting, he asked
for permission to attend her. He argued at length to be allowed
to represent his client. At this point, Knowlton admitted the
meeting was an inquest, and Jennings was refused admission
and asked to leave.

Massachusetts Attorney General Albert Pillsbury had put
himself into the case, and it is safe to say he advised Hilliard
and Knowlton they could not carry off the subterfuge.

A bulletin was issued by Knowlton at the end of Monday,
stating, "Inquest continued to 10 o'clock." Nothing, he said,
was developed for publication.

From the minute the first cry of "Murder!" had gone out on Thursday morning, commerce and industry virtually came to a halt in Fall River. Hundreds, thousands, had choked off Second Street so that passage by carriage was impossible except in the early morning hours or late at night. Many of the mills and businesses had shut down in the afternoon because workers never returned from their lunch hours.

It had been much the same since, and this was the sixth day. Crowds continued to mass on Second Street, gazing at the house and hoping some member of the mystery cast might enter or leave. On every corner, groups would gather, checking to be sure they knew the latest gossip or to exchange new theories.

When the word went out on Tuesday that an inquest was to be held before Judge Blaisdell that morning at 10:00, crowds instantly rushed to Court Square and, within minutes, it and all the approaching streets were clogged with the curious.

The Old Court House, as it was called in 1892, had been built in 1857 and named the Second District House. It was a squat, gloomy, and forboding building of grayish native stone. It housed Fall River's two firefighting units, mammoth horse-drawn Metacomet and King Philip fire engines. Immediately to the rear of the first floor was the police lockup. The remainder of the floor was used as a city stable.

The second and third floors were shared by the police and the court. There were sleeping quarters for off-duty policemen and offices for the judges, clerks, and lawyers. Crowning the building was a cupola for the fire alarm bell which was tolled by means of a rope extending to the street below.

Promptly at 10:00, a hack approached and fervor reached the pandemonium stage. Most of the convention had not seen any of the principals since the hour of the murders, and a glimpse of someone involved was the least they would settle for. But if they hoped to spy Lizzie—and surely they did—they were to be disappointed.

The hack contained Officer Patrick Doherty and the servant girl Bridget Sullivan.

She was immediately rushed into the presence of Knowlton, Marshal Hilliard, Medical Examiner Dolan, State Police Officer Seaver, and Dr. Coughlin, the mayor of Fall River. One can only imagine the panic the young, immigrant servant must have felt to be surrounded by such an august group. Indeed, reports were that she was "deeply distressed," broke frequently into sobs, and was barely coherent.

She was ushered first into Hilliard's office, where she was questioned for an hour or more before the group moved into the district court room and the inquest was officially begun before Judge Blaisdell.

She told of the breakfast scene, of washing windows, of ultimately lying down in her room, and of Lizzie's frantic summons from the bottom of the backstairs. Her testimony, as far as is known, revealed nothing she had not told the police before.

Back to square one. Perhaps the afternoon session with Lizzie would produce more:

Q. (Mr. Knowlton) Give me your full name.
A. Lizzie Andrew Borden.
Q. Is it Lizzie or Elizabeth?
A. Lizzie.
Q. You were so christened?
A. I was so christened.
Q. What is your age, please.
A. Thirty-two.
Q. How long had your father been married to your step-mother?
A. I think about 27 years.
Q. How much of that time have they lived in that house on Second Street?
A. About 20 years last May.
Q. Have you any idea how much your father was worth?
A. No sir.
Q. Have you ever heard him say?
A. No sir.
Q. Have you ever formed an opinion?
A. No sir.
Q. Do you know something about real estate?
A. He owns two farms in Swansea, the place on Second Street and the A. J. Borden building and corner and the land on South Main Street where McMannus [read *McManus*] is, and then a short time ago he bought some real estate further south that formerly, he said, belonged to a Mr. Birch.

Q. Did you ever deed him any property?

A. He gave us some years ago, Grandfather Borden's house on Ferry Street and he bought that back from us some weeks ago. He gave us $5000 for it.

Q. Did you pay him anything when you took a deed from him?

A. No sir.

Q. Did you ever know of your father making a will?

A. No sir.

Q. Did he have a marriage settlement with your stepmother?

A. I never knew of any.

These were District Attorney Knowlton's first questions of Lizzie when she took the stand at the inquest at 2 P.M. that afternoon. They were queries that plumbed for a motive, one of the elements that he would have to prove to a jury if he had a prayer of getting a conviction.

It would be the position of the prosecution that Lizzie's motive had been greed and the dread that her father might be planning to leave his considerable estate to Abby. If that was allowed to happen, Emma and Lizzie would face more years of privation and, even worse, total subservience to their dour stepmother.

Gossip that there had been protracted arguments within the family over money and property was easy to come by. *Proof* was another thing. Knowlton was experienced in the ways of criminal prosecution, and he surely knew that, absent witnesses and hard evidence, the motive for the slayings had to be a clear and substantial one.

Q. Did you ever know of your father making a will?

A. No sir.

Q. Did he ever mention the subject of a will to you?

A. He did not.

Q. Do you know of anybody that your father was on bad terms with?

A. There was a man that came there that he had trouble with. I don't know who the man was.

Q. Tell all you saw and heard.

A. I did not see anything. I heard the bell ring and Father went to the door and let him in. I did not hear anything for

some time, except just the voices: then I heard the man
say, "I would like to have that place. I would like to have
that store." Father says, "I am not willing to let your business go in there." And the man said. "I thought with your
reputation for liking money, you would let your store for
anything." Father said, "You are mistaken." Then they
talked awhile and then their voices were louder and I
heard father order him out.

Q. Beside that, do you know of anybody that your father had
bad feelings toward or who had bad feelings toward your
father?

A. I know of one man that has not been friendly with him:
they have not been friendly for years.

Q. Who?

A. Mr. Hiram C. Harrington.

Hiram was Andrew's brother-in-law, married to his sister,
Laurana. The root of their dislike for each other was not surely
known, only that it had begun years before and had festered
like the Hatfield-McCoy feud.

With their diverse personalities and ambitions, it is easy to
imagine they would be as immiscible as oil and water. Harrington was a blacksmith, with no aspiration to be anything but
a blacksmith. He had saved nothing and invested nothing because he earned little more than what was needed for
absolute necessities. As Andrew saw it, he was not worthy of
Laurana.

At some point years before, there had been "hard words"
between them, and from that day, Hiram was not welcome in
the Borden house, nor was Andrew ever known to visit his
sister unless he knew Hiram was not at home.

On the day after the murders, Hiram spoke freely with
reporters, and he patently enjoyed the limelight. He aired his
version of what had happened at Andrew's house and left little
doubt that he thought Lizzie was the villain.

Implying an intimacy with Lizzie that he certainly never had,
Harrington told how he had had a long "interview" with her,
another fabrication. A reporter who had been present when
Harrington came to the Borden house said he had been inside
exactly three minutes. "Mr. Harrington is embittered against

the family," he told his editor, "and does not hesitate to make startling statements."

"Money, unquestionably money," was the motive for the murders, he said. "I would not be surprised at the arrest any time of the person to whom in my opinion suspicion strongly points. . . ."

While others present on the morning of the murders had described Lizzie variously as crying, deeply agitated, or on the verge of fainting, Harrington had said she was "very composed, showed no signs of any emotion nor were there any traces of grief upon her countenance."

Unfortunately for her and as untrue as it was, this image would hound Lizzie forever. Victorian ladies were supposed to get the vapors, tremble, and swoon at times of adversity. The 1892 public, and the writers who have written about her since, will not forgive her for her shyness, her strong sense of propriety, and her unwillingness to show her deepest emotions in public.

Asked if he knew whether there were dissensions in the Borden family, Harrington was quick to say there were, although, he added, "it has been always kept very quiet." Not any longer. Harrington was getting his own back for all of Andrew's slights.

"For nearly ten years," he said, "there have been disputes between the daughters and their father and stepmother." The disputes were bitter, he added, and Lizzie did most of the "demonstrative contention." She was haughty and domineering and of a "repellant disposition," and he had heard many bitter things she had said of her father.

He concluded his statement with a left-handed swipe at Lizzie. "I am positive," he added unctuously, "that Emma knows nothing of the murder."

For a man who wasn't allowed in the house while Andrew was alive and who was not even invited to the funeral when he died, his insight into family intimacies was extraordinary.

Q.   Do you know of anybody that was on bad terms with your stepmother?
A.   No sir.
Q.   Or that your stepmother was on bad terms with?
A.   No sir.

Q. Did *you* ever have any trouble with your stepmother?
A. No sir.
Q. Have you, within six months, had any words with her?
A. No sir.
Q. Within a year?
A. No sir.
Q. Within two years?
A. I think not.
Q. When last that you know of?
A. About five years ago.
Q. What about?
A. Her stepsister, half-sister.
Q. What name?
A. Her name now is Mrs. George W. Whitehead.

This, the prosecution would claim, was where it all began, the rumored dissension in Andrew's home, Lizzie and Emma's supposed hatred of their stepmother, and the awful prospect that she, not they, might become Andrew's heir.

Abby's stepsister Sarah had married George W. Whitehead, and it was neither a prosperous nor prospering union. They shared half a nondescript house with Abby's mother, Mrs. Gray. Mrs. Gray wanted to sell her half, but the few prospective buyers wanted the whole house or nothing. Fearing that her stepsister might find herself homeless in her declining years, Abby had importuned Andrew to buy the house.

To Andrew, $1500 was not a great sum and, since he had never done anything for Abby except marry her and thereby obtain a free housekeeper, he had arranged the purchase and put the house in Abby's name.

This was the genesis of the Abby-as-heir theory, if the prosecution was correct. Knowlton attempted to drive that point home:

Q. Then you have been on pleasant terms with your stepmother since then?
A. Yes sir.
Q. Cordial?
A. It depends on one's idea of cordiality, perhaps.

Q. According to *your* idea of cordiality?
A. Quite so.
Q. What do you mean by "quite so?"
A. Quite cordial. I do not mean the dearest friends in the world, but very kindly feelings and pleasant.
Q. You did not regard her as your mother?
A. Not exactly, no; although she came here when I was very young.
Q. Were your relations toward her that of daughter and mother?
A. In some ways it was and in some it was not.
Q. In what ways was it not?
A. I did not call her mother.

There it was again, the sentence that convinced Deputy Fleet that Lizzie was a murderer. Later, too late, she would say she meant no disrespect, that she was under the shock of the hour and had responded to relentless questioning by other police-men before Fleet. She did not say so, but it is probable that Fleet's belligerence had not encouraged amicable responses.

It seems the thought never came to anyone that, while a child at the age of four would have no hesitancy in calling the wife of her father "mother," an adult might without venom or hatred, prefer to call her by her Christian or married name.

It is equally odd that no one took exception to the fact that Emma, who was a child of 14 at the time of the marriage, not only would not call her "Mother," but would not even acknowl-edge that she was "Mrs. Borden." The only way Emma would ever address her was "Abby." In Victorian New England, such impudence from a child was unknown.

Q. What dress did you wear the day they were killed?
A. I had on a navy blue, sort of bengaline or India silk skirt with a navy blouse. In the afternoon, they thought I had better change it. I put on a pink wrapper.
Q. Did you change your clothing before the afternoon?
A. No sir.
Q. Where was your father when you came down on Thursday morning?
A. Sitting in the sitting room in his large chair.

Q. Where was your mother? Do you prefer me to call her Mrs.
    Borden?
A. I had as soon you called her mother. She was in the dining
    room with a feather duster dusting.
Q. Where was Maggie?
A. Just come in the backdoor with the long pole and brush
    and getting her pail of water. She was going to wash the
    windows around the house. She said Mrs. Borden wanted
    her to.
Q. Did you get your breakfast that morning?
A. I did not eat any breakfast. I did not feel as though I
    wanted any.
Q. What was the next thing that happened after you got
    down?
A. Maggie went out of doors to wash the windows and father
    came out into the kitchen and said he did not know
    whether he would go down to the post office or not. And
    then I sprinkled some handkerchiefs to iron.
Q. Did your father go downtown?
A. He went down later.
Q. How long a job was that—ironing the handkerchiefs?
A. I did not finish them. My flats were not hot enough.
Q. Where were you when he returned?
A. I was down in the kitchen.

It may be that her memory for this detail of where she was
when Andrew returned home was simply faulty, or it may be
that it was a vital part of some important deception. No one has
ever been able to say which, but Lizzie and Bridget disagreed in
their answers.

Under relentless questioning, Lizzie said, variously, that she
was in the kitchen, dining room, or upstairs. She settled finally
on the kitchen. Bridget's unshakeable remembrance was that
she was upstairs. She remembered because Andrew had trouble with the front door locks, and when Maggie had also fumbled opening them, she had exclaimed "Oh, pshaw!" or
perhaps a more pungent expletive, and she had heard Lizzie
laugh upstairs.

The significance of their differing remembrance is not
known, but, apparently, there was one.

Right now, however, Knowlton was intent on placing Lizzie upstairs at the time he would maintain that Abby had been murdered. Lizzie did not hesitate to say she had been upstairs.

Q. Did you go back to your room before your father returned?
A. I think I did carry up some clean clothes.
Q. Did you stay there?
A. No sir.
Q. Did you spend any time up the front stairs before your father returned?
A. No sir.
Q. Or after he returned?
A. No sir. I did stay in my room long enough when I went up to sew a little piece of tape on a garment.
Q. How long had you been there?
A. I had only been upstairs just long enough to take the clothes up and baste the little loop on the sleeve. I don't think I had been up there over five minutes.
Q. Had you any knowledge of Mrs. Borden going out of the house?
A. She told me she had had a note, somebody was sick, and said, "I am going to get the dinner on the way," and asked what I wanted for dinner.
Q. Did you tell her?
A. Yes, I told her I did not want anything.
Q. Did you hear her come back?
A. I did not hear her go or come back but I suppose she went.
Q. When you found your father dead you supposed your mother had gone?
A. I did not know. I said to the people who came in, "I don't know whether Mrs. Borden is out or in; I wish you would see if she is in her room."
Q. You supposed she was out at the time?
A. I understood so; I did not suppose anything about it.
Q. Did she tell you where she was going?
A. No sir.
Q. Did she tell you who the note was from?
A. No sir.
Q. Did you ever see the note?
A. No sir.

Q. Do you know where it is now?
A. No sir.
Q. She said she was going out that morning?
A. Yes sir.

With that question, the inquest was adjourned until 10 A.M. the following day.

The crowd outside shuffled and grumbled; they had expected an arrest and here was another delay. The reporters were equally disappointed and adjourned to the taprooms to come up with a rehash to send their editors.

By now, every major paper in every major city in New England and on the East Coast had at least one representative on the grounds, some accompanied by a photographer or artist. The only wire service, the Associated Press, had their man present, and some had come from as far away as New Orleans and San Francisco. They numbered at least a hundred. Word of the mystery had even reached London and the Continent.

The newspapers, like the people of Fall River, were divided into pro-Lizzie and anti-Lizzie camps. In Fall River, the *Globe* kept up its daily call for the arrest of Lizzie. The *Springfield Republican*, on the other hand, took a different view:

All through the investigation carried on by the Fall River police, a lack of ability has been shown seldom equalled, and causes they assign for connecting the daughter with the murder are on a par with their other exhibitions of lack of wisdom. Because someone, unknown to them and too smart for them to catch, butchered two people in the daytime on a principal street of the city, using brute force far in excess of that possessed by this girl, they conclude that there is probable reason to believe that she is the murderess. Because they found no one walking along the street with his hands and clothes reeking with blood, they conclude that it is probable, after swinging the axe with the precision of a butcher, she washed the blood from her hands and clothes.

Regardless, it was 5 P.M.; the inquest had shut down, and tomorrow was another day.

6

Locked Up!

R AIN! THANK THE LORD!
The August heat broke on the second day of the inquest. Instead of sweltering in humidity, the crowds of curious now carried umbrellas and wore Wellingtons. By 10:00 A.M. they had filled the square. They had expected the arrest of someone on Monday and had been practically guaranteed one on Tuesday. Now it was Wednesday. Surely it would come today.

At 10:05, Lizzie was reminded that she was still under oath and took the stand again.

Q. When you went out to the barn, where did you leave your father?

A. He had laid down on the sitting room lounge, taken off his shoes, and put on his slippers, and taken off his coat, and put on the reefer.

Reefers, double-breasted, sleeveless garments, were the less dressy equivalent of a smoking jacket. It is a commentary on

Andrew's rigid formality that even on the hottest day of the year, he donned his reefer rather than relax in shirtsleeved comfort in the privacy of his home.

Lizzie's statement that he had taken off his shoes and donned slippers is one of the anomalies of her testimony. When he died, Andrew was wearing black congress gaiters, ankle-top shoes with elastic gussets in the sides. Changing into slippers was perhaps what he normally did when he took his noon nap, and Lizzie may simply have assumed that was what he had done on this day. If there was a dark motive behind this misstatement, no one ever fathomed it. Knowlton ignored it and pressed on. He was far more interested in Lizzie's movements that morning, minute by minute.

Q. Whereabouts in the barn did you go?
A. Upstairs.
Q. How long did you remain there?
A. I don't know. Fifteen or 20 minutes.
Q. What doing?
A. Trying to find lead for a sinker.
Q. Can you give me any information how it happened at that particular time you should go into the chamber of the barn to find a sinker to go to Marion with to fish the next Monday?
A. I was going to finish my ironing. My flats were not hot. I said to myself, "I will go and try to find that sinker. Perhaps by the time I get back the flats will be hot." That is the only reason.
Q. Had you got a fish line?
A. Not here; we had some at the farm.
Q. Had you got a fish hook?
A. No sir.
Q. Had you got any apparatus for fishing at all?
A. Yes, over there.
Q. Had you any sinkers over there?
A. I think there were some. It is so long since I have been there. I think there were some.
Q. You had no reason to suppose you were lacking sinkers?
A. I don't think there were any on my lines.

Q. Where were your lines?

A. My fish lines were at the farm here.

Q. What made you think there were no sinkers at the farm on your lines?

A. Because some time ago when I was there I had none.

Q. How long since you used the fish lines?

A. Five years, perhaps.

Q. You left them at the farm then?

A. Yes sir.

Q. And you have not seen them since?

A. Yes sir.

And on and on and on. The questions concerning the sinkers, lines, and poles went on for over an hour. It must have seemed to the few allowed into the inquest that Knowlton was being paid by the question. What was the point in all this haggling over such a minor matter? After all, the purpose of the inquest was supposedly to look into the deaths of two prominent citizens, not to dawdle with fish hooks and sinkers.

But Knowlton was planting the seeds of a crop he hoped to harvest later before a jury. Lizzie's trip to the barn had to be trivialized and, if possible, discredited altogether. If he could convince a jury that she had fabricated the visit entirely, she would then be placed inside the house at the time Andrew was killed. Unlike Morse's alibi, Lizzie's was vulnerable to ridicule even if Knowlton could not actually disprove it.

For another hour he walked her through the events of the morning. The story she and Bridget had told a dozen times was repeated in minute-by-minute detail. Few questions were new. One was:

Q. Did you have an apron on Thursday?

A. Did I what?

Q. Have an apron on Thursday?

A. No sir, I don't think I did.

Q. Do you remember whether you did or not?

A. I don't remember sure, but I don't think I did.

Q. You had aprons, of course?
A. I had aprons, yes sir.
Q. Will you try and think whether you did or not?
A. I don't think I did.
Q. Will you try and remember?
A. I had no occasion for an apron on that morning.
Q. If you can remember, I wish you would.
A. I don't remember.
Q. That is all the answer you can give me about that?
A. Yes sir.

Nothing in that exchange to help. Knowlton then switched to the subject of axes and hatchets and how much Lizzie knew about either.

Q. Did you have any occasion to use the axe or hatchet?
A. No sir.
Q. Did you know where they were?
A. I knew there was an old axe down cellar; that is all I knew.
Q. Did you know anything about a hatchet down cellar?
A. No sir.
Q. Where was the old axe down cellar?
A. The last time I saw it it was stuck in the old chopping block.
Q. Was that the only axe or hatchet down cellar?
A. It was all I knew about.
Q. When was the last time you knew of it?
A. When our farmer came to chop wood.
Q. When was that?
A. I think a year ago last winter; I think there was so much wood on hand he did not come last winter.
Q. Do you know of anything that would occasion the use of an axe or hatchet?
A. No sir.
Q. Do you know of anything that would occasion the getting of blood on an axe or hatchet down cellar?
A. No sir.
Q. I do not say there was, but assuming an axe or hatchet was found down cellar with blood on it?
A. No sir.

Q. Do you know whether there was a hatchet down there before the murder?

A. I don't know.

Q. You are not able to say your father did not own a hatchet?

A. I don't know whether he did or not.

Q. Did you know there was found at the foot of the stairs a hatchet and axe?

A. No sir, I did not.

Q. Assume that is so, can you give me any explanation of how they came there?

A. No sir.

Q. Assume they had blood on them, can you give any occasion for there being blood on them?

A. No sir.

In courtroom jargon, this line of questioning is called a fishing expedition. The questions mean nothing in themselves, but they open up the opportunity for the witness to unwittingly reveal something that *could* be of interest. In this exchange, apparently neither side gained anything. Lizzie did not deny all knowledge of axes and hatchets, only a vagueness about how many and where they were.

In describing Andrew's return from downtown, she once again said he had taken off his congress boots. This time, she said she *saw* him do it. Since she obviously had not, it is strange that Knowlton made no effort to pin her down on this point. If, instead of making an honest mistake, she was deliberately lying, this would have been an excellent opportunity to catch her out. But, Knowlton passed over her description and it was not mentioned again.

Lizzie was recalled for the third time the following day, Thursday. Knowlton took up immediately the Bence testimony that she had gone to Smith's drugstore to purchase prussic acid the day before the murders.

Q. Your attention has already been called to the circumstance of going into the drugstore of Smith's, on the corner of Columbia and Main Streets, by some officer, has it not, on the day before the tragedy?

A. I don't know whether some officer has asked me, somebody has spoken of it to me. I don't know who it was.

Q. Did that take place?

A. It did not.

Q. Do you know where the drugstore is?

A. I don't.

Q. Did you go into any drugstore and inquire for prussic acid?

A. I did not.

Knowlton had now questioned Lizzie for a total of 12 hours. In his mind, as he would later put it, her testimony had been "a confession," a conclusion that was in for hard sledding. A few more questions and he would be through.

Q. Was the dress that was given to the officers the same dress that you wore that morning?

A. Yes sir.

Q. The India silk?

A. No, it is not an India silk. It is silk and linen. Some call it bengaline silk.

Q. Miss Borden, of course you appreciate the anxiety that everybody has to find the author of this tragedy, and the questions that I put to you have been in that direction. I now ask you if you can furnish any other fact, or give any other, even suspicion, that will assist the officers in any way in this matter?

A. About two weeks ago—

Q. Were you going to tell the occurrence about the man that called at the house?

A. No sir. It was after my sister went away. I came home from Miss Russell's one night and as I came up, I always glanced towards the side door as I came along by the carriage way, I saw a shadow on the side steps. I did not stop walking but I walked slower. Somebody ran down the steps, around the east end of the house. I thought it was a man because I saw no skirts and I was frightened, and of course I did not go around to see. I hurried to the front door as fast as I could and locked it.

During the three days she had been questioned, others had been called and quizzed: Bridget, Drs. Bowen and Dolan, Eli Bence, Adelaide Churchill, Emma, Harrington, Morse, and others. The crowds outside had never diminished; every arrival or departure of a carriage was the cause of sensation. It was now the seventh day since the murders.

When Knowlton had asked his last question and heard Lizzie's answer, he asked her to wait across the hall in the matron's room and not to leave the building.

A hurried conference was held in Hilliard's office down the hall. The warrant he had in his pocket was scrapped and a new one hastily written and dated so he could maintain that she was not under duress or jeopardy when she had been questioned. It is probable that he then regretted having lost his composure once during that interrogation, snapping at Lizzie, "You did not answer my question, and you will, if I have to put it to you all day." That would make it difficult to maintain that she had voluntarily testified.

With the new warrant signed by Judge Blaisdell, Knowlton and Hilliard left the courthouse, hailed a carriage, and set off for the residence of Attorney Jennings. They informed him that they were prepared to arrest her and asked if he would like to be present. He would.

The three returned to the courthouse and proceeded to the matron's quarters, where Lizzie was lying on a couch.

"I have here a warrant for your arrest," Hilliard told her, "issued by the judge of the District Court. I shall read it to you if you desire, but you have the right to waive the reading of it."

Jennings, tight-lipped, advised Lizzie, "Waive the reading."

"You need not read it," she told the marshal.*

---

*Typical of Porter's biased treatment of events is his description of this scene. On two consecutive pages, he wrote that "Upon the face of the prisoner there was a pallor . . . her eyes were moist with tears . . . " and she was "almost prostrated." He added, "She gave way to her feelings and sobbed as if her heart would break. Then she gave up to a violent fit of vomiting and the efforts to stop it were unavailing." In the very same paragraph, however, he wrote of her "unemotional nature" and said "she did not shed a tear." On the same page, he also noted that all during the "open, fair, and impartial" trial, she had been "defended by her chosen counsel." Actually, the trial had been *closed* and her counsel *barred* from the courtroom.

The warrant for her arrest made no reference to the murder of Abby; she was accused only of murdering Andrew.

The word flashed in an instant to the mob packed in front of the courthouse. Each time the doors opened, they surged forward and were pushed back by the police. Emma was the first to appear, suffering intensely, it was said, but Lizzie was not allowed to leave. She was searched by the matron and held.

There was no suitable jail cell in which to place her, so sheets and covering were hastily procured, and she was left alone in the matron's quarters—with the door firmly locked.

The news was flashed around the world by telegraph, and the *Globe* printed the triumphant headline:

LOCKED UP
LIZZIE BORDEN AT LAST IN CUSTODY

7

A Square of Seven and One-Half Feet

A T 9:15 THE NEXT MORNING, Friday, the twelfth, a hack pulled up at the side door of the courthouse. Emma and John Morse alighted and went up the stairs. The Reverend Buck was already in attendance with Lizzie in the matron's quarters.

At 9:30, Attorney Jennings entered the courtroom, asked for a sheet of paper, and sat, writing furiously.

Lizzie entered at 9:45, dressed as she had been the day before, in a dark blue suit and a pert black hat with a tiny spray of red flowers on the front. Emma had brought her a small valise of fresh clothing, but there had not been time to change that morning.

Jennings rose and addressed the court:

"Your Honor, before the prisoner pleads, she wishes to present the following:

Bristol ss. Second District Court. Commonwealth vs. Lizzie A. Borden. Complaint for homicide. Defendant's plea.

And now comes the defendant in the above entitled complaint and before pleading thereto says that the Honorable Josiah C. Blaisdell, the presiding justice of the second district court of Bristol, before which the complaint is returnable, has been and believes is still engaged as the presiding magistrate at an inquest upon the death of said Andrew J. Borden, the person whom it is alleged in said complaint the defendant killed, and has received and heard and is still engaged in receiving and hearing evidence in relation to said killing and to said defendant's connection therewith which is not and has not been allowed to hear or know the report of, whereof she says that said Honorable Josiah C. Blaisdell is disqualified to hear this complaint, and she objects to his so doing, and all of this she is ready to verify.

But before Jennings could argue his motion, the warrant had to be read and Lizzie's plea entered. The warrant was a linguistic nightmare of "saids" and "aforesaids."

Commonwealth of Massachusetts, To Augustus B. Leonard, clerk of the second district court of Bristol, in the county Bristol, and Justice of the Peace:

Rufus B. Hilliard, city marshal of Fall River, in said county, in behalf of said Commonwealth, on oath, complains that Lizzie A. Borden of Fall River, in the county of Bristol, at Fall River, aforesaid, in the county aforesaid, on the fourth day of August, in the year of our Lord 1892, in and upon one Andrew J. Borden, feloniously, willfully and of her malice aforethought, did make assault and that the said Lizzie A. Borden, then and there with a certain weapon, to wit, a hatchet, in and upon the head of the said Andrew J. Borden, then and there feloniously, willfully and of her malice aforethought, did strike, giving unto the said Andrew J. Borden, then and there, with the hatchet aforesaid, by the stroke aforesaid, in manner aforesaid, in and upon the head of the said Andrew J. Borden, one mortal wound, of which said mortal wound the said Andrew J. Borden then and there instantly died. And so the complainant aforesaid, upon his oath aforesaid, further complains and says that the said Lizzie A. Borden, the said Andrew J. Borden in manner and form aforesaid, then and there feloniously, willfully and of her malice aforethought did kill and murder.

It was signed by Marshal R. B. Hilliard.

"The prisoner must plead in person," said Judge Blaisdell. In response to the clerk's question as to how she pled, Lizzie stood and replied:

"Not guilty."

The clerk, apparently unsure what she had said, asked the question again. This time, Lizzie spoke louder, accenting the word *not*.

The formalities over, Jennings rose to argue his motion that Judge Blaisdell should recuse himself. It was the kind of motion lawyers customarily make, doubting they will prevail. He would be arguing a point of equity, that it was palpably unfair to a defendant to face the same judge at arraignment who was still presiding over the "inquest" that sent her there, and where counsel was prohibited to represent her.

He pressed his view by pointing out, "Your Honor sits here to hear this case, which is returnable before you, when you have already been sitting on the case in another capacity. By all the laws of human nature, you cannot help being prejudiced from the character of the evidence which has been submitted to you. The Constitution does not allow a judge to sit in such a double capacity, and it guarantees a defendant from a prejudiced hearing."

The position argued equity, not law, and Knowlton pointed this out. He knew of more than 20 cases that had been handled in this same manner and, he said, "It is your Honor's duty to hear this complaint."

Judge Blaisdell agreed. "The statutes make it my imperative duty to hold an inquest," he said, "and upon the testimony introduced at that hearing, to direct the issuance of warrants."

"Then," Jennings said, "we are ready for trial."

The audacity of proposing an immediate trial caught Knowlton off guard, and he moved for a continuance.

"We are anxious to proceed at once," Jennings said. "We ask for a trial at the earliest possible moment."

Again, Knowlton pleaded that he was not ready, and an agreement was reached setting August 22nd as the day for the preliminary hearing. Since murder was not a bailable offense, Judge Blaisdell remanded Lizzie to the county jail in Taunton.

Court Square was in a frenzy as the proceedings of the morning broke up. Word spread at once that Lizzie would be taken to Taunton on the 3:40 train, and the crowd was divided as to which would give the better coign of vantage, the square or the railroad station. They were evenly divided.

At 3:20, the prisoner appeared at the side door, accompanied by the Reverend Buck, Marshal Hilliard, and State Officer Seaver. Clerk Leonard handed up her small valise of clothing and the carriage moved off.

It was a straight run from the courthouse to the station, and the route was lined as for a coronation. Most of the crowd, however, was destined to disappointment as the hack took a circuitous route of side streets. A squad of police pushed back the crowd that was on the platform waiting for the train, which was already ten minutes late. Lizzie waited in the carriage with the Reverend Buck until the "all aboard" call was given.

Dressed in her favorite color, blue, and with her face partially hidden by a matching veil, she alighted and entered the last coach supported by the marshal and the Reverend Buck. The blinds were drawn and the train pulled away.

It was a run of less than 30 minutes to Taunton, where another mob waited.

The matron of the county jail was the wife of the sheriff Andrew J. Wright, who had been Hilliard's predecessor as marshal of Fall River. As a child, Lizzie had played in their yard with their daughter, Isabel. Her welcome to the now-famous prisoner was cordial but strained.

Lizzie was taken at once to the cell that would be her home for the next ten months, a square of seven-and-one-half feet. The furniture: a chair, a bed, and a washbowl.

It is safe to say that during those ten months, every reporter and artist assigned to the case clamored to interview the prisoner. All were refused save one, a Mrs. McGuirk, with whom Lizzie had served in charitable causes in Fall River. Her interview was published in the *New York Recorder* on September 20:

"I know I am innocent and I have made up my mind that, no matter what happens, I will try to bear it bravely and make the best of it."

The speaker was a woman. The words came slowly, and her eyes filled with tears that did not fall before they were wiped away. The woman was Lizzie Borden, who had been accused of the murder of her father, and personally has been made to appear in the eyes of the public as a monster, lacking in respect for the law, and stolid in her demeanor to such an extent that she never showed emotion at any stage of the tragedy, inquest or trial, and, as far as the government would allow they knew, had never shown any womanly or human emotion of any sort since the public first crossed the threshold of the Borden house.

I was anxious to see if this girl, with whom I was associated several years ago in the work of the Fall River Fruit and Flower Mission, had changed her character and become a monster since the days when she used to load up the plates of vigorous young newsboys and poor children at the annual turkey dinner provided during the holidays for them and take delight in their healthy appetites.

I sought her in the Taunton jail and found her unchanged, except that she showed traces of the great trial she has just been through. Her face was thinner, her mouth had a patient look, as if she had been schooling herself to expect and to bear any treatment, however unpleasant, and her eyes were red from the long nights of weeping. A dark shade now protects them from the glaring white light reflected from the walls of her cell.

"How do you get along here, Miss Borden?" I asked.

"To tell the truth, I am afraid it is beginning to tell on my health. This lack of fresh air and exercise is hard for me. I have always been out of doors a great deal, and that makes it harder. I cannot sleep nights now, and nothing they give me will produce sleep. If it were not for my friends, I should break down, but as long as they stand by me I can bear it. They have been, with few exceptions, true to me all through it, and I appreciate it. If they had not, I don't know how I could have gone through it all. I certainly should have broken down. Some things have been very unpleasant, but while everyone has been so kind to me I ought not to think of those. Marshal Hilliard has been very gentlemanly and kind to me in every way possible.

"The hardest thing for me to stand here is the night, when there is no light. They will not allow me to have a candle to read by, and to sit in the dark all the evening is very hard; but I do not want any favors that are against the rules. Mr. Wright and his wife are very kind to me and try to make it easier to bear, but of course, they must do their duty.

"There is one thing which hurts me very much. They say I don't show any grief. Certainly I don't in public. I never did reveal my feelings and I cannot change my nature now. They say I don't cry. They should see me when I am alone, or sometimes with my friends. It hurts me to think people say so about me. I have tried very hard to be brave and womanly through it all. . . .

"It is a little thing, I suppose, but it hurt me when they said I was not willing to have my room searched. Why, I had seen so many different men that day and had been questioned about everything till my head was confused and in such a whirl that I could not think. I was lying down and Dr. Bowen was just preparing some medicine for me when a man came to my room and began to question me. I knew he was a policeman because he had brass buttons on his clothes. I asked the doctor:

'Must I see all these people now? It seems as if I cannot think a moment longer, my head pains me so.'

He went out. When he returned he said I must see them, and then the policeman came back with another man. They spoke about my mother, and that was the time I said, 'She is not my mother, but my stepmother.' I supposed, if it was necessary that I must talk to them just then, I must tell as near as I could what was right. . . .

"If people would only do me justice, that is all I ask, but it seems as if every word I have uttered has been distorted and such a false construction placed on it that I am bewildered. I can't understand it."

There was not a trace of anger in her tones—simply a pitiful expression. She recovered herself with an effort and we said "goodbye."

For the first time in print, a different Lizzie had been shown, not at all what the *Globe* had told their subscribers she was, and they hit back the next day:

The flap-doodle, gush, idiotic drivel, misrepresentations, and in some instances, anarchic nonsense, which is being promulgated by women newspaper correspondents, WCTU conventions, and other female agencies in connection with the Borden murder just now, may originate in good intentions but do not strengthen Lizzie Borden's case much in the opinion of the public. The Commonwealth of Massachusetts will, for the present, adhere to the forms of law in conducting cases, regardless of the clamor or criticism of any petticoat propaganda.

Linked with this choleric attack against women in general, the *Globe* (probably Edwin H. Porter), in the same edition, manufactured and printed as fact a story alleging that Lizzie had, six months before the murders, consulted a Providence attorney with questions about property disposal in case of a death. The next day, police denied all knowledge of any such contact.

Reporters from other papers canvassed every attorney in Providence and found that none of them had been contacted. The more honest papers branded the story as false and the *Globe* never mentioned it again.

So much for flap-doodle and misrepresentations.

The ubiquitous Judge Blaisdell, who had presided at the inquest and the arraignment, was to sit as well at the preliminary hearing on Monday, August 22. Just as she had gone to the Taunton jail, wearing blue and escorted by the Reverend Buck and Marshal Hilliard, Lizzie returned, wearing the same dress and with the same escorts. She arrived on the 11:00 train, and by noon the crowds had reassembled before the courthouse. Again, they were due for disappointment. Again, Knowlton told Blaisdell the Commonwealth was not prepared and asked for three more days. Attorney Jennings raised no objection and the postponement was granted.

Lizzie was put in the charge of Matron Reagan and remained in Fall River for the three days.

The preliminary hearing lasted six days, and 23 persons testified. It was a dress rehearsal for the trial in superior court. Since the prosecution's case was duplicated at the trial, it will be treated, along with the defense, in the following chapters.

At the conclusion of the testimony, both Jennings and Knowlton argued their viewpoints with great intensity. Jennings was first:

"I must say I close this case with feelings entirely different from those I have ever experienced at the conclusion of any case. This man was not merely my client, he was my friend. I had known him from boyhood days, and if three short weeks ago anyone had told me that I should stand here defending his youngest daughter from the charge of murdering him, I should have pronounced it beyond the realm of human credibility. . . .

"I suggest that even the learned district attorney himself cannot imagine that any person could have committed that crime unless his heart was as black with hatred as hell itself."

(Porter, who had stated repeatedly that Lizzie had shown no emotion of any kind since the hour of the murders, acknowledged in his book that at this point Lizzie's tears flowed freely and her form was convulsed. In a later paragraph, however, he reverted to form and said she showed no emotion.)

Jennings attacked the prosecution's failure to show motive or means in their presentation.

It was almost impossible, he said, "for a person to commit these crimes without being almost covered with blood, from the waist upward in the case of Mr. Borden, and from the feet upward in the case of Mrs. Borden."

The police, he said, developed a theory that the murders had been committed by someone in the house and set about "proving" it. The "inquisition" of Lizzie had been an outrage.

"Here was a girl they had been suspecting for days. She was virtually under arrest and yet, for the purpose of extracting a confession from her to support their theory, they brought her here and put her on the rack, a thing they knew they would have no right to do if they placed her under arrest.

"Day after day the same questions were repeated to her in the hope to elicit some information that would criminate her. Is it a wonder," he asked, "there are conflicting statements?"

"They haven't proved that this girl had anything to do with the murder. They can't find any blood on her dress, on her hair, on her shoes. They can't find any motive. They can't find the axes and so I say I demand the woman's release."

"Don't," he begged, "put the stigma of guilt upon this woman, reared as she has been and with a past character beyond reproach. Don't let it go out in the world as the decision of a just judge that she is probably guilty."

As Jennings sat down, there was a moment of silence, then a ripple of applause that swelled to a crescendo. No effort was made to silence it. Tears filled the eyes of the spectators. Lizzie openly wept and court adjourned.

Knowlton must have been thankful for the two-hour recess. There was time for the passion of Jenning's argument to subside. He opened by agreeing with Jennings that, "The crime of murder touches the deepest sensibilities of feeling. There is the deepest feeling of horror about it, and above all, in the unnaturalness that brings the thrill of horror to every mind."

Of the parricide, he said, "There was not a man, woman, or child in the world of whom we could not have said, they would have done it. But it was done. There is no motive for murder," he admitted. "There is *reason* for it, but no motive."

As to why the police had directed their inquiries toward Lizzie, it was simply because she was the one who benefitted by the deaths. They had found, he said, the only person in the world with whom Abby was not in accord.

Since Jennings had chastised the police for not looking more diligently for the murderer outside the home, Knowlton vigorously protested that they had done that; that they had followed every lead no matter where it went, every rumor, no matter how inconsequential it seemed.

He had not alluded to the demeanor of the defendant, he said, and would not do so now. But he promptly did, in his very next sentence:

"While everybody is dazed, there is but one person who, throughout the whole business, has not been seen to express emotion," and he was relieved that, "these facts do not point to a woman who expressed any feminine feeling."

This, despite the fact that her sensitivity to the events that had brought her to this point had been demonstrated over and over.

"We are constrained to find that she has been dealing in poisonous things," he concluded, "that her story is absurd and that hers and hers alone has been the opportunity for the commission of the crime." And, to take the edge off the applause that had greeted Jennings's remarks, he added:

"Yielding to clamor is not to be compared to that only and greatest satisfaction, that of a duty well done."

There was no applause when he sat down; only deathly silence. Judge Blaisdell then ended the proceedings.

"The long examination is concluded and there remains but for the magistrate to perform what he believes to be his duty," he said. "It would be a pleasure for him, and he would doubtless receive much sympathy if he could say, 'Lizzie, I judge you probably not guilty. You may go home.' But upon the character of the evidence presented through the witnesses who have been so closely and thoroughly examined, there is but one thing to be done—painful as it may be. The judgment of the court is that you are probably guilty and you are ordered committed to await the action of the superior court."

Judge Blaisdell was later to say that he was satisfied the government had not produced enough evidence to warrant a conviction, nor perhaps the finding of an indictment, but he felt satisfied that enough had been shown to warrant holding the defendant for the grand jury, which could consider the entire case against her and report on the evidence.

Lizzie stood and listened to the clerk read the decision ordering her back to the Taunton jail to await the action of the grand jury scheduled to meet on November 7.

On November 15, the grand jury took up the charges against Lizzie. In the two months between the preliminary hearing and the grand jury session, Knowlton had been in daily contact with Attorney General Pillsbury. There were meetings, telephone calls, and letters dealing with every facet of the case. The private conversations cannot be known, but it is apparent from the letters that were preserved that Knowlton had no confidence in the Commonwealth's case and was debating with the attorney general over some method by which they would be justified in not taking it to the grand jury. Reluctantly, they concluded that the preliminary hearing decision precluded that avenue.

The grand jury took up the charges against Lizzie on November 15 and listened to the Commonwealth's case as outlined by an unenthusiastic Knowlton. Pillsbury had written:

"I still favor holding back all that can be prudently held back especially as I now think that what you have absolutely determined to put in will make the case as strong to the public as if everything went in." It was bad advice. The grand jury adjourned six days later without taking any action.

In the meantime, Lizzie's and Emma's former friend, Alice Russell, had wrestled with her conscience and come to the conclusion that Lizzie was guilty of the murders. She met with Knowlton and agreed to be a witness for the prosecution. In a flurry of activity, Knowlton called the jury into session again and presented for the first time the story of the dress-burning Miss Russell had witnessed. Whatever else he may have told the jury is not known, but on December 1, they voted 20 to 1 to return three indictments, one for the murder of Andrew, another for the murder of Abby, and a third charging her with the murder of both. They had deliberated for ten minutes.

Pillsbury wrote Knowlton a letter of congratulations for his work on "this accursed case."

Lizzie was returned at once to the Taunton jail, and Jennings renewed his plea to Pillsbury that she be allowed to furnish bail; that there was no threat she might flee the country.

Pillsbury dismissed the request and wrote Knowlton: "Jennings spent the afternoon with me Friday on the question of bail, but I think I have quieted him."

To the president of the Women's Christian Temperance Union, he sent off a waspish response to her similar plea for bail:

"I have received your request to have Lizzie A. Borden admitted to bail with full appreciation of your feelings and of all the suggestions which you make in support of the request, all of which, however, with many other circumstances, have already been carefully considered. I cannot properly make any further reply than to ask that you give the prosecuting officers credit for some knowledge of the circumstances of the case, and of their own duty; and that you will extend to them the consideration which is due to public servants who are trying faithfully and conscientiously to discharge their duty without fear or favor."

As the months ground on and no date was set for Lizzie's trial, Jennings repeatedly wrote Pillsbury asking that it be done. The best he received was a curt "I am not at present able to give you any information upon the subject."

In December, Jennings asked if the trial could be set in Taunton, where Lizzie was being held.

"She is very urgent in this desire, and I trust it can be brought about without seriously interfering with the arrangements of the government."

Pillsbury's one-sentence response was, "I don't suppose anybody on the part of the government has so much as thought about it and of course it will be for the court to determine."

Finally, on May 8, 1893, six months after the grand jury vote, Lizzie was taken to New Bedford and arraigned before Judge J. W. Hammond of the superior court. She pleaded "not guilty" to each of the three indictments, and her trial was set for the fifth day of June—in New Bedford.

By now, no one could be found in Fall River who was not totally convinced either of the guilt or of the innocence of Lizzie

Borden. The murders and her indictment were dinner conversation nationwide.

Murder has ever been a subject of great mystique. It is not the death that attracts and hypnotizes, for death is a commonplace occurrence. It is the sheer *audacity* of murder; the *taking* of a life; the supreme crime. A chilling fillip is added when there is a grotesquery to ponder and when there is no solution advanced that cannot be struck down by advancing still another solution.

The Borden murders did not involve sordid criminal offenders, drunks, or street brawlers. Murders in that element were frequent and only to be expected. Had Andrew and Abby been murdered by a vagrant or a man Andrew had victimized by his penury, the case would have passed from public concern in a matter of weeks. Though they were pillars of Fall River, the Bordens were unknown outside the city limits. What kept interest fever-hot was the conflict between the two competing convictions: Lizzie *must* have done it—yet *couldn't* have done it.

The public had six months in which to compare notes with their neighbors, perfect their theories, and rail against or praise the officials in charge of the case.

But Knowlton and Pillsbury, the two authorities who were left with the case now that the police had unearthed all the evidence they could, realized that they were enmeshed in a trap; that it was highly doubtful they could convict their prisoner.

Knowlton approached Pillsbury with an idea that might get them off the hook: suppose Lizzie could be examined by outstanding medical authorities and found to be insane! Jennings could then plead her *non compos mentis* and the Commonwealth could plea bargain with her and avoid a trial. Pillsbury agreed, and Knowlton and Hilliard dispatched officers throughout the city to see if anyone could be found who would say they had thought the Bordens were crazy. District policeman Moulton Batchelder reported back to Knowlton with his findings:

Captain James C. Stafford of New Bedford said he knew Lizzie's mother well and she was a peculiar person but he had never heard of any of the Bordens or Morses being insane.

A Mrs. Holland said the same, though she had always thought they were peculiar.

Abraham G. Hart of the Fall River Savings Bank said he didn't know much about Lizzie but didn't think either the Bordens or the Morses were insane.

Southard H. Miller, longtime friend of Andrew, who had commented to a newspaperman on the day of the murders, told of his lifetime friendship with the family and his opinion that, though somewhat peculiar, none of them was insane.

Rescome Case said he had never heard that any one of them was insane, but he thought some of them were worse than insane!

John S. Brayton knew of no streak of insanity, and neither did Mrs. William Almy, widow of one of Andrew's former partners. David Sewall Brigham, ex-city marshal of Fall River, didn't know of insanity in the family but offered the comment that Lizzie had a bad disposition.

George A. Patty went further: "Lizzie is known to be ugly," he said, and Mrs. George Whitehead agreed.

On his own, Pillsbury attempted to enlist the help of Dr. George F. Jelly, a Boston psychiatrist, and Dr. Edward Cowles of the McLean Asylum in Somerville, Massachusetts. Dr. Jelly wrote a two-sentence turndown:

"I have received your letter of today. I do not think that the indications of insanity which you mention, are sufficiently strong or tangible enough to enable me to express any opinion."

Dr. Cowles's response was equally as negative:

"I will say that my inferences are *against* a theory of insanity in the person charged with the crime, from anything I have so far read concerning her conduct before or after the event."

Knowlton reported his meager findings to Pillsbury. Undaunted by all the negative reports, they invited Jennings to Pillsbury's office in Boston to see if he could be talked into a sanity examination. Pillsbury wrote Knowlton:

"Jennings was here today, evidently indisposed to consent at first, but more inclined before he left, I think. He went away saying that he must see Adams and that he would let us hear from him as soon as possible."

Jennings did not fall into the trap. He wrote Pillsbury the next day:

"Since my talk with you, I have been seriously considering your proposition and have come to the conclusion that I cannot consent to unite with you in the examination proposed. I asked Adams's opinion on the advisability of the course proposed, without expressing any opinion of my own, and also on my return hence, that of Mr. Holmes who, to a certain extent, represents the Borden girls, without informing him that I had consulted Adams. Both came to the same conclusion: that, in view of all the circumstances, we could not do anything which suggested a doubt about her innocence and that the course proposed would not be wise or expedient on our part."

Jennings: 1; Knowlton and Pillsbury: 0.

In December, Pillsbury became ill and was confined, first in the hospital and later, at home. He wrote Knowlton that, in all probability, he would be unable to direct the trial against Lizzie in June. In Massachusetts, the attorney general was charged to lead the team of prosecutors in cases of such magnitude as this one, and Pillsbury's illness was depressing news.

Knowlton, in a letter dated April 24, wrote of his despair:

"Personally, I would like very much to get rid of the trial of the case and fear that my own feelings in that direction may have influenced my better judgment. I feel this all the more upon your not unexpected announcement that the burden of the trial would come upon me."

We have no way of knowing what they had discussed when they repeatedly reviewed the case, but it is apparent from Knowlton's letter that it was his opinion they should have quashed the indictment, but he feared the uproar from the public and was opting to pass the buck to a jury.

"I confess, however, I cannot see my way clear to any disposition of the case other than a trial. Should it result in disagreement of the jury, there should be no difficulty in disposing of the case by admitting the defendant to bail; but a verdict either way would render such a course unnecessary. The case has proceeded so far and an indictment has been found by the grand inquest [read *grand jury*] of the county, that it does not seem to me that we ought to take the responsibility of discharging her without trial, *even though there is every reasonable expectation of a verdict of not guilty.*"

The italics are the author's, to emphasize the callous admission that they had no compunction about stigmatizing Lizzie forever by bringing her to trial even though they had every reasonable expectation of acquittal. This was what the Reverend Jubb had prayed they would not do in his sermon after the murders, and what Jennings had pleaded Judge Blaisdell not do when he addressed the court at the preliminary hearing.

"I am unable to concur fully in your views as to the probable result. I think that it may well be that the jury might disagree upon the case. But even in my most sanguine moments, I have scarcely expected a verdict of guilty. The situation is this: nothing has developed which satisfies either of us that she is innocent, neither of us can escape the conclusion that she must have had some knowledge of the occurrence."

In short, although they can't prove Lizzie is guilty, she can't prove she is innocent, therefore she should be brought to trial— an incredible interpretation of the assumption of innocence. Even Knowlton, at this point, does not accuse her of the murders, only that she "had some knowledge" of the occurrence. Nor does he now accept any of the responsibility for the grand jury's indictment. Reaffirming his reluctance in presenting the case to them, he continued:

"She has been presented for a trial by a jury which, to say the least, was not influenced by anything said by the government in the favor of the indictment.

"Without discussing the matter more fully in this letter, I will only say as above indicated that I cannot see how any other course than setting the case down for trial, and trying it, will satisfy that portion of the public sentiment, whether favorable to her or not, which is worthy of being respected.

"June seems to be the most satisfactory month, all things considered. I will write more fully as to the admission of her confession after I have looked the matter up."

What Knowlton was referring to when he wrote of her "confession" cannot be fathomed. Certainly, Lizzie had not confessed to anything. It could have been a typographical error or an error in dictation. If it was a reference to her testimony at the inquest, that was anything but a confession.

Had a copy of this remarkable letter fallen into Attorney Jennings's hands, there would never have been a Lizzie Borden trial—or, if one was unavoidable, it would not have lasted longer than it would have taken him to read it to the jury. It is an unprecedented look behind the scenes at what can only be called reprehensible tactics by the Commonwealth.

But, there *was* a Lizzie Borden trial, and it was set for June 5 in New Bedford.

8

Confessions, Cranks, and Trickey Business

B Y NOW THERE HAD BEEN A FULL MOON in Massachusetts, and the avalanche of confessions and crank letters piling up on District Attorney Knowlton's desk threatened to swamp him. On the very top was this one just in from Boston:

"You are fooling your time away," it said, "trying to place the deed of the Borden family upon the young lady Miss Lizzie Borden as I can satisfy you if you could only get hold of me that she is not guilty.

"No power will ever hang me for the deed for I shall blow my brains out. But, before I do, I shall clear Miss Borden in some way without showing the Fall River police that they are in any way smart. I had a motive and swore that I should kill the Bordens and kill I have, but I hope no innocent person will suffer for my crime. I could tell you all the particulars if I could have my revolver at my head to not give you a chance to hang me. I slept in the barn the night before. After the deed, I jumped the fence, flew down to the pond [?] and washed my face and hands. The police will find my coat and pants buried [?] about ten feet out in the pond, and my old black slouch hat, all covered with three large stones. . . . "

From Albany, New York, came another "confession," even more bizarre:

"The killing of old man Bordon [sic] and his wife was not perpetrated by any member of his family as is generally supposed. But they were put out of the way by an illegitimate son whom Bordon refused to recognize after the mother of his offspring died a number of years ago in a certain Massachusetts insane asylum of a broken heart.

"That son is now 25 years of age. He was not known to any member of the family save the old man and woman."

The letter went on to say that the writer was that illegitimate son, and that Andrew had been bribed into paying him each year for the past 25 years and was supposed to have made a final payment of $5,000 but had reneged. Whereupon the writer had killed Andrew and Abby with a lather's hatchet, which he had then dropped overboard from a Fall River steamer.

"No use to track for me," the letter concluded, "for it will be an utter impossibility to do so. At the hour this letter is mailed, I shall take a train for hundreds of miles away."

For which ending, it can be imagined, Knowlton was truly thankful. Marshal Hilliard received a similar letter and wrote Knowlton that it was strange the illegitimate son hadn't known how to spell the Borden name. He had spelled it "Bordon" throughout.

A lad of 16, named Alfred A. Smith, wrote from the Massachusetts Reformatory, where he was serving a term for breaking and entering and larceny, to say that he had been passing the Borden home on the morning of the murders and had seen a woman looking out an upstairs window and she had hastily backed away at sight of him. He had passed back up the street some time later and the same thing happened again. On a third trip, he had found a hatchet and a pair of bloodstained gloves just inside the fence. He had sold the hatchet for ten cents and had thrown away one of the gloves, but he thought the other one was home in a bureau drawer. Needless to add, it wasn't. Spiritualists had been in touch also. One wrote from Lynn, Massachusetts, to say she was in communication with the dead and had been told there was a closet at the end of the "sopha" where Andrew had lain (there wasn't) and that a man had been secreted there until the opportunity to murder. The weapon was a broad blade claw hammer and he had "thrown it in the cellar."

Another seer wrote from Boston to say that in a vision she had seen the bloodstained "effects" of the Bordens hidden under the floor in a lower room covered by a carpet. Her visions, the writer assured Knowlton, were "inspirational," and he would do well to give them a trial.

In the file marked "cranks" were a number of letters from a correspondent calling himself "Justice." He alternately berated the police, who " . . . deserve knocking on the head for their stupidity," and advised Knowlton how the investigation should be conducted:

1. Dr. Bowen should be taken by the neck and flung into a cell. [Reason not given.]
2. Had he considered that Lizzie had dressed as a man while committing the murders so her clothes would show no bloodstains and her escape would go unnoticed?
3. The murderer had secreted himself under a bed.
4. The murder weapon was buried in the garden among the flowers and vegetables.

And on and on.

A Toledo, Ohio, dentist knew the murderer had chloroformed the victims before murdering them. A former warden of the New York Pasematta Convict Prison advised that he knew Lizzie had worn a dress or wrap and used gloves that would "take but a moment to destroy." More than a dozen people wrote that the murder weapon was not an axe but the flatiron Lizzie had used to iron her handkerchiefs. Letters came by the dozen advising Knowlton to look for the missing weapon in the well, in the stove flue, in the piano, under the floor, in the walls, in the oven, and every other conceivable place already searched.

Wasn't there an old-fashioned privy where the weapon could be "deposited," a Dedham, Massachusetts, writer wanted to know. There wasn't. From Brooklyn, New York, came a letter saying the solution to it all could be found in Albert P. Southwick's new novel, *The Catherwood Mystery*. (It was signed with the initial *S*). The same writer advised, too, to look in the chimney.

The owner of a Ouija board penned an eight-page conversation he had had with the board in which every question had been clearly answered.

Religion and racism were prominently mentioned in correspondence to Knowlton.

"Your chances will not be hurt for the attorney generalship," one letter said, "by doing your duty, even if it does hang an Irishman." And "Beware of Jesuits," warned a Brattleboro, Vermont, writer. This was, he assured Knowlton, the opinion of most of the New England states.

Many wrote to congratulate the police on the job they had done. At least half thought Knowlton and Hilliard were heroes, but one postal card signed "Voter" said one thing was certain, Knowlton would never be district attorney again. "The people of Bristol county will tend to that next November after the mean, underhanded part you have taken in the Borden case."

For every crank letter Knowlton received, Marshal Hilliard could count three.

Within a week, "confessions" had come from Minneapolis ("I killed them for sixty dollars!"); Boston ("I did it! I said I would and I did!"); New York ("I killed Mrs. Borden first and waited several days to get a chance at the old man's money."); Circleville, Ohio ("I myself done the deed with an Indian tomyhawk!"); Chicago ("I taken them by my own hand. Spair the fair maiden!"); Rochester, New York ("I can if necessary furnish proof although I die on the gallows—although I much prefer the mode of execution in vogue in this state, that of electrocution."); Chicago ("I took the revenge for a harm done to me nearly hav a score of years ago by that old perjurer and outrager!"); and Springfield, Massachusetts ("Catch me if you can, old boy! I am too sharp for you!").

A writer from Brockton, Massachusetts, said he had not done it but he knew who did. Just write him and he would tell all.

Letter unsigned. A writer from Providence, Rhode Island, would, for $85,000, "place in your hands the circumstances and actors in this fearful drama." Far cheaper was the offer from Mrs. S. A. Douglas of River Point, Rhode Island, who described herself as "a person born with the qualifications of a detective." She would come to Fall River and obtain a confession for eight or ten dollars a day.

Bridget was the villain, wrote "A Friend." "True Americans will learn in time never to employ a catholic!" Newport, Rhode Island, agreed: "I have seen enough of Roman Catterlicks to believe they can do poisonous, murdersome deeds against Protestants." A New Yorker wrote that the "Portugee" they were looking for was Mr. C. Norlander, a Swedish newspaperman living around the corner on Third Avenue.

Hilliard's crank collection included letters urging him to blame "The Anarchists," just on general principles, or a "secret alien order" the writer knew about. Another wrote from New York that Lizzie had contacted him some years ago, offering a large sum of money if Andrew and Abby could be electrocuted.

Three writers said the solution was simple. All Hilliard had to do was to look in the eyes of Andrew and Abby. Everyone knew that the last image seen before death was frozen on the victim's retina!

If none of these confessions and suggestions worked, he could enlist the help of an astrologer who only needed to know the birth dates of Andrew, Abby, and Lizzie to determine if the planet Saturn had been on a spot in the heavens occupied by the sun or the moon at the time of the murders.

Mrs. Alexander of Rochester, New York, wrote to say she "had the charm" and could make Andrew and Abby say who had murdered them! Mr. M. T. Richardson, publisher of the *Boots and Shoes Weekly*, was a competent phrenologist and only needed a good photograph of Lizzie's head to determine if she would tend to murder under favorable conditions. So could a writer from Boston, and so could Theo VanWyck of Mount Vernon, New York, if he had a photograph of Lizzie's hand, for he was an expert at palmistry.

If all else failed, wrote John S. Adams of Boston, just look for a man named Dominick Flynn and "keep a red eye on him."

But the zany highlight of the Borden case did not come from the flood of crank letters and confessions that any major crime generates. It was provided by *The Boston Globe*, the largest newspaper in New England. Their star crime reporter, aptly named Henry Trickey, had been on the scene from the day after the murders.

This was the twentieth anniversary of *The Boston Globe*. Just a month before the trial it had printed a special edition commemorating the date, and it had contained an unprecedented 183 columns of advertising, exulting in its position of having the largest circulation in all New England.

Working for a Massachusetts paper rather than an out-of-state one gave Trickey an inside track with the police, none of whom were publicity-shy. He was particularly tight with officers Medley and Mullaly, Assistant Marshal Fleet, and a private investigator with questionable credentials, E. D. McHenry. McHenry was probably hired by the Fall River police in some capacity, but after what became known as The Trickey Affair, everyone ran for cover and denied knowing him.

According to *The Boston Globe*'s story, McHenry had approached Trickey and told him that Marshal Hilliard had given him the task of copying the affidavits of 25 witnesses who would testify against Lizzie. It was the Commonwealth's entire case, and, for $1,000, Trickey could have copies—exclusively.

Sensing a major scoop over all his competition, Trickey handed over $30.00, all he had on him at the moment, and took the next train to Boston to pick up the rest. *The Boston Globe* put up the other $970.00, and Trickey was back on the train the next afternoon.

For a week, McHenry hemmed and hawed and dodged him, but finally produced a collection of papers, accepting $400.00 more from Trickey.

Back on the train, Trickey took his scoop back to Boston. With no verification whatsoever, *The Boston Globe* stunned the nation the following day with a story that occupied the entire center of their front page. The headline screamed

LIZZIE BORDEN'S SECRET
MR. BORDEN DISCOVERED IT AND HOT WORDS FOLLOWED
STARTLING TESTIMONY OF 25 NEW WITNESSES

EMMA WAS KICKED DURING THAT QUARREL
FAMILY DISCORD AND MURDER

It was a wild and ludicrous story, but, *The Boston Globe* assured their readers, the information "here published for the first time, is corroborated in a most convincing manner":

> The *Globe* is enabled to lay before its readers not only every fact of importance now in the government's possession, but as well to describe how and by whom the information was secured by the patient and unceasing toil of the police. The evidence is forthcoming from 25 people, all of whom stand high in the community and have no motive for speaking maliciously about the defendant.

Column after column was given over to the details of the 25 "affidavits"; each was quoted in full.

John H. Murphy, Bedford Street, would testify, for instance, that he was standing on the sidewalk close to the Borden home and had seen Lizzie open the window of the room in which Abby had been killed. The time was such that, at that very moment, "she must have been standing over the mutilated remains of her stepmother."

Mrs. Gustave Ronald and Mr. Peter Mahaney were also standing in front of the Borden house at 9:40 that morning and they had both heard a "terrible cry or groan." Looking up at the open guest room window of the Borden home, they had both seen Lizzie in plain view, her head covered with a rubber hood. Augustus Gunning, described as a lodger at Mrs. Churchill's home, would testify that he, too, saw the hooded Lizzie at the window.

"These witnesses," *The Boston Globe* said, "fix Miss Borden at her mother's side almost at the minute when she probably was killed."

The most damning evidence would come, however, from the testimony of Mr. and Mrs. Frederick Chace and their daughter Abigail, who had been guests of the Bordens the night before the murders. They had overheard a quarrel between Lizzie and Andrew. Andrew had raged:

"You can make your own choice and do it tonight! Either let us know what his name is or take the door on Saturday and when you go fishing, fish for some other place to live, as I will never listen to you again. I will know the name of the man who got you into trouble!"

Lizzie's reply was, "If I marry this man, will you be satisfied that everything will be kept from the outside world?"

"I would rather see her dead than have it come out," Andrew had grumbled to their guests. When asked if he knew the name of the man who had gotten Lizzie into trouble, he said, "No; but I have my suspicions and have had all along. If I am right, I will never recognize this man in the world. She has made her own bed, so let her lie upon it."

It was dialogue straight out of a penny thriller, but a Mr. G. Romaine Pittson would also swear that Andrew had discussed Lizzie's "condition" with him just a few days earlier.

Almost as condemning was the testimony Mrs. George Sisson would give about a conversation she had overheard at the funeral between Lizzie and Bridget. Lizzie had snapped at Bridget, "Are you a fool or a knave? Why don't you say how much money you want to keep quiet?" (Actually, Bridget had not even attended the funeral.) Mrs. Sisson would also say that Andrew had told her he had made out a will leaving Lizzie and Emma $25,000 each and all else to Abby, and third, that Lizzie had offered to sell her for $10 the watch that had been stolen in the daylight robbery of the Borden home. And Bridget, the fantasy continued, would swear that Lizzie had called her aside on the afternoon of the murders and had whispered to her, "Keep your tongue still and don't talk to these officers and you can have all the money you want."

McHenry himself would take the stand and testify that for days he had secreted himself under Lizzie's bed in the jail quarters and had listened to the conversations that went on between Lizzie and the Reverend Buck, Attorney Jennings, police matron Reagan, Emma, and all other visitors. To make his vigilance more comfortable, he had removed a portion of a wall in the adjoining bathroom, replaced the wall with muslin cloth, and had himself a clear view into Lizzie's cell at all times.

From behind his muslin curtain, he had overheard a heated quarrel between Lizzie and Emma in which Lizzie railed that Emma wanted to see her hanged and would not keep her secret. The argument culminated with Lizzie kicking Emma three times, pelting her with biscuits, and calling her a damned bitch!

By now, the story had become such a fantasy, one has to wonder if *anyone* at *The Boston Globe* read it—even the youngest, most inexperienced copyboy—before it was set in type!

The evening edition added more lurid details as the editors boasted about their scoop:

ASTOUNDED!
ALL NEW ENGLAND READ THE STORY
GLOBES WERE BOUGHT BY THE THOUSANDS
LIZZIE BORDEN APPEARS IN A NEW LIGHT
BELIEF IN HER INNOCENCE SHAKEN
EXCITEMENT RUNS HIGH IN FALL RIVER
POLICE THINK THE SCOOP A CORKER

Not by any stretch of the imagination did the police think "the scoop a corker." The thrust of McHenry's story was that the Fall River police had admitted bafflement, virtually removed itself from the investigation, and turned it all over to McHenry, who had experienced little difficulty in coming up with 25 witnesses and solving the case.

Even as *The Boston Globe*'s evening edition hit the streets screaming their "corker," the story was already beginning to unravel. Inspector Harrington of the Fall River police was the first to fire off a telegram to the paper saying the entire testimony attributed to him was a lie.

Attorney Jennings issued an immediate statement calling the story a tissue of lies, citing the fact that many of the addresses of the "witnesses" were vacant lots or were nonexistent. Many of the witnesses could not be identified in the city directory; others reported they had never been questioned and had certainly made no statements. Dr. Bowen, Lizzie's physician, telegraphed to say she had no "secret." By nightfall, responsible parties at *The Boston Globe* began to realize they may have been had by a giant hoax.

In the next issue, they began backtracking, but they were still not yet willing to admit they had been duped by the most intricate fiction any newspaper had ever swallowed. Admitting

no responsibility for publishing without the slightest verification, they pointed the finger at McHenry:

DETECTIVE MCHENRY TALKS
HE FURNISHED THE GLOBE WITH THE BORDEN STORY
IT HAS BEEN PROVED WRONG IN SOME PARTICULARS

McHenry stuck to his guns, saying "the names of the witnesses were given wrong for obvious reasons," but without
saying what the obvious reasons were. The facts, he said, were
all correct. They weren't, and by now, *The Boston Globe* attorneys convinced management to bite the bullet and admit they
had been snoockered. It would be a miracle if the paper could
withstand the lawsuits.

The center section of Tuesday's front page carried the retraction and apology in boldface type:

THE LIZZIE BORDEN CASE

. . . The *Globe* feels it its duty as an honest newspaper to state that it
has been grievously misled in the Lizzie Borden case. It published
on Monday a communication that it believed to be true evidence.
Some of this remarkably ingenious and cunningly contrived story
was undoubtedly based on facts. The *Globe* believes however that
much of it is false and never should have been published. The *Globe*
being misled has innocently added to the terrible burdens of Miss
Lizzie Borden. We hereby tender our heartfelt apology for the inhuman reflection on her honor as a woman and for any injustice the
publication reflected on her. . . .

As retractions and apologies go, it was good enough, but had
Lizzie instituted libel action, as Attorney Jennings urged, in all
probability she would have owned *The Boston Globe* when the
smoke cleared. Perhaps with that in mind, *The Boston Globe*
continued apologizing the next day:

HONEST AMEND
GLOBE APOLOGY PLEASED ITS READERS
REGRETS SPREAD BROADCAST AT FALL RIVER
MCHENRY'S ACTS CONDEMNED BY FAIR-MINDED CITIZENS

The editorial page contained additional apologies. But this was not the end of the fiasco.

In addition to bribing McHenry, Trickey had also offered Bridget a thousand dollars if she would leave the country. Bridget reported it to Knowlton, and the same grand jury that indicted Lizzie handed down an indictment of Trickey for tampering with a government witness. The indictment was kept secret for a while because Trickey had fled the scene for parts unknown. Word of the indictment leaked, and *The Boston Globe* ate crow again on Saturday, December 3, commenting:

> It is reported, on what seems indisputable authority, that Henry G. Trickey was the person named and that he is accused of tampering with a government witness . . . and this witness was offered inducements to leave the country.

Attorney General Pillsbury was incensed over the tampering charge and instructed Knowlton to hunt down Trickey at all costs. Two days later *The Boston Globe* found him:

HENRY G. TRICKEY DEAD
TRIED TO BOARD A MOVING TRAIN AND FELL

Not satisfied with this quick and easy solution, Pillsbury instructed Knowlton to send someone to examine the corpse to be sure it was Trickey. It was.

In the meantime, Detective McHenry was hounded out of his detective business office in Providence and fled to New York. He bombarded Hilliard, Knowlton, and Pillsbury with incoherent letters blaming everyone connected with the investigation, contending Trickey had committed suicide and pleading for payments for his services. As far as is known, however, he went unpaid for one of the slickest scams ever perpetrated.

9

Meantime, Back in the Real World

O N JUNE 5, 1893, the day set for Lizzie's trial, New Bedford, Massachusetts, though teeming with industry, fishing, and cotton weaving, could be described as a beautiful city, with its well-cared-for roads liberally arbored with magnificent elms, its residences like gems set in well-clipped lawns, hospitable in appearance, cordial in welcome.

For years it enjoyed and deserved the reputation of being the epitome of New England propriety and comfortable consistency. Its people were content to find recreation in the central park, entertainment and instruction in churches of a dozen denominations and in an opera house where lecturers came and where the best dramatic companies presented their plays and musicals. It was, in short, a quiet, gentle place of rest and comfort.

On this day, as they had at Fall River, the crowds began gathering early, and by 9:00 A.M., the courthouse on County Street was surrounded by the curious. Many remained all day in hope of sighting someone associated with this high drama. By the next day, it would be necessary to throw up a temporary fence around the trim, columned brick building to hold them back. Every boarding house, bed-and-breakfast, and hotel was full. The passage of ten months since the murders of Andrew and Abby had done nothing to slake public interest.

At exactly 11:28 A.M., Andrew Wright, high sheriff of Bristol county, now acting as bailiff, rapped to silence the mob crowded shoulder to shoulder in the second floor courtroom. With great aplomb, he swung open the door to the chambers of the justices and escorted to the bench, one at a time, the three justices who would preside over the trial.

Associate Justice Caleb Blodgett was first, the youngest of the trio, with neatly trimmed whiskers, alert blue eyes, and a penchant for the white neckties then in fashion.

Associate Justice Justin Dewey was next, a scholarly man with a large head thickly covered with silver-gray hair that fell casually over his forehead. Tall and angular, he carried his years comfortably.

Finally, Sheriff Wright held the center chair for Chief Justice Albert Mason, like Dewey, dignified, silver-haired, and benign. His great underjaw was emphasized by a full, square-cut beard.

At separate facing tables sat the counsels for the defendant and the Commonwealth. Andrew Jennings and Melvin O. Adams represented Lizzie. Their leader, ex-Governor George D. Robinson, would not be present until Wednesday. Hosea M. Knowlton, district attorney for the second district, and William H. Moody, district attorney for the eastern district, were seated for the Government.

Lizzie was next to enter.

She was dressed in black save for a blue plume of feathers in her hat, two blue velvet rosettes in her hair, and an enamelled pansy pin at her throat. Her nut-brown hair was pulled back into a soft, long roll behind her head. In her kid-gloved hands she held a tiny nosegay of blossoms and a bombazine fan. One correspondent, conditioned by the stories of Lizzie the Vile and seeing her now for the first time, wrote:

She is no Medussa or Gorgon. There is nothing wicked, criminal, or
hard in her features. She was modest, calm, and quiet, and it was
plain to see that she had complete mastery of herself and could make
her sensations and emotions invisible to an impertinent public.

Because the oppressively hot courtroom was filled with 145
prospective jurors (three had been excused by death or illness),
40 or more newsmen, a handful of Lizzie's supporters, and the
officers of the court, no spectators were admitted on this first
day. Seating capacity had been increased by an additional 50
chairs, and 25 had been set aside for the press corps, but even
that was not enough to accommodate the crowd. Another 15
chairs were hastily added but, still, reporters found themselves
scribbling their notes on pads resting on their knees, while
other reporters lined the walls.

The prospective jurors were farmers or merchants; all were
bearded and at least middle-aged. Both sides had agreed there
would be no young men on the jury and none from Fall River.
This being 1893, women had not been considered. Twenty-
seven more years would have to go by before women's suffrage
would be recognized by the Congress.

The time consumed today in the selection of a jury is sharply
contrasted with how it was done in 1893 in Massachusetts.
While today, jury selection has been turned into a tug-of-war
between opposing counsels probing for hidden prejudices and
for balance by race, color, creed, age, demographics, and per-
ceived personalities, the selection of Lizzie's jurors was entirely
in the hands of Judge Mason. Tradition was that if the judge
considered the prospective juror to be sane and solid, he indeed
was. Each counsel was permitted to challenge 22 of them
peremptorily, with or without cause. Jennings challenged 15,
and each time, Lizzie was required to stand in her place in
the dock and say the single word, "challenge." Moody challenged 12.

By 5:00, 108 of the jurors had been questioned by Judge
Mason and 12 were chosen for the task. They were William F.
Dean, Louis B. Hodges, and John C. Finn of Taunton, Frank G.
Cole of Attleboro, Charles I. Richards of North Attleboro,
George Potter of Westport, John Wilbur of Somerset, Frederick
C. Wilbar of Raynham, Lemuel K. Wilber of Easton, William

Westcot of Seekonk, Augustus Swift of New Bedford, and Allen H. Wordell of Dartmouth. Justice Mason appointed Mr. Richards to act as foreman.

Someone on Knowlton's staff had prepared for him six-line descriptions of each of the men who would hear the case. Their comments and his handwritten opinions are revealing:

Of Frank G. Cole, it was noted that he was a Republican and unmarried. "All these jewelers are intelligent men and read papers . . . a good straight man." Knowlton added, "Grand Army." John C. Finn was described as an Irishman but very intelligent. Augustus Swift was a Protestant and a deep believer in circumstantial evidence. Knowlton noted, "Good man. With us."

Charles I. Richards, the foreman, would be "a string-straight man no matter what anyone said." George Potter was an American and a Universalist, but he was a Mason. He had limited education but was credited with common sense. Knowlton was cautioned that Lemuel K. Wilber didn't believe in capital punishment but his wife thought Lizzie was guilty.

Judge Mason advised them their pay would be $3 per day, plus board and lodging, for the duration of the trial.

At some time the next day, he told them, they would take the short train ride to Fall River to familiarize themselves with the physical makeup of the Borden home and property.

Then, it was 5:00, and court was adjourned for the day.

Knowlton had made up his mind some time between Christmas, when Attorney General Pillsbury was stricken, and the day of the trial that he was going to take as little part in it as he reasonably could. His associate, District Attorney Moody, was neither as experienced nor as familiar with the nuances of the case, but he was a competent, energetic man. He would carry the brunt of the presentation. For the first seven days, Knowlton yielded it all to Moody.

At 9:00 A.M. on day two, the jury was instructed to stand together as good men and true and hearken to the evidence. Moody rose to tell them what the Commonwealth believed to be that evidence. The Essex county district attorney walked to the railing that fenced in the jury and spoke in a low, confidential manner commensurate with the melancholy of the moment. He was obviously constrained and ill at ease.

"Upon the fourth day of August of the last year," he said, "an old man and woman, husband and wife, each without a known enemy in the world, in their own home, upon a frequented street in the most populous city in this county, under the light of day and in the midst of its activities were, first one, then, after an interval of an hour, another, killed by an unlawful human agency.

"Today, a woman of good social position, of hitherto unquestioned character, a member of a Christian church and active in its good works, the own daughter of one of the victims is at the bar of this court accused by the grand jury of this county of these crimes.

"There is no language, gentlemen, at my command which can better measure the solemn importance of the inquiry which you are about to begin than this simple statement of facts."

He spent the next two hours expanding on this "simple statement of facts."

Opening statements by counsel on both sides are not, of course, evidence, but are summations of what each hopes to prove. Exaggerations as to the strength of their positions are commonplace, and the worth of upcoming evidence is accented by what is said and what is not said. Each side vies to convince the jury that theirs is the true version of the happening, hoping that what their cases lack in hard evidence they can make up for with histrionics and obfuscation. The opening minutes of any trial are often the most important. Setting the tone, winning the jury's trust and confidence, sincerity, and demeanor are all of greater import than the minutiae of the evidence to come.

Moody walked the jury through the minutes of that fatal day, pausing along the way to accent those things important to the Commonwealth's case. He spoke of the animosity and the hatred the prosecution would maintain permeated the house on Second Street, and he pointed out that Lizzie would not call Abby her mother.

He told of the sickness the family had suffered the day before and the day of the murders and promised they would prove that Lizzie had tried to purchase prussic acid the very day before.

He described the house and grounds in detail, though the jury had come to the courtroom that day prepared to journey there that afternoon for their own inspection of the premises.

Minute by minute, he timed the day of the murder as the prosecution thought it had played out. The doors with locks on every one were described, as were the details of Bridget's window-washing and the gruesomeness of the mutilated bodies. "There was blood spattered in every direction," he said, "and it is probable spatters would be impressed on the clothing of the assassin." This was a statement he would later hedge as the subject became one of the focal points of the trial.

Once having proved all the things they were prepared to prove, Moody concluded, "we shall ask you to say whether any other reasonable hypothesis except that of the guilt of the prisoner can account for the said occurrences which happened upon the morning of August 4."

"The time for idle rumor," he said, "for partial, insufficient information, for hasty and inexact reasoning, is past."

From the first minute that morning in court, Lizzie had sat erect and almost motionless, her eyes fixed on Moody, attentive to his every word as he addressed the jury. She held her tightly folded fan as a baton, lightly touching her cheek. During Moody's graphic description of the multiple wounds and the contents of the victims' stomachs, she visibly paled and covered her eyes with her handkerchief. All eyes were on her now as Moody stood away from the jury rail.

An "eye-witness" reporter, sitting a few feet from her, detailed the scene:

Two or three minutes had passed and Lizzie had not moved. The fan and arm that held it up dropped into the prisoner's lap. Her head was back against the rail, her eyes were shut, her mouth was open and her breast heaved with very long breaths.

"Lizzie Borden is asleep!" was the whisper that galloped through the courtroom. Deputy Sheriff Kirby, who sat beside her, took friendly alarm at such disrespectful behavior and tried to waken her before the court should see her. He shook her arm. Her head rolled over so that her cheek rested on the rail at right angles to the line of her body. A purple cast came over her face. City Missionary Jubb of Fall River sprang to his feet and began to fan her.

A deputy sheriff came quickly with a glass of water. After a little, she regained partial consciousness. Mr. Jubb ordered somewhat sharply to find her smelling salts. Then she put both hands on the arms of the chair and fell back against the railing, not half over her faint. Mr. Jubb was applying the smelling salts and was so much in earnest that her breath went from her and she put up her hand to push the bottle away. In another minute her eyes opened. Sheriff Wright, in the meantime, began rapping on his desk for order. The people crept back into their seats and the episode ended with Miss Borden leaning her head against the rail, with her eyes shut.

Headlines in all the papers next day screamed of her fainting, but, since such a public display of distress and emotion did not jibe with the carefully crafted image of Lizzie, Edwin Porter does not mention it in his history of the Borden murders. *The New York Times* did, however, in their news columns, and further editorialized:

> The trial of Lizzie Borden on a charge of murdering her father and stepmother opened at New Bedford yesterday with the process of selecting jurors. This trial is likely to be followed with peculiar interest on account of the extraordinary character of the case and the mystery in which the murder has been enveloped from the moment of its discovery. The probability would seem to be overwhelmingly against the young woman who is charged with it unless she was insane, but the crime itself affords the only evidence of her insanity and that plea has been repelled by her counsel. On the other hand, not the slightest evidence has been found so far as has yet appeared to the public of the perpetration of the crime by any one else, and circumstances have seemed to point to the guilt of the accused. The development of the evidence before the court will be watched with unusual interest.

This, in a paragraph, was what the Lizzie Borden drama was all about: she couldn't have "done it" unless she was insane, which she wasn't; but there was no evidence that anyone else could have done it! It was on this proposition that the Commonwealth had built its case. The fatal flaw was not the thundering incompetence of the police or the prosecution, but their arrogant assurance that the vast and ignorant unwashed would never perceive this flagrant dichotomy between what *might* have been and what *must* have been.

It was now 11:10, and a brief recess was called following Lizzie's fainting spell. When all were again settled, Moody called the trial's first witness, civil engineer Thomas Kieran. He gave a protracted description of the Borden house and detailed the size and location of the rooms as well as the relationship between the house, the barn, and the neighboring homes.

Attorney Jennings was well aware that the prosecution would attempt to make much of the fact that, during the morning hours, Lizzie had gone upstairs to her room and had passed the guest room going and coming. Since the door of the room was known to be open, why had not Lizzie seen Abby? She was lying "in plain view from the hall," Moody had said.

On cross-examination, Kieran admitted that he had conducted a series of tests while measuring the Borden home to determine what could be seen when opposite the guest room door as one mounted or descended the stairs. He had even had one of his assistants lie where Abby had fallen.

"Then I went downstairs and came up the stairs in the middle of the stairs, as I would if I had been trying to see this man," he said.

Moody was on his feet immediately, protesting this evidence, but his objections were overruled.

Kieran continued, stating that when he mounted the steps as one ordinarily would, he could not see his assistant even though he knew he was there. Only by pausing on one certain step and gazing along the floor line, could he see the much taller man's feet protruding. From the hallway and from the door of Lizzie's room, he could see nothing.

It was a small point, but an important one. First blood had been drawn by Jennings, and on this triumphant note for the defense, court adjourned for the trip to Fall River.

On day three, the trial settled down to business. Photographer James A. Walsh identified the official photographs he had taken of the bodies of the victims and the premises, and they were introduced into the record. The second witness was the shadowy John Vinnicum Morse.

He told how he had arrived the day before the murders, had his midday meal with Andrew and Abby, and then visited their Swansea farm, returning at 8:30 that night. He had not seen Lizzie during the noon meal, during the evening, or the following morning. He had left soon after the mutton breakfast and before Lizzie had come downstairs. He offered no explanation for arriving for a visit of several days without any luggage.

He had left the Borden house at about 8:45 in the morning, he said. He first stopped by the post office and then went along to Weybosset Street, about a mile away, to visit his niece.

When he returned to the house about 45 minutes after the cry of "Murder!" had been raised, he said he had not noticed the scores of curiosity seekers gathered in front of the house. Nor had he noticed burly Charles Sawyer in his red plaid shirt standing guard at the side door. He had strolled around to the backyard, eaten some pears picked up from the ground, and only then went into the house where "someone informed me that something had happened."

The "something" was merely the murder of Andrew and Abby.

He was followed to the stand in rapid succession by Abraham G. Hart, treasurer of the Union Savings Bank, John P. Burrill, cashier of the National Union Bank, Everett M. Cook, cashier of the First National Bank, Jonathon Clegg, a hat maker, and Joseph Shortsleeves and James Mather, carpenters, who traced Andrew's movements downtown on the morning of the murders, from 9:30 until he returned home at 10:45.

In his opening statement to the jury, Moody had said Lizzie's motive for the parricide had been to prevent Andrew from changing his will to favor Abby. This presupposed there had been a will. As an officer of the court, Jennings advised the judges and jury that he had been Andrew's lawyer for many years and had never been asked to write a will for him, and none existed. Hart, Andrew's confidant at the Union Savings Bank, confirmed he had never heard of a will either. Knowlton sat silent and offered no challenge to this vital testimony, but neither did he allow it to change his tack. He continued to maintain that this was Lizzie's motive.

After lunch, Bridget Sullivan took the stand for the prosecution, but as the newspapers would say the next day, she testified for the defense.

She had worked for the Bordens for more than three years and her duties included cooking, washing, ironing, and cleaning the downstairs rooms and her own. The elders and the daughters each took care of their own rooms. For four hours, she described every detail of the morning of August 4.

She arose, she said, at 6:15, with a sick headache. The first thing down, she took in the daily milk can from the back stoop and put out the clean one, along with a pan to receive the iceman's daily 25-pound cake of ice.

By 6:30, she was building her fire of wood and coal and preparing a breakfast of mutton soup, reheated mutton (for the third time), johnnycakes, cookies, bananas, and coffee.

(Someone was later to say there were two things about the Borden murders that, once heard, could never be forgotten: the jingle about 40 whacks and this breakfast menu served on the hottest morning of the year!)

When she came down, John Morse was already sitting in the dining room reading a newspaper. Mrs. Borden was next down the backstairs, followed by Mr. Borden about five minutes later. He had with him his slop jar, which he emptied in the back yard, and returned with a basket of pears picked from the ground around the trees. After he had washed his hands in the kitchen sink, the three had sat down for breakfast.

After eating heartily, Morse had left by the backdoor and Andrew had invited him back for "dinner," customarily served at 12:00 noon. Andrew washed his teeth in the kitchen sink, drew a basin of water, and went up the back stairs to his room.

Lizzie came down about five minutes later, Bridget said, and settled for a breakfast of black coffee and a cookie. As for herself, Bridget retired to the back yard to be sick. Again, the dreadful breakfast! After about 10 minutes, she returned to the kitchen, locked the screen door, and was met by Mrs. Borden, who told her she wanted all the downstairs windows washed, inside and out. It would be the last order Bridget would receive from her mistress.

From the cellar she got her pail and from the kitchen closet, her brush. The handle was out in the barn and she went to get it. She had told Lizzie she would be working outside and the screen door could be locked after her because there was water in the barn she could use.

Lizzie had taken down the ironing board and put irons on the stove to heat. She asked Bridget if she planned to go out that afternoon.

"There is a cheap sale of dress goods at Sargent's this afternoon at eight cents a yard," Lizzie had said, but Bridget told her she wasn't feeling well and probably wouldn't be going.

No, she hadn't seen anyone outside while she was going to and from the barn on six or seven trips for more water. She couldn't see the side door or the front door most of the time and someone could have entered either one without her knowing it, and, no, she hadn't seen anyone delivering a note to Mrs. Borden.

As for what Lizzie had worn that morning, it had been a blue dress with a sprig in it.

The window washing had taken about an hour-and-a-half, and she had come back into the house to rest a bit. Mr. Borden had returned from downtown and she had been lying down for just a few minutes when the city hall bell rang 11 times. The next thing was Lizzie's cry, "Maggie, come down!"

She told of trying to get Dr. Bowen from across the street and of running to Alice Russell's house.

Bridget's description of the morning had brought out nothing new—if you failed to note the time discrepancy, as both Knowlton and Robinson did.

George Dexter Robinson rose for the cross-examination, and it can be said without bias that, from this point, he would remain the dominant figure of the trial.

His was a commanding persona but without the overpowering air of dominance common to men of substantial build and weight. His moustache was neatly trimmed and his dress impeccable.

He had graduated with honors from Harvard at the age of 22. Three had apparently been his lucky number. He had been elected three times to the state legislature, three times to the House of Representatives in Washington, and three times governor of Massachusetts. He had taken the state capitol from Benjamin F. Butler, "Beast Butler" of Civil War notoriety.

He was a masterful politician, which title can only be earned by those with an infallible understanding of what moves the emotions of voters or, in this case, jurors. When riding the circuit searching for votes, he instinctively knew that his choice of a horse was more important than what his votes might be in the next assembly. If it were too fine an animal, the hardscrabble Massachusetts farmer would resent the ostentation. At the same time, an inferior nag would indicate he had no knowledge of horseflesh, and that would be worse.

As he visited over fences or chatted in parlors, Robinson, at some point, would invariably inquire as to the time. No matter what his constituent's Ingersoll showed, Robinson would adjust his watch to agree.

He showed the world the image he wanted it to see: that of an amiable, honest backwoodsman, a friend whenever one was needed. His handicap was a good family background, money, and a Harvard education.

Lizzie, it is said, had great trust in him from the moment he had laid an avuncular hand on her arm and said, "Don't you worry, little girl. Everything's going to be all right."

Right now, his principal task in cross-examining Bridget was to destroy the prosecution's description of 92 Second Street as a cauldron of hatred and anger. He knew the adage that there are no family secrets from the servants.

Bridget had been an impressive witness, not at all a frightened, ignorant servant girl, as might have been expected. For three hours she had stood in a witness box that was barely two feet square. Two hours into her grilling by Moody, Justice Dewey had motioned for the bailiff to bring a chair for her but she had waved it away. Her responses to Moody's questions had been crisp, positive, and courteous. She had stood erect and seldom even rested her hands on the protecting rail. She could have been Hester Prynne in the pillory.

Q. You were called Maggie?
A. Yes sir.
Q. By Miss Emma and Miss Lizzie?
A. Yes sir.
Q. But that was not unpleasant to you?
A. No sir, it was not.
Q. Not at all offensive?
A. No sir.
Q. Did not cause any ill-feeling or trouble?
A. No sir.
Q. Did you have any trouble there in the family?
A. No sir.
Q. A pleasant place to live?

A. Yes sir, I liked the place.
Q. And for aught you know, they liked you?
A. As far as I know, yes.
Q. It was a pleasant family to be in?
A. I don't know how the family was. I got along all right.
Q. You never saw anything out of the way?
A. No sir.
Q. You never saw any conflict in the family?
A. No sir.
Q. Never saw the least—any quarelling or anything of that kind?
A. No sir, I did not.

She added that Lizzie and Abby always spoke civilly to each other and that meals were taken together, though not always, since the daughters usually did not get up until 9:00, long after the elders.

Q. How was it [the conversation] this Thursday morning after they came downstairs?
A. I don't remember.
Q. Didn't they talk in the sitting room?
A. I heard her talk as she [Lizzie] came along.
Q. Who spoke?
A. Miss Lizzie and Mrs. Borden.
Q. Talking in the sitting room?
A. Mrs. Borden asked some question and she answered very civilly.
Q. When you heard them talking, they were talking calmly, the same as anybody else?
A. Yes sir.
Q. There was not so far as you knew, any trouble that morning?
A. No sir, I did not see any trouble with the family.

She was reminded that at the preliminary hearing, she had said they had discussed some Christmas plans and that, when asked if she knew of any trouble between Miss Lizzie and her mother, she had replied, "No sir, never a word in my presence." Robinson had clearly made his point but pressed Bridget one more time:

Q. Now if nothing had happened that morning, Miss Sullivan, nothing unusual had happened that day, would there be any reason why you should remember that Thursday more than any other day?

A. Why, no, there was no reason that I should remember that day any more than any other day. . . .

If there had been murderous hatred between Lizzie and Abby, it had been totally hidden for three years from their daily servant. Bridget had said nothing damaging to Lizzie, and her calm manner on the stand must have been sympathetically viewed by the jurors.

The third day of the trial ended on that note, and both sides retired to neutral corners.

The Boston *Advertiser* editorialized:

Up to this point the government has distinctly failed to convict Lizzie Borden. The opinion deepens that it will not fasten the guilt upon her. The duty of the government is to prove absolutely that Lizzie Borden committed these murders or she ought to, and will, go free.

10

The High Sheriff
and Day Four

O F THE GREAT ENTOURAGE OF NEWSMEN gathered for the sensational trial, the stand-out performer was easily Joe Howard, a voluble, robust writer who self-styled himself as journalism's first syndicated columnist. His comings and goings were attended with almost as much zeal as were those of the principals of the trial. His daily recounts were spirited, bombastic, opinionated, and avidly read by hundreds of thousands of subscribers to dozens of Eastern newspapers.

His ebullient description of day four is an excellent example of his flamboyant, nonconforming style:

> Human nature, with all its trimmings of vanity, superstition, self-conceit, and itch for notoriety, has been admirably illustrated today in the presence of a tremendous audience, which was rapped into silence by jolly-hearted, stern-visaged, virile-fisted Sheriff Wright at

the cheerless hour of 9 o'clock this morning. The country roads were alive with farmers' teams from early dawn, hurrying toward the courthouse, each occupant bearing an expectant look of curious hope to be sightseers. I was glad to find that the sheriff, in imitation of the final distribution of the peoples of the earth, like the shepherds of the olden times who divided the sheep from the goats, had the men on one side and the women on the other.

Sheriff Wright was his favorite target for teasing. He was a bustling little beaver of a man, who knew with perfect certainty that the sole reason for his being on the earth in this year of our Lord was to ensure the decorum of the second district court of the Commonwealth of Massachusetts. And Joe Howard knew it, too:

There is no question of deportment with the audience. It is the audience of a New England country town, an audience of factory hands, fishermen, sea-going lads, lawyers, and businessmen and all kinds of women, good and bad, homely and beautiful, vulgar and gentle, that are born to gladden and trouble the earth. They keep very quiet. They sit very still. They feel themselves not only under the subduing spell of this tragic cause, but under the eagle, arching glance of one, with whom among all these, there is a question of deportment. This is the high sheriff of Bristol county, the highest sheriff there ever was; so high that he has to bob when he walks under the moon. Except when occupied in stately procession precedent to the movement of their honors the court, and when engaged in glancing around the courtroom to see that no unhappy wretch is daring to breathe without having previously consulted him, the high sheriff of Bristol county is engaged in retrospection. He is happy when, with stately tread, with his high silk hat fixed firmly on his head and his swallowtailed coat of Websterian blue flapping its tails like a streamer from a flagpole, with enough brass buttons on it to fit out a regiment of Haitian generals, he precedes the honorable, the justices of the superior court of the state of Massachusetts as they enter the room and take their places behind the bench. He is happy when, with darkening frown, he glances around and indicates to some unhappy deputy his august displeasure. But the golden moments of his life come when he is introspective; when, seated behind his desk, in the full gaze of the multitude, he thinks real thoughts, all about himself. Then is the high sheriff of Bristol county in a condition of positive, supreme peace and satisfaction.

It was a fitting description of the setting for day four.

If it had been round four of a championship fight, the referee and judges would undoubtedly have scored it a draw. The government put their two star witnesses on the stand and gained points with each, but counterpunches by the defense held the damage to a minimum, even landed a few punches of its own.

Dr. Seabury Bowen, a physician for 26 years, had lived across the street from the Bordens for 22 of those years and had been their family doctor for 12 of them. He took the stand first on the morning of June 8 and told how he had been sent over to the Bordens by his wife on the morning of August 4 last.

He had made a cursory examination of the two bodies of his old acquaintances, and it was apparent that both victims were beyond medical help. Mr. Borden's face was so terribly mangled, he said, it was hardly to be recognized by one who knew him as well as he did.

Lizzie had asked him to send a telegram to Emma, who was away visiting in Fairhaven, and he had gone the few blocks to the telegraph office, sent the message, and returned, only to be told by Mrs. Churchill that Mrs. Borden's body had been discovered upstairs.

District Attorney Moody asked what Lizzie was wearing when he first went into the house. At the inquest, he had said, "It is pretty hard work for me. Probably if I could see a dress something like it, I could guess, but I could not describe it. It was sort of drab, not much color to it to attract my attention. A sort of morning calico dress, I should judge."

Moody tried desperately to move Bowen off-center as to what "drab" was, but the good doctor wouldn't budge. He knew nothing about women's dresses and less about feminine colors and designs.

On cross-examination, Counsel Melvin O. Adams asked about Lizzie's emotional state. The ladies present, Bowen said, his wife, Mrs. Churchill, and Miss Russell, had been "fanning and working over her. I don't know exactly what—rubbing her wrists and rubbing her head." She had, he said, thrown herself on a lounge in the dining room, and he had finally told the ladies to take her to her room. He had given her a preparation called Bromo-Caffeine to quiet her "nervous excitement" and another dose to take an hour later.

Q. Did you have occasion to prescribe for her on account of this mental distress and nervous excitement, after that?
A. Yes sir.
Q. When was it?
A. Friday.
Q. Was the prescription or medicine the same as the other?
A. It was different.
Q. What was it?
A. Sulphate of morphine.
Q. In what doses?
A. One eighth of a grain.
Q. When?
A. Friday night at bedtime.
Q. The next day you changed that?
A. I did not change the medicine but doubled the dose.
Q. That was on Saturday?
A. On Saturday.
Q. Did you continue the dose on Sunday?
A. Yes sir.
Q. Did you continue it on Monday?
A. Yes sir.
Q. And on Tuesday?
A. Yes sir.
Q. How long did she continue to have that?
A. She continued to have that all the time she was in the station house.
Q. After her arrest, was it not?
A. And before.
Q. In other words, she had it all the time up to the time of her arrest, the hearing and while in the station house?
A. Yes sir.
Q. Does not morphine, given in double doses to allay mental distress and nervous excitement, somewhat affect the memory and change and alter the view of things and give people hallucinations?
A. Yes sir.

There was an audible stir of excitement in the courtroom at this information, and the jury would be reminded in Robinson's summation that Lizzie had been under heavy sedation by this opium derivative all the time she had been questioned by the police and interrogated at the inquest.

No, he had not seen any bloodstains on Lizzie's person and had had ample opportunity to notice if any had been.

The widow Adelaide Churchill was called next. She was returning from the grocers when she saw Bridget, "white and going rapidly" across the street to Dr. Bowen's house. She had put down her groceries and looked out her kitchen window to see what was happening.

She saw Lizzie leaning against the door jamb, looking excited and agitated. The widow said she had called out, "What is the matter?"

"Oh, Mrs. Churchill, do come over," Lizzie cried. "Someone has killed father!"

After a report of the morning's happenings was drawn from her, the questions turned to what Lizzie had been wearing.

Q. Will you describe the dress that she had on while you were there?
A. It looked like a light blue-and-white groundwork. It seemed like calico or cambric and it had a light blue-and-white groundwork with a dark, navy-blue diamond printed on it.
Q. Was that the dress she had on this morning? [Showing her the dark blue dress Lizzie had given the police.]
A. It does not look like it.
Q. Was it?
A. This is not the dress I have described.

Score one for the prosecution.

Alice Russell, a longtime friend of the Bordens, was next, now a witness against Lizzie. She had volunteered to the police that she had seen Lizzie burn a skirt on the Sunday afternoon following the murders, and Knowlton had promptly told newsmen that her testimony at the trial would assure Lizzie's conviction. Moody called her now to make good on that promise.

Joe Howard, the columnist, described her as "very tall, angular, and thin, with a lofty forehead and pale blue eyes and holds her mouth as though 'prism' and 'prunes' were its most frequent utterances. With crossed arms, she emphasizes her replies with little taps with a bombazine fan."

She spoke first of Lizzie's visit to her home on the evening before the murders; how she appeared to be agitated and depressed, saying she feared for her father's life as well as her own. Could she give a description of the dress Lizzie had worn the next morning?

Her answer was a curt, "None whatever."

The important subject of the dress burning was next. What exactly had she seen?

"I went into the kitchen and I saw Miss Lizzie at the other end of the stove. I saw Miss Emma at the sink. Miss Lizzie was at the stove and she had a skirt in her hand, and her sister turned and said, 'What are you going to do?' and Lizzie said, 'I am going to burn this old thing up. It is covered with paint.'

She had left the kitchen, saying, "I wouldn't let anybody see me do that, Lizzie."

Score another for the prosecution.

However . . .

There is a maxim that every law professor tries to drum into his students from the first day: never ask a witness a question unless you already know the answer. Moody failed to heed that cardinal rule when he interrupted Robinson's cross-examination to ask:

Q. Miss Russell, will you tell us what kind of a dress—give us a description of the dress that was burned, that you testified about, on Sunday morning?

A. It was a cheap cotton Bedford cord.

Q. What was its color?

A. Light-blue ground with a dark figure—small figure.

Q. Do you know when she got it?

A. I am not positive.

Q. Well, about when she got it?

A. In the early spring.

Q. Was your attention called to it at the time she got it, in any way?

A. She told me that she had got her Bedford cord and she had a dressmaker there and I went over there one evening and she had it on, in the very early part of the dressmaker's visit, and she called my attention to it, and I said, "Oh, you have got your Bedford cord." This is the only time I saw it until this time.

Q. Until the time it was burned?

A. Yes sir.

Q. To make it clear, between the time you saw it on Miss Lizzie Borden and had the talk about it in the spring, you did not see it again until the Sunday morning after the homicide?

A. I never remember of ever seeing it and I am quite sure I did not—that I never did.

Moody sat down, apparently blissfully unaware that he had destroyed his own witness. By asking these additional questions, he had unwittingly wiped out one of the prosecution's principal claims; that Lizzie had burned on Sunday the dress she had worn on Thursday morning.

Miss Russell had said she could give no description whatsoever of the dress Lizzie had worn on the morning of the murders. Her description of the dress burned in the kitchen stove was, on the other hand, detailed. It was the Bedford cord, and she emphatically stated four times that she had not seen it from the day in the spring when it was first worn until the Sunday morning it was burned. Therefore, she was testifying she had *not* seen it on the morning of the murders and it was *not* the dress Lizzie had worn!

It was not even necessary for Robinson to call the jury's attention to the fact that Miss Russell had said Lizzie burned a "skirt," not a dress.

Score a major one for the defense.

It would be illuminating to know what impression Assistant Marshal John Fleet made on the jury. A cold reading of the trial transcript, coupled with the comments of many of the reporters, leaves the impression of belligerence, even arrogance. Clearly, he was the only witness to engage Robinson in combat. That he won is extremely doubtful, since the truth and accuracy of his testimony was itself doubtful.

First of all, he was, as is said, ahoist his own petard. He had directed the efforts of the Fall River police in the numerous full scale searches of the Borden house, barn, and grounds on Thursday, Friday, and Saturday. They had, so they said, done everything short of stripping off the wallpaper and taking up the carpet. He was now going to have to explain to the jury why no bloodstained dress had been found and why it had taken them five days to decide on what the murder weapon was. For a known fact, Lizzie had not left the house after the murders, and there had been a very few minutes from the time of the Borden's death until the police had received the first phone call, so where were the clothes and hatchet if she was the murderer? When had there been time for the murder and all the events that must have taken place before that call was received at headquarters?

There is a lesson to be learned by any fledgling lawyer from the adroit way the ex-governor handled these two witnesses, Miss Russell and Assistant Marshal Fleet, who were both hostile but of different temperaments. The rule is never to provoke a hostile witness for fear of what he may blurt out. The wily Robinson observed that caveat carefully when questioning Lizzie's former friend, but masterfully defied it in dealing with Fleet. He was aware that some time after the murders, Miss Russell had come to her own conclusion that Lizzie was guilty, and he dealt with her gently. His approach suggested that what she had to say was of no importance, when, to her, this was the high point of her life.

Fleet was a different opponent, a professional with professional motives. Robinson deliberately exasperated the witness to show the jury his hostility and prejudice.

Although he had arrived on the scene at 11:45, he had not spoken to Lizzie until she had retired to her room. She had told him the now-familiar story of her father returning from downtown, going to the sitting room and, ultimately, at her suggestion, lying down on the sofa because he appeared to be feeble. She had told him of her trip to the barn and that Morse had been a guest the night before. She did not think he had anything to do with the murders, nor did she think Bridget was involved. The fact that Lizzie had absolved them of any suspicion, when it would have been to her advantage to encourage that thought were she herself the murderer, seems to have made no impression on him. He *had* been struck, however, by Lizzie's saying that Mrs. Borden was not her mother, but her stepmother. That remark, innocent or vituperative, seems to have convinced Fleet of her guilt and galvanized his every action from that point. He had had no time for Lizzie's mourning. He had asked for an immediate search of her room.

He and Officers Minnehan and Wilson had found nothing. He had then gone to the cellar to take part in the search there. Officer Mullaly had shown him two axes and the hatchets Bridget had led him to. In addition to those four weapons, Fleet testified that he had discovered a box on a shelf and in it had found the hatchet head they would later claim to be the murder instrument. This, in direct contradiction to testimony that *Bridget* had taken down the box and showed it to Mullaly. This would not be the only time Fleet's description of events would be in conflict with others'.

He described the hatchet as "covered with a heavy dust or ashes." Moments later he said it was not dust, but ashes. The handle had been broken and it appeared to be a recent break. At the time, he apparently had not thought it was the murder weapon, since he had left it in the box and put it back on the shelf. The two axes and both hatchets had been sent to Harvard for laboratory examinations. None showed signs of bloodstains. The only other possible weapon then, was the hatchet head, so the police had then seized upon it as the instrument of death.

Then came the embarrassing questions about the searches of the house.

Most of Thursday afternoon had been taken up with searches of the house, barn, and grounds. Five people had conducted the search on Friday: Fleet, Marshal Hilliard, Captain Desmond, Medical Examiner Dolan, and State Detective Seaver. Jennings had insisted on being present to be sure there was no hanky-panky. The Borden house was a small one, and places to secrete bundles of clothing or murder weapons were few. The Friday search had taken more than four hours, and on Saturday the same team spent an additional five hours.

Apparently in an effort to lessen the appearance of incompetence, Fleet did not even mention the searches that had taken place on Thursday and Friday. He indicated that the first search had been on Saturday.

He admitted they had found a basket in the barn loft containing "lead and iron" that could be used to make sinkers. He had paid little attention to it, even though Lizzie had described just such a container in her inquest testimony. He was obviously not looking for anything favorable to Lizzie.

At first, he indicated that the search on Saturday had been a cursory one, even though taking that tack only accented incompetence on the part of the police. After all, finding the weapon and bloodstained clothing was an absolute necessity before accusing anyone. Robinson doggedly pursued the subject, forcing Fleet to do an about-face and admit the searches had been meticulous and detailed.

Whereas his first reply to Robinson's question as to how thorough the search had been was to say he had not examined the various dresses very closely, Robinson pinned him down to a description of the room-by-room search. Fleet finally admitted that he had taken each garment out, examined the outside, and turned each one inside out. He had found no bloodstains of any kind.

Robinson battled Fleet with the same fervor in reference to the handleless hatchet. At the inquest and again in his direct testimony, he had maintained that the hatchet was covered with ashes, that were put there after it had been washed, for the purpose of making it appear unused for a long period of time. Robinson forced him to admit there was an ash heap in the cellar big enough to fill 50 baskets, and that the dust on the other items in the box might have come from ashes as well.

How clear it was to the jury that Fleet's only concern in the investigation had been to build a case against Lizzie Borden we can't know. That he had "managed" his testimony to fit his convictions must have been transparent. By now, the fame of George Washington's little hatchet was eclipsed by the one found in the Borden cellar.

Since the first day of the trial, a cow had roamed the field adjacent to the courthouse, and through the open windows had punctuated even the most distressing testimony with mournful moos protesting the oppressive heat, the lack of fresh vegetation, or milking hands. Robinson was through with Fleet and turned back toward his seat. As if to accent the end of the day, the cow lowed long and plaintively.

Sheriff Wright rapped a pencil on his desk, calling for silence. The justices turned to him querulously and the spectators burst into laughter.

It was 5:15 and day four was adjourned.

The New London, Connecticut, *Day* commented:

> Although the Lizzie Borden case is yet in its early stages, it is already apparent that the prisoner stands in no danger of conviction. The web of circumstantial evidence which the state has been weaving for ten months, has been rent in various places by ex-Governor Robinson.

The Worcester, Massachusetts, *Spy* echoed that view and added:

> Lizzie Borden has not yet been acquitted, but it certainly looks as if the Fall River police were going to be disappointed in their hunger for a "pound of flesh." That warrant for her arrest was a stroke of forehandedness that quite overreached itself.

And the Worcester, Massachusetts, *Telegram* warned:

> If the government can show that it was justified in arresting this girl, it had better be about it.

North Main Street, Fall River, as Lizzie knew it.

The A. J. Borden Building, nearing completion on the morning of the murders.

Lizzie Borden.

Andrew Jackson Borden.

Emma Lenora Borden.

Abby Durfee Gray Borden.

Lizzie Andrew Borden.

Andrew J. Borden, as his body was found.

Abby Borden, as her body was found.

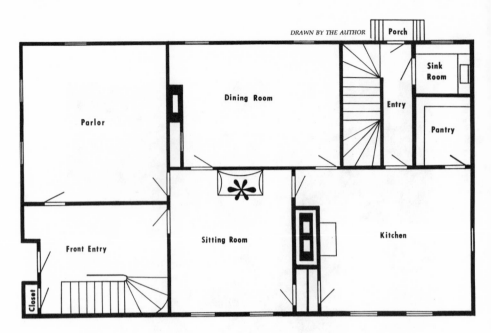

Plan of the first floor of the Borden house.

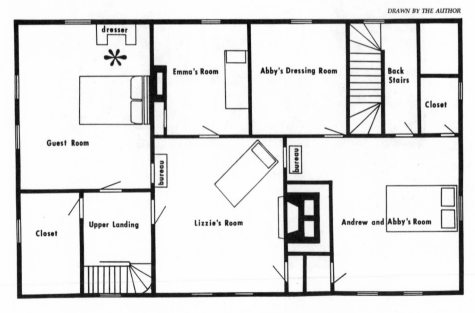

Plan of the second floor of the Borden house.

The guest room.

Front view, 92 Second Street.

Rear view, 92 Second Street.

From *Boston Globe*, August 11, 1892

SECOND STREET AND THE BORDEN HOME (1) 92 Second Street—
the Andrew Jackson Borden residence. (2) The barn. (3) The side entrance
(see also below). (4) Mrs. Churchill's home—generally called the Buffinton
house. (5) Residence of Dr. Seabury Bowen. (6) The Chagnon house. (7)
Home of Dr. Kelly. North and south are as shown.

Side entrance, 92 Second Street.

ANDREW J. JENNINGS,
COUNSELOR AT LAW,
SECTION G, GRANITE BLOCK.

FALL RIVER, MASS., Nov 22 1892.

Hon A. E. Pillsbury
Attorney General

My Dear Pillsbury

Since my talk with you I have been seriously considering your proposition and have come to the conclusion that I cannot consent to unite with you in the examination proposed. I asked Adams opinion on the advisability of the course proposed without expressing any opinion of my own and also on my return home that of Mr Holmes who to a certain extent, represents the Borden girls, without informing him that I had consulted Adams. Both came to the same conclusion, that in view of all the circumstances we could not do anything which suggested a doubt of her innocence and that the course proposed would not be wise or expedient on our part

Sincerely yours
Andrew J Jennings

Attorney Jennings's letter to Attorney General Pillsbury declining his proposal to have Lizzie submit to an insanity examination or to a plea of "not guilty by reason of insanity."

Hosea M. Knowlton. Arthur E. Perry.
Counsellors at Law.
OFFICE:
38 North Water Street.

Long Distance Telephone.

(Dictated.) New Bedford, Mass., November 22, 1892.

Hon. A. E. Pillsbury,

Attorney-General.

Dear Sir:-

I did not have time to write so
fully as I desired about the sanity business. I could do nothing whatever with Jennings. He took exactly the position I feared he would,
and seemed to regard it as some sort of a surrender if he consented
to anything. We can make some investigations into the family matters
without him, but it will not be so thorough as it would be if we had
his assistance.

I note your suggestions about form of indictment, which I will
adopt if we ever get so far; of which, however, I am far from certain.

Yours Truly,

*District Attorney Knowlton's letter to Attorney General Pillsbury in which
he expresses his doubt there is sufficient evidence for an indictment since
Attorney Jennings refuses to have Lizzie examined for insanity.*

Hosea M. Knowlton.   Arthur E. Perry.

Counsellors at Law.
OFFICE:
38 North Water Street.

Long Distance Telephone

(Dictated.)   New Bedford, Mass. April 24, 1893.

Hon. A.E Pillsbury, Attorney General:

My Dear Sir:-

I have thought more ˜about the Lizzie Borden case since I talked with you, and think perhaps it may be well to write you, as I shall not be able to meet you probably until Thursday, possibly Wednesday afternoon.

Personally I would like very much to get rid of the trial of the case, and fear that my own feelings in that direction may have influenced my better judgment. I feel this all the more upon your not unexpected announcement that the burden of the trial would come upon me.

I confess, however, I cannot see my way clear to any disposition of the case other than a trial. Should it result in disagreement of the jury there would be no difficulty then in disposing of the case by admitting the defendent to bail; but a verdict either way would render such a course unnecessary.

The case had proceeded so far and an indictment has been found by the grand inquest of the county that it does not seem to me that we ought to take the responsibility of discharging her without trial, even though there is every reasonable expection of a verdit of not guilty. I am unable to concur fully in your views as to the probable result. I think it may well be that the jury might disagree upon the case. But even in my most sanguine moments I have scarcely expected a verdict of guilty.

The situation is this: nothing has developed which satisfies either of us that she is innocent, neither of us can escape the conclusion that she must have had some knowledge of the occurrence. She has been presented for trial by a jury which, to say the least, was not influenced by anything said by the government in the favor of the indictment.

WIthout discussing the matter more fully in this letter I will only say as above indicated that I cannot see how any other course than setting the case down for trial, and trying it will satisfy that portion of the public sentiment whether favorable to her or not, which is worthy of being respected.

June seems to be the most satisfactory month, all things considered. I will write more fully as to the admission of her confession after I have looked the matter up.

Yours Truly,

H.M.Knowlton.

District Attorney Knowlton's letter to Attorney General Pillsbury in which he stated he had no hope of obtaining a conviction of Lizzie.

The other discovery is still more important; on one of the cuts in Mrs. Borden's skull, near the right ear, there is a very small but unmistakable deposit of the gilt metal with which hatchets are ornamented when they leave the factory; this deposit (Dr. Cheever confirmed the observation fully) means that the hatchet used in killing Mrs. Borden was a <u>new</u> hatchet, not long out of the store. Perhaps this is not new information, either to you or Dr. Dolan; it was new to me and seemed important enough to justify immediate conveyance to you. The shining deposit can be seen with the naked eye; it is plainly visible with the use of a lens, when once its situation is indicated.

Very truly Yours

F. W. Draper.

Mr. Knowlton.

Extract of Dr. Francis W. Draper's letter advising District Attorney Knowlton that the handleless hatchet could not have been the murder weapon.

INDICTMENT.

COMMONWEALTH
VS.
LIZZIE ANDREW BORDEN.

MURDER.

Commonwealth of Massachusetts.

BRISTOL SS. At the Superior Court begun and holden at Taunton within and for said County of Bristol, on the first Monday of November, in the year of our Lord one thousand eight hundred and ninety-two.

The Jurors for the said Commonwealth, on their oath present,—That Lizzie Andrew Borden of Fall River in the County of Bristol, at Fall River in the County of Bristol, on the fourth day of August in the year eighteen hundred and ninety-two, in and upon one Andrew Jackson Borden, feloniously, wilfully and of her malice aforethought, an assault did make, and with a certain weapon, to wit, a sharp cutting instrument, the name and a more particular description of which is to the Jurors unknown, him, the said Andrew Jackson Borden feloniously, wilfully and of her malice aforethought, did strike, cut, beat and bruise, in and upon the head of him, the said Andrew Jackson Borden, giving to him, the said Andrew Jackson Borden, by the said striking, cutting, beating and bruising, in and upon the head of him, the said Andrew Jackson Borden, divers, to wit, ten mortal wounds, of which said mortal wounds the said Andrew Jackson Borden then and there instantly died.

And so the Jurors aforesaid, upon their oath aforesaid, do say, that the said Lizzie Andrew Borden, the said Andrew Jackson Borden, in manner and form aforesaid, then and there feloniously, wilfully and of her malice aforethought did kill and murder; against the peace of said Commonwealth and contrary to the form of the statute in such case made and provided.

A true bill.

HENRY A. BODMAN,

HOSEA M. KNOWLTON, Foreman of the Grand Jury.

District Attorney.

Bristol ss. On this second day of December, in the year eighteen hundred and ninety-two, this indictment was returned and presented to said Superior Court by the Grand Jury, ordered to be filed, and filed; and it was further ordered by the Court that notice be given to said Lizzie Andrew Borden that said indictment will be entered forthwith upon the docket of the Superior Court in said County.

Attest:—

SIMEON BORDEN, Jr.,
Asst. Clerk.

A true copy.
Attest: *Simeon Borden* Clerk.

Indictment of Lizzie Borden by the grand jury (never shown before).

The handleless hatchet introduced as the murder weapon.

Bridget Sullivan.

Andrew J. Jennings.

Sarah Morse Borden and daughter, Emma Lenora.

Lizzie's neighbor, Miss Adelaide Churchill.

Rufus B. Hilliard, marshal of Fall River.

DR. WILLIAM A. DOLAN

Fall River medical examiner.

ELI BENCE

Druggist who said Lizzie asked for prussic acid.

JOSIAH BLAISDELL

Judge who presided at the inquest and the preliminary hearing.

DR. SEABURY BOWEN

First doctor to examine the bodies.

The grand jury.

The trial jury.

The Taunton jail where Lizzie was held for ten months.

David Kent

Maplecroft (above) and 92 Second Street (below) as they are today.

The Borden family monument, Oak Grove Cemetery.

11

▄▄▄▄▄▄▄▄▄

The Hoodoo Hatchet

*T*HE HEADLINE IN *The New York Times* of June 10 encapsulated
what took place on the fifth day of the trial:

BREAK IN THE STATE'S CASE
POLICE WITNESSES IN BORDEN CASE DISAGREE
ONE OF THEM SWEARS THAT HE SAW THE PIECE OF
HATCHET HANDLE ALLEGED TO BE MISSING IN THE VERY BOX
WHERE THE HATCHET WAS FOUND.

Or as Joe Howard would say it, "The fifth day of the trial of
Lizzie Borden for her life was marked by the most dramatic
sensation in its record. The tattered web which the legal spiders
of the Commonwealth have been weaving around her had one
of its strongest threads snapped by a sudden and totally unexpected blow that left it sagging at one side. The government's
witnesses did not agree. One stuck to the outlined programme

in his testimony and another followed him with a startling disclosure. Then the first witness was called back and made to confirm his apparent insincerity."

Captain Philip Harrington followed Fleet to the witness stand as day five began. On the day of the murders, he had been a foot patrolman; he had since jumped all ranks and had been made captain. The Fall River *Globe* had found him to be an excellent source of "inside information," particularly because he leaked his stories exclusively to them.

His description of events from the time he arrived at 12:15 was meticulous, even to describing which hand he had used to open each door and where each person had been standing (or sitting) when he had spoken to them.

He had been the fourth or fifth person (depending on whose account was accurate) to interrogate Lizzie about what had taken place. She had told him of her father's return from the post office and his sitting in the dining room for a moment and then stretching out on the sofa in the sitting room. She recounted her trip to the barn, where she had been for 20 minutes, and said she had seen no one and heard nothing while there.

Downstairs, he had noticed Dr. Bowen with some note paper in his hand, standing near the stove. He had seen the word "Emma" written on one corner, but Bowen had dropped the paper in the grate. He had asked Bowen what the paper was and had been told it was nothing—a personal note he had taken from his pocket—something about his daughter going somewhere.

Robinson, fearing the impression might be left that Bowen had burned the missing note, objected, saying, "I cannot let this go in the record unless you (Knowlton) give me an assurance that it has nothing whatever to do with the case." Knowlton acknowledged, "It has nothing to do with the case at all."

A defense attorney's most important job in any trial is to try to discredit the prosecution's witnesses. By creating a doubt about the accuracy or truthfulness of any portion of testimony, however insignificant, a doubt can be planted in a juror's mind about the accuracy or truthfulness of all of it. Robinson spotted such a deviation in Harrington's testimony.

On direct questioning, he testified that all the windows in the barn were closed. Robinson, in cross-examining, read his testimony given at the district court, in which he had said one of the windows was open. A flustered Harrington quickly recanted and admitted one of the windows had been open. It was a minor point and meaningless as evidence, but worth making, since it helped establish that everything being said in the trial was not necessarily the gospel.

Successful once, Robinson pressed on, leading Harrington to swear he had particularly noted that Andrew's shoes were laced. Robinson produced one of the official photographs showing the shoes had no laces; that they were congress gaiters with elastic sides. Harrington's airy response was, "The photograph is wrong."

Robinson turned away, shaking his head. There would be other, better opportunities to question witness credibility when the next two witnesses were called.

When Officer Michael Mullaly took the stand next, he gave no sign that he was a powder keg about to explode. A younger man than most of the other officers, he was lean, trim, and in the best physical condition, just the kind of officer you would want walking the beat in front of your house.

His first questions of Lizzie had been to determine what valuables Andrew might have had on his person. He was told to look for a silver watch and chain, a wallet with money in it, and a gold ring on his little finger. A check showed all were accounted for. Robbery, then, was clearly out as a motive.

He had then asked about axes and hatchets. Lizzie said there were both in the house and had summoned Bridget to show him where they were. She had led the way to the basement and showed him two claw hatchets and two axes. From a niche in the chimney, she had taken down a box and showed him also a hatchet head. Fleet had come down a few minutes later, and Mullaly had shown him the trove of weapons. He had then conducted a general search of the house and yard but had found no other weapons or signs of blood anywhere.

Since Fleet had said *he* was the one who had found the box containing the hatchet head, Robinson enjoyed the opportunity to cross-examine Mullaly and get him to repeat that it was Bridget, not Fleet, who had pointed out the box. One more occasion to point out that police witnesses were not infallible; one more chance to gig Fleet for his brusque manner on the stand. What he got next from Mullaly was of far greater value than both of these minor satisfactions.

Asked to describe the contents of the box Bridget had shown him, Mullaly said it contained odd bits of metal, a doorknob, some hinges, and the handle of the hatchet head.

"Mr. Fleet not only took out the blade but the handle also." Mullaly's words fell like a bombshell at Robinson's feet.

"What?" he bellowed.

"In addition to the bit of wood stuck in the eye of the hatchet, there was another piece as well," Mullaly said.

Q. Another piece of what?
A. Handle.
Q. Where is it now?
A. I don't know.
Q. Was it a piece of the same handle?
A. It was a piece that corresponded with that. [Pointing to the piece of wood that had been in the hatchet head.]
Q. The rest of the handle?
A. It was a piece with a fresh break in it.
Q. The other piece?
A. Yes sir.
Q. Was it a handle to the hatchet?
A. It was what I call a hatchet handle.
Q. Well, did you take it out of the box?
A. I did not.
Q. Did you see it taken out?
A. I did.
Q. Who took it out?
A. Mr. Fleet took it out.
Q. You were there?
A. I was there.
Q. Anybody else?
A. Not that I know of.
Q. Did Mr. Fleet put it back, too?
A. He did.

Let's follow Joe Howard's newspaper account of this dramatic moment:

The feelings of the counsel for the Commonwealth may be imagined. They sat rigid in their chairs like statues. Governor Robinson ordered the witness to stand where he was until Fleet could be found. He was to have no chance to tell the marshal what he had been saying. Mr. Jennings was all over the room at once. He sent his office assistant to the foot of the courthouse stairs to see that no one spoke to Fleet. He sent a shrewd detective from Cambridge to stand at the head of the stairs and see that Mullaly had no chance to say a word to his chief. At the same instant, a friend of the police seated in the courtroom slipped from a chair within the bar and went unostentatiously out into the hall.

District Attorney Knowlton, leader for the government, felt the glare of the ex-governor's eyes.

"Where is the handle?" the governor asked.

"I don't know," said Mr. Knowlton. After another pointed inquiry he said, with a voice unlike his own, "I never heard of it before."

Mr. Knowlton, who is best described as a man of round-headed, vigorous Cromwellian figure, soon found his voice and his feet. He suggested the court detail an officer to go to the Borden house and see if the missing handle is there now and Mr. Robinson protested.

"I only suggest it in the interest of justice," Mr. Knowlton replied.

"I want justice too, but not in that way," said the ex-governor.

Robinson asked the court's permission to recall Fleet immediately, and the justices agreed. Mullaly was asked to stand down while Fleet was brought back to the stand. Knowlton wanted to question Fleet first, but the court ruled against him. Robinson bore down:

Q. Will you state again what you found at the time you looked in (the box)?

A. I found a hatchet head, the handle broken off, together with some other tools in there and the iron that was inside there. I don't know just what it was.

Q. You did not find the handle, the broken piece, not at all?

A. No sir.

Q. You did not see it, did you?

A. No sir.

Q. You did not see it?

A. No sir.

Q. Did Mr. Mullaly take it out of the box?

A. Not that I know of.

Q. You looked in so that you could have seen it if it was there?

A. Yes sir.

Q. You have no doubt about that, have you, at all?

A. What?

Q. That you did not find the other piece of the handle that fitted on there?

A. No sir.

Q. You saw no piece of wood with any fresh break in the box, around the box or near it?

A. No sir, not that I am aware of. I did not see any of it.

There was an audible stir among the spectators, and the jurors exchanged looks. It was obvious to everyone: Fleet was lying under oath.

Eyewitness testimony is, and has always been, subject to human error, but since this hatchet was presented as the most important item of physical evidence, any fact about it, no matter how trivial, would not be overlooked or casually forgotten by the police. During the inquest and the preliminary hearing, they had maintained that one of the other hatchets or one of the axes had been the murder weapon. When all of them had been eliminated by the Harvard examinations, only then had they turned to the handleless hatchet. Now it strained credibility too far to ask the jury to believe Mullaly must have only *imagined* finding a handle.

According to the defense, a handle was vital to the theory. Without one, the head alone could not be seriously regarded as a lethal weapon in the hands of a woman of no notable strength.

The public and, more important, the jury, was left to ponder the significance of the missing handle and the reason it had been broken at the time of the murder, if indeed it had. The police wanted to create the assumption that it had been broken off and disposed of because it was stained with blood that could not be quickly washed away. That would not, however, explain why there was no blood on the wooden piece still stuck in the head. If the handle had been stained, certainly the piece nearest to the spurting that resulted from the 28 blows would also be.

As *The New York Times* had said, Mullaly's testimony had been the "break" in the state's case. Typical of the biased record in Porter's *The Fall River Tragedy*, Mullaly's sensation was dismissed with a single sentence and is not even mentioned in Pearson's 433-page *The Trial of Lizzie Borden*.

Earlier, Adelaide Churchill had stoutly maintained that the dress Lizzie had turned over to the police was not the one she had worn when Adelaide had first run over that morning. Left unchallenged, her testimony could do serious damage to the defense. She was recalled in the afternoon and quizzed again. Robinson asked her to say what Bridget was wearing, and Adelaide responded, positively, it was a light-colored calico.

Bridget had said she was wearing a dark indigo blue dress. Robinson read Bridget's testimony to that effect but, like Harrington with the shoelaces, Adelaide was not to be persuaded; Bridget had been wearing a light-colored calico.

The impression was unavoidable: if Adelaide had been wrong about what Bridget had worn, she could also be mistaken about Lizzie's apparel.

As far as Porter's "history" is concerned, there was no sixth day of the trial; he omitted it entirely. Perhaps he did so because it was another day of setbacks for the prosecution.

Faced with the conflicting testimony concerning the hatchet handle and the now-confused description of Lizzie's dress, the prosecution hoped to get back on track with the help of Lieutenant Francis L. Edson. He had been one of the six men who had ransacked the Borden house on Monday after the Harvard laboratory had reported negatively on the axes and hatchets sent to them. It was the defense, however, that benefitted from his description of the events of that Monday.

From the beginning of the investigation, the police had not believed that Lizzie had been in the loft of the barn when Andrew had been killed. If the prosecution could convince the jury of that, Lizzie would be pinned down inside the house at the minute of his death. It would prove opportunity, one of the three legs of the mythical triad necessary to convict: motive, means, and opportunity.

He had been sent to pick up the hatchet head, Edson said. He had also picked up a basket of odds and ends in the barn and taken it back to the station for inspection and inventory. On cross-examination, Robinson drew from him a list of the basket's contents: sheet lead, a doorknob, and an assortment of metal pieces. The basket was just as Lizzie had described at the inquest and lent credence to her story of being up in the loft rummaging in that very basket.

Officer William Medley also centered the court's attention on the loft. Asked to describe what he had noticed during his examination, he spoke positively and in detail. In the following quotations, he refers to the floor of the *barn* but is speaking of the *loft* floor:

"I went upstairs until I reached about three or four steps from the top, and while there, part of my body was above the floor— above the level of the floor—and I looked around the barn to see if there was any evidence of anything having been disturbed and I didn't notice that anything had or seemed to have been disturbed and I stooped down low to see if I could discern any marks on the floor of the barn having been made there. I did that by stooping down and looking across the bottom of the barn floor. I didn't see any and I reached out my hand to see if I could make an impression on the floor of the barn and I did, by putting my hand down—and found that I made an impression on the barn floor.

Q.   Describe what there was on or about the floor by which you made an impression.
A.   Seemed to be accumulated hay dust and other dust.
Q.   How distinctly could you see the marks which you made with your hand?
A.   I could see them quite distinctly when I looked for them.
Q.   Go on and describe anything else which you did.
A.   Then I stepped up on the top and took four or five steps on the outer edge of the barn floor, the edge nearest the stairs, then came up to see if I could discern those, and I did.
Q.   How did you look to see if you could discern those foot steps which you made?
A.   I did it in the first place by stooping down and casting my eye on a level with the barn floor, and could see them plainly.

Q. Did you see any other footsteps in that dust than those you made yourself?

A. No sir.

Medley's testimony was potentially devastating to the defense. In his zeal to present the worst possible scenario against Lizzie, Pearson quoted Medley's testimony word for word in his account of the trial. It is the *only* testimony on day six that he quoted. All other witnesses were dismissed by merely listing them.

The prosecution must have been delighted with Medley's description of what he had *not* found in the loft. They had suffered heavy losses with both the dress and the hatchet, but had apparently won the battle of the barn. Readers are asked to remember Medley's description and the detail with which he pictured what he had done. What seemed on day six to be a solid victory for the prosecution took on a different dimension when the defense presented its case.

Once again, the subject came up as to who had found the hatchet head and what had been done with it. By now, nobody was certain; not the police and certainly not the jury.

Medley confidently said he had picked it up on that Monday, carefully wrapped it in *brown* paper and took it to Marshal Hilliard. Egged on by Robinson, he demonstrated exactly how he had wrapped it, using a piece of paper courteously furnished by Robinson.

Captain Dennis Desmond took the stand next to describe how *he* had found the hatchet and carefully wrapped it in a *newspaper*, and he demonstrated exactly how he had wrapped it, using a piece of newspaper courteously furnished by Robinson.

Desmond was not able to say whether it was *The Boston Globe* or the *Providence Journal* he had used. It was, however, just about the only humorous moment in the trial; two serious-faced officers, each under oath, solemnly swearing he had done something only one of them could have done. We can't know whether the jury regarded it as an instance of deliberately false testimony or harmless braggadocio.

Push came to shove as the court prepared to adjourn until Monday, at which time the prosecution proposed to offer into evidence the testimony Lizzie had given at the "inquest." Robinson, of course, was opposed. A written statement setting out the parameters of the arguments was agreed upon. Summarized:

1. The declarations offered are the testimony, under oath, of the accused in a judicial proceeding.
2. The defendant was not then under arrest, but three days before the time of giving such testimony, was notified she was suspected of committing the crimes, and the house, including the defendant, were thereafter, until her arrest, under the constant observation of police officers.
3. That she was duly summoned by a subpoena.
4. That before she so testified, she requested to have counsel present, which request was refused.
5. That when her testimony was concluded she was not allowed to leave the courthouse, but was placed under arrest.
6. Prior to said inquest, a warrant charging her with the Bordens' murder was issued but not served.
7. That before giving her testimony, she was not cautioned that she was not obligated to testify to anything which might incriminate herself.

The next day was Sunday. When court reconvened on Monday, this would be the compelling issue. It is safe to say both sides believed that the court's ruling as to the admissibility of Lizzie's testimony would presage who would win the final victory.

12

The Harvard Cover-up

O N SUNDAY, the Woonsocket, Rhode Island, *Reporter* editorialized:

> After a week's testimony on the part of the prosecution in the Borden murder trial, the indications are that the accused young woman will never be convicted. The defense, if the layman can judge, has much the best of the case so far, for there has been no direct evidence fastening the atrocious crime upon the prisoner, and leading witnesses have, in several important instances, been flatly contradictory. As the case now stands, a disagreement is the most the government can expect, while public sentiment already clamors for an acquittal.

And in the ebullient words of Joe Howard, "We stand on the hither verge of a sensational week, having passed through one of exceeding trial to nerves and physiques, not to mention moral sensibilities. It is not too much to say that everyone connected with the case, not even excepting the learned judges upon the bench, was heartily glad when the hour for adjournment came on Saturday, affording many an opportunity to go home and refresh their overtaxed energies by a day of rest."

Though no one mentioned it, the 12 men who made up the jury were probably the most in need of refreshment. What some had probably looked upon as a lark in the beginning had turned into a virtual nightmare for all.

As one reporter described their ordeal:

> Up at 6 o'clock in the morning, breakfast at 7, tramp to the courthouse at 9, there to sit on their oak bench until 1, tramp through broiling sun to the hotel for dinner in silence, march back again in a column like a press-gang; hammered at until 5 by the learned brothers at the bar, back to the hotel in lockstep for supper and at 8 locked in their rooms, sworn not to discuss the days events. No refreshments, alcoholic or otherwise permitted. Their recreation: a cribbage board and three worn decks of cards.

And how to describe the breathtaking heat of 100 or more degrees inside that cramped courtroom, packed with 50 more sweating people than its capacity; with every window open to the lowing of the court cow and with not even a ceiling fan to stir the fetid air?

This was day seven.

It was the contention of the defense that Lizzie's three days of testimony at the so-called inquest had been obtained while she was under virtual arrest, and she had not been told that anything she said could be used against her. In the language of the 1990s, she had not been "Mirandized."

Knowlton sat, still silent, at the prosecution's table. William H. Moody spoke for the prosecution.

He argued that the "inquest" had been properly called and held under the public statutes of the Commonwealth. He attacked Robinson's complaint that Lizzie's attorney had not been allowed to be present by citing the provisions of Massachusetts law that stipulated that inquiries "may be private" and "any and all may be excluded." But this evaded the question as to whether or not the "informal examination of witnesses," as it had been announced, had been an "inquest" when it had taken place.

The central question now was, he said, "whether there is anything in the circumstances—which would take the declarations there made by her out from the general rule that any act or declaration of the defendant—is competent and admissable."

He argued that *what* Lizzie had said was not important; that it was not a confession. And, besides, there was a difference between a confession and statements that might be evidences of guilt. While Article 12 of the Massachusetts Declaration of Rights and the Fifth Amendment to the U.S. Constitution clearly state that no one shall be compelled to furnish evidence against oneself, Lizzie had not been compelled; her declarations had been voluntarily given. In short:

" . . . upon an inquiry into the death of a person, if one then under suspicion and informed that he is then under suspicion, responds to the subpoena of the state, and in the eye of the law voluntarily gives testimony at that inquiry, if he is subsequently arrested—what he said at the inquiry is admissable against him."

It was a callous argument, the position that, if one were foolish enough to testify against oneself after being told they were under suspicion, then it was admissable.

Robinson's reply was a broadside and began with a condensate of the facts:

1st. The homicides were committed August 4.

2nd. The defendant's testimony was given August 9 to 11.

3rd. The defendant was accused of the crimes by the mayor August 6.

4th. The defendant was kept under police observation from August 6 till arrest. "The house was surrounded"; she knew the police were around her.

5th. The defendant on or before August 9 was subpoened to testify at the "inquest."

6th. The defendant requested counsel—denied.

7th. The defendant was not properly cautioned.

8th. A warrant for her arrest was issued August 8, *before* she testified.

9th. The defendant was arrested at the conclusion of her testimony.

"In other words," Robinson said, "the practice that was resorted to was to put her really in the custody of the city marshal, beyond the possibility of any retirement, or any release or any freedom whatsoever, keeping her with the hand upon the shoulder—she, a woman, could not run—covering her at every moment, surrounding her at every instant, empowered to take her at any moment, and under those circumstances, taking her to that inquest to testify.

"She was taken by the city marshal and with no advisor to warn her that she did not have to unless she wanted to, was made to stand for three sweltering days of grilling, unaware of the pregnant fact that all the while, the marshal had a warrant for her arrest in his pocket.

"The police said, 'We will hold the paper in our pockets and get what we can from her and later, if we decide to arrest her, we will put away that paper and arrest her on another.' "

It was worse, he said, than any burned dress.

"And that went on for three days, with no intimation to her from anybody who was authorized to make it—nay, we may say, who was *bound* to make it, that she had any rights at all. Denied counsel, neglected as far as the court acted or the district attorney, to tell her that she ought not to testify to anything that might tend to criminate herself, she stood alone, a defenseless woman, in that attitude.

"If *that* is freedom, God save the Commonwealth of Massachusetts!"

It was vintage Robinson. Moody had spoken laboriously for 45 minutes, citing precedents back to and including English law. But, within the first five minutes of his reply, Robinson had added the emotional ingredient, fair play, and that's what the argument was all about.

Moody's only reply in rebuttal was that Robinson's argument was magnificent, but it was not law.

The chief justice called the noon recess at 11:15 and court resumed at 12:40.

The conduct of the inquest, he said when court reconvened, was not this court's concern, only the admissability of what had been said there.

"The common law," he continued, "regards this species of evidence with distrust. Statements made by one accused of crime are admissable against him only when it is affirmatively established that they were voluntarily made.

"The common law regards *substance* more than form. The principle involved cannot be evaded by avoiding the form of arrest if the witness at the time of such testimony is practically in custody. From the agreed facts and the facts otherwise in evidence, it is plain that the prisoner at the time of her testimony was, so far as relates to this question, as effectually in custody as if the formal precept had been served; and, without dwelling on other circumstances which distinguish the facts of this case from those of cases on which the government relies, we are all of opinion that this consideration is decisive and the evidence is excluded."

The New York Times heralded the decision in headlines the following day:

BIG GAIN FOR LIZZIE BORDEN
HER TESTIMONY AT THE INQUEST NOT TO GO TO THE JURY
BRILLIANT ARGUMENT IN HER BEHALF BY EX-GOV ROBINSON

The defense won a decided advantage today when the court excluded as evidence the testimony given by Lizzie Borden at the inquest held soon after her father and stepmother were murdered in Fall River. There have been several breaks in the prosecution's case, none so bad as the one made by the decision as to the prisoner's evidence at the inquest. The decision will go a great way toward making Lizzie Borden a free woman.

Fall River Medical Examiner William A. Dolan took the stand as principal witness for the prosecution in the afternoon session of day seven.

He described in gruesome detail the various wounds on the heads of the two victims and the beheading that had taken place at Qak Grove Cemetery on the day of the funeral. He brought along plaster casts of the heads, and they were introduced into evidence.

In the words of *The New York Times* reporter, "It was a hard day for the prisoner." She learned for the first time what had taken place when the burial service had been halted, and she wept openly. At one point, she had to be helped from the courtroom.

Dolan told how he had been passing the Borden home and had been summoned inside very soon after Andrew's body had been discovered. By then, Dr. Bowen had covered the body with a sheet. He had found Andrew's hands still warm and bright red blood still oozing from the wounds about his head and face. He had then gone upstairs and looked at the body of Mrs. Borden, touched her head and hands, and found them much colder than Andrew's.

Because of the talk about possible poisoning, he had removed the stomachs of both bodies and collected samples of the milk delivered that morning and the day before. He had gone with officers to the basement and was shown two axes and two hatchets. All these items had been sent off to the Harvard Medical School for examination.

Two hairs had adhered to the head of one of the hatchets, and there were spots on the axes that looked like blood.

He then produced the plaster cast of Andrew's head, each wound outlined in blue ink.

Q.   How many wounds did you find on his head?
A.   Ten on the fleshy part.
Q.   And what was the condition, generally speaking, of the skull of Mr. Borden as to being crushed in?
A.   From in front of the ear, commencing about 1 1/2 inches in front of the ear, to probably 1 1/2 inches behind the ear, the bone was all crushed in.

For almost an hour, Dolan measured each of the wounds in the plaster skulls of Andrew and Abby and enumerated the bloodstains found about the bodies, as to number and size. Taking into account the contents of the stomachs and the color of the blood around the wounds, it was his opinion that Mrs. Borden died first, from one-and-a-half to two hours before Andrew had suffered a similar fate.

Asked if wounds such as he had described on both bodies could have been inflicted with a hatchet by a woman of ordinary strength, his terse answer was yes.

On cross-examination, Attorney Adams went on the offense by reading back to Dr. Dolan his testimony at the preliminary hearing:

Q. In your opinion, would that hatchet that you saw furnish an adequate cause of these incised wounds?
A. Yes sir.
Q. The wounds in both cases?
A. Yes sir.

Adams asked Dolan if he wished now to change that testimony.

A. I do; yes sir.
Q. In what respect?
A. That is, *providing* the cutting edge of that axe is a certain distance—a certain length.
Q. Hadn't you measured it at that time?
A. No sir, I had not.
Q. Have you measured it since?
A. No sir.

It was a startling admission that he had identified the handleless hatchet as the murder weapon without ever doing the one necessary thing, measuring the blade. The absurdity of it was not lost on the jury, especially when, a few questions later, Dolan admitted that some of the wounds were five inches in length, an inch-and-a-half wider than the blade of the hatchet introduced as the murder weapon.

Needless to say, all of this information was deleted from Porter's "Bible."

When court convened for the eighth day of the trial, Dr. Dolan took the stand again to complete his testimony. This time, instead of a plaster cast of Andrew's skull, he brought the real thing. A horrified Lizzie was mercifully allowed to sit in the hallway during its exhibition in the court.

Of all the mysteries connected to the Borden murders, the most profound was revealed in the first few questions put to Dr. Dolan by Attorney Adams. Discussing the nature of the blows to the heads of Andrew and Abby, Adams put these questions to Dolan:

Q. You think the assailant swung the instrument from left to right, don't you?
A. Yes sir.

Q.   And all these wounds can be fairly accounted for by blows from left to right?
A.   Yes sir.
Q.   That is to say, by a left-handed person?
A.   Yes, by a left-handed person.

Lizzie was right-handed.

The questioning took another turn at this point, and it was never mentioned again, either in examinations, cross-examinations, or in Robinson's summary.

This, it would seem, would have been almost certain vindication of Lizzie, had it been pursued. In none of the accounts of the Borden murders has this astounding point ever been mentioned or speculated on, but the trial transcript is explicit and, by repetition of the question, cannot be regarded as a stenographic error.

Why this specter of a left-handed killer was not seized upon by the defense, we can now never know. One can almost hear Robinson heaping scorn on the prosecution, acting out for the jury a right-handed person clumsily swinging a hatchet with the left hand; ridiculing the idea that such an act could possibly have taken place!

Instead, the left-handed killer remains one of the most baffling of all the Borden mysteries.

On redirect examination, the prosecution made a valiant effort to explain how a three-and-a-half-inch hatchet could have made wounds two inches long. The answer was, Dolan said, because the whole cutting edge hadn't been brought into play. How, he was asked, could a three-and-a-half-inch hatchet make a four-and-a-half-inch wound? By sliding and by also crushing its way in. It was all very clear until Adams, in re-cross-examination, asked his first question:

"From the appearance of an injury having various lengths like one, two, three, four and five inches, you are hardly able to determine the length of the cutting edge giving them, are you?" Dolan's reply: "No sir."

Dr. Edward Stickney Wood, the physician and chemist who had headed the forensic team of examiners at Harvard, was called to the stand, and it is believable that Dr. Dolan was glad to turn over the hotseat to him. Wood was a red-faced, gray-haired, stalwart, and handsome man who looked like an army officer browned by long duty on the plains.

Knowlton had, from the first day, yielded the prosecution's case to Moody. He had occupied the leader's chair at the prosecution's table but throughout the week's proceedings he had only occasionally exchanged quiet confidences with Moody. He had followed the questioning and cross-questioning with interest and attention, but it was apparent that his fire did not burn with intensity. For good reason, he now rose to take charge.

Four days before the trial began he had received a letter from Dr. Frank W. Draper, who had taken part with Dr. Dolan in the autopsy of both bodies at the Oak Grove Cemetery. Draper, educated at the Harvard Medical School, had been in practice for 24 years. He was one of the medical examiners for Suffolk county, that is, Boston. In addition, he was Professor of Legal Medicine in the Harvard Medical School, a position formerly called Professor of Medical Jurisprudence.

Among his duties as Boston's medical examiner, he had been called upon in nearly 3,500 cases of death, when homicide was suspected or charged. He was not new to testifying in court.

On May 31, he conferred with Dr. David W. Cheever, and Draper wrote a four-page letter detailing what their testimony would be when called to the stand. Dr. Cheever was also a graduate of the Harvard Medical School with follow-up studies in Paris. He had been an instructor at his alma mater for 23 years and had been professor of surgery for 21. He was also on the staff of the Boston City Hospital. They were, he wrote, in entire accord on these facts:

1. That the cause and manner of the deaths were the same in both cases, namely, fracture of the skull and injury to the brain by blows on the head.
2. That the weapon was an edged tool of some weight, like a hatchet.
3. That the length of the edge of the weapon was about 3½ inches.
4. That Mrs. Borden was killed by blows inflicted from behind, the assailant standing astride the body.

5. That Mr. Borden was killed by blows given by the assailant standing at the head of the sofa just within the door.
6. That the assailant was right-handed and used his right hand, or, if using both hands, that the left hand was foremost, or in front of the right hand, on the handle.
7. That Mrs. Borden died first, and that the supposition of an hour's interval is not inconsistent with the facts relating to the stage of digestion, the body temperature, and the condition of the blood in the two cases.
8. That the deaths were not instantaneous.
9. That a woman would have sufficient physical strength to inflict the blows, assuming that she was of normal adult vigor.

"I write," he continued, "especially to inform you of two important discoveries which I made upon a careful examination of the two skulls. On Mr. Borden's skull, I found that the blow just in front of the ear left its mark on the base of the skull within the cavity."

That blow, he wrote, cut directly through the carotid artery and was necessarily and immediately fatal from hemorrhage.

All well and good, Knowlton must have thought as he read this summary. Nothing unexpected. Then came the bombshell: "The other discovery is still more important. On one of the cuts in Mrs. Borden's skull near the right ear, there is a very small but unmistakable deposit of the gilt metal with which hatchets are ornamented when they leave the factory; this deposit (Dr. Cheever confirmed the observation fully) means that the hatchet used in killing Mrs. Borden was a *new* hatchet, not long out of the store."

The shining deposit, he continued, could be seen with a magnifying glass or, for that matter, with the naked eye.

This must have been to Knowlton, the proverbial last straw. As he had written Attorney General Pillsbury, the case against Lizzie was fatally weak, and he had no hope of convicting her. Now, at the last minute, here came a letter from two unimpeachable authorities—his own expert witnesses—saying the hatchet on which the police and the prosecution had built their case was not the murder weapon at all—old, dull, and rusty as it was!

If Drs. Draper and Cheever were allowed to state their findings from the witness box, there would be no purpose in even continuing the trial. The prosecution had surely lost the dress as physical evidence. They had relied for a motive on a five-year-old quarrel over an insignificant piece of property, and now, with the hatchet discredited, about the only thing left was the fact that somewhere along the line, Lizzie stopped calling Abby "Mother."

These must have been the thoughts running through the mind of the astute but realistic prosecutor as he approached the railing to question Dr. Edward S. Wood. Since the subject would now center around the Harvard examinations of the bodies, clothing, and suspected instruments, he certainly wanted no testimony from Wood mentioning the discovery of Drs. Draper and Cheever.

Wood acknowledged that he had been Professor of Chemistry at Harvard for the past 16 years. His specialty was poisons and bloodstains, and he had been called on to testify in several hundred trials such as this one.

He had, he said, examined the two containers of milk and had found no evidence of any poison in either of them. In his opinion, Abby had preceded Andrew in death by approximately three hours, twice the 90 minutes Dolan had estimated.

Questioning turned then to the hatchets, axes, and clothing he had also received, and his answers were entirely negative.

The claw-hammer hatchet had several stains on the handle, the side, and the edge, all of which appeared to be bloodstains, but chemical and microscopic tests gave absolutely negative results. Both axes had stains that appeared to be blood, but the tests proved negative with them also.

Knowlton hoped for a positive answer to his next question: "Did you make an examination to be able to determine whether it was reasonably possible that that hatchet could have been used in inflicting the wounds that you have described and then have been washed soon afterwards, so that traces of blood might or might not be found upon it?"

Woods replied that it could not have been washed quickly on account of the cavities in between the head and the handle. This put a crimp in the prosecution's picture of Lizzie hastily rinsing blood from the hatchet and dipping it in ashes to simulate dust. Positing that she had spent 10 or 15 minutes scrubbing it wouldn't stand up.

The hair, labeled "taken from the hatchet," was without question animal hair, and probably was from a cow.

There was a brown "smooch" that looked like blood on the skirt Lizzie wore, but it wasn't. There was another lower down, but neither was it blood. There *was* one stain of blood about the size of a small pinhead, eight inches from the hem, that was consistent with the characteristics of human blood. Nothing was found on her shoes or stockings.

On cross-examination, Adams asked if he was able to say that the pinhead spot on Lizzie's petticoat did not come from her menstrual flow and Wood replied that he could not; that it might have.

Adams asked if the character of the blood was satisfactory for the determination that it was even human blood. The professor's answer was an enigmatic, "If it is satisfactory at all, it is." Perhaps it was all of no importance. The prosecution's picture of this tiny speck coming as a result of the slayings was now blurry indeed because any splatter would have come on the front of Lizzie's garments, not the back. The prosecution had not attempted to show that the speck was the blood type of either of the victims and did not go beyond the phrase "consistent with human blood." As to whether it had penetrated the garment from the outside rather than the inside, their only answer was that it was "more distinct" on the outside, an entirely different matter. All this over a speck measuring one three-thousandth of an inch.

Finally, the questioning turned to the important matter of the spatterings of blood on the walls and furniture near each body. It was important to the defense to establish the volume, distance, and variety of these spatters, since it had been established by the state's own expert that Lizzie had none on her person or clothing. Knowlton, in redirect examination, tried to denigrate their importance by asking Wood:

Q.   Have you had occasion to consider the subject of the spattering of blood when blows are struck in the manner in which you have heard these blows described?
A.   Yes sir.
Q.   What can you say as to that generally?
A.   It might spatter in any direction and might not spatter in every direction.

Q. That is, there is no rule at all?

A. No sir.

Q. What happens? Does it spatter or spurt?

A. Spatters. When any blunt surface strikes a pool of blood, of course it will spatter in that direction, varying according to accidental circumstances.

Q. Would there be any way in which you could determine whether any given surface near the wounds would receive the spattering or not, or how much?

A. No.

It should be remembered that Wood was a witness for the prosecution and, as such, couched his testimony in a way to help their case. The answers to Knowlton's questions were correct, technically, but fall far short of what objective testimony would have been.

As one familiar with bloodstains and the human anatomy, Wood knew that, in both cases, the aortic artery had been severed. There is great pressure in this main trunk artery and, when severed, blood does not *flow* from it; it *spurts* and *gushes.* The chances are overwhelming that anyone standing nearby would be showered with it.

Adams pressed Wood for better answers:

Q. Assuming that the assailant stood behind Mr. Borden when these injuries were given and received, have you formed an opinion whether he would be spattered by blood to any extent?

A. I have thought that he must be spattered with blood, but I don't think it is absolutely necessary that he should.

Q. You have expressed that opinion, have you not?

A. Yes.

Q. And you give that opinion, taking into mind the bloody spots you saw on the wall and parlor door?

A. I beg your pardon. I will correct what I just said. Your question was if the assailant stood behind him, at his head. *I don't see how he could avoid being spattered.*

This was more like it. Adams pressed again:

Q.   What part of the body would receive these spatters?
A.   Above the position of the head, or from this level up. [Pointing with his hands]
Q.   From the waist up?
A.   Yes sir.
Q.   Assuming that the assailant of Mrs. Borden stood over her when she was lying down on the floor, face downward, and taking into account the spatters of blood which you saw, have you formed an opinion as to whether her assailant would be spattered with blood?
A.   I don't see how the assailant could avoid being spattered in that place.
Q.   What portion of the body would receive the spatters in your opinion?
A.   From the lower portion of the body and upward.

Thus, the assailant would have been spattered with blood *from the waist up* while slaying Mr. Borden and *from the waist down* in the case of Abby.

The forensic expert called by the prosecution thus had described a blood-drenched assailant, yet every witness who had been with Lizzie that morning saw no blood on her dress, her face, her hands, or in her "immaculate" hair.

A pleased Robinson and Adams took their seats at the defense table.

Dr. Draper took the stand next.

At first, he used plaster casts of the two skulls and verified the marks that showed the wounds upon them.

In the dock, Lizzie put her head down almost on the back of her defender, the ex-governor. Not satisfied with the plaster casts, Knowlton apologized to the court but insisted that the skull itself be brought in for the witness to use. Columnist Joe Howard described the macabre scene:

It was Mr. Borden's skull. It was done up in a white handkerchief and looked like a bouquet such as a man carries to his sweetheart. A pile of law books was arranged high on the table in front of jury and made a stand for the skull to rest upon. The professor uncovered the skull and put it on this heap of learning, but the jaw came separately in his hand. When the doctor put it in its place by lifting the rest of the skull, he moved the two parts so that the mouth opened and shut like the silent jaws of a ghost. To see that jaw wag made the spectators wonder what it would say if it could talk.

Sentence by sentence, Knowlton led Draper through a detailed description of each gash in the skull, what damage it had done, its width and length. Mercifully, Lizzie, on the point of collapse, was escorted from the courtroom and allowed to sit where she could not be seen but could hear whatever she chose to hear.

We can never know, so there is no profit in speculating, what arguments Knowlton had used to persuade Draper to change his testimony that the murder weapon had been a new hatchet with gilt metal that had come off when the first blow had been struck. That his contradictory testimony was a cover-up is obvious. Knowlton put it squarely to him:

Q. [Showing him the handleless hatchet head] Are you able to say whether that hatchet head is capable of making those wounds?
A. I believe it is.

And later, in re-direct examination, Knowlton pressed the point as to "whether in your opinion those wounds that you found could have been inflicted by that hatchet?" Draper's response: "In my opinion they could."

Dr. Cheever, who followed Draper to the stand, was asked the same question. He replied, "This hatchet [holding the handleless hatchet head] could have caused the wounds."

It might be argued that neither doctor had, technically, perjured himself. In response to Knowlton's two questions, Draper had said it "could" have made the wounds in the skull. He had not said that it "had." The same is true of Dr. Cheever's testimony. Knowlton may have found a way to frame his questions so that neither respondent would have to perjure himself when replying. If that was, indeed, Knowlton's solution to his dilemma, it did nothing to protect the Harvard professors from an equally serious charge, a sin of omission rather than commission, that of witholding evidence known to them. In either event, it was a manipulation that brought no credit to revered Harvard University or the Commonwealth Knowlton represented.

It was nearing 5:00 P.M. when Dr. Cheever stepped down. The day had been a total loss for the prosecution, and court adjourned day eight.

13

The Prosecution Rests

*J*UNE 14—DAY NINE—temperature: 98 degrees with the humidity rising.

Still, every seat in the New Bedford courtroom was filled. Something intriguing was happening: women occupied most of the seats, a phenomenon never before witnessed in staid New England courts. Nor were these witnesses to the drama idle housewives or shop girls seeking titillation. They were, in the main, well-dressed matrons from the upper level of society, dressed in silks and soft cottons, sporting picture hats from the better milliners of Boston.

Two extraneous matters had come suddenly into importance.

First, Lizzie's condition. After her fainting spell on opening day, occasioned by the graphic descriptions of the wounds on the heads of the victims, she had, on two other occasions, become faint and had to be led from the courtroom; once at the display of Andrew's skull and once from the oppressive heat. There was speculation as to whether, if there was more of the blood and horror show yet to come, she would be able to remain in the suffocating courtroom and witness it. If not, could the trial continue without her?

Second, on the previous day when the grisly photographs of Andrew's slashed face had been distributed to the jury again, juror Louis B. Hodges of Taunton had swayed in his seat and was saved from collapse by the assistance of a fellow juror. He was vigorously fanned by another juror while a third fetched a glass of water and he attempted to drink. Judge Mason called a five minute recess while Hodges was taken into the hall and given smelling salts and support by the other jurors. He returned after the recess and sat, visibly weak and shaken, for the remaining six hours of testimony. Speculation: would the trial stand up on appeal if only 11 jurors could make it through the rest of the ordeal?

The court came to order promptly at 9 A.M. The court cow no longer lowed in the field. Sheriff Wright turned away a reporter's question as to whether he had had a hand in the cow's absence.

City Marshal Rufus Hilliard took the oath and stood in the witness box. He detailed how he had received a call telling him of some trouble at the Borden house on the morning of August 4 and how he had dispatched first, Officer Allen and, soon after, Officers Doherty, Mullaly, Medley, and Wilson, and Assistant Marshal Fleet. He himself had gone to the house in the middle of the afternoon.

He had participated in the day-long search on Saturday, and it had been a thorough one, from basement to attic. No, he had not spoken to Lizzie, but he had picked up the dress she had worn on the day of the murders.

Mayor John W. Coughlin was next. He had accompanied the marshal to the Borden house on Saturday evening. He described the mob collected around the house, filling the sidewalk and the streets. It had been difficult, he said, trying to reach the house in their carriage without running over someone. They had made their way through, however, and had assembled the family in the parlor for a conference. Lizzie had been there, along with Emma and John Morse. It had been a somber occasion.

"I have a request to make of the family," he had said, "and that is that you remain in the house for a few days, as I believe it would be better for all concerned if you did so."

Lizzie had spoken up immediately. "Why? Is there anybody in this house suspected?"

The mayor had replied, referring to John Morse's rescue from a mob the night before, "Well, perhaps Mr. Morse can answer that question better than I, as his experience last night, perhaps, would justify him in the inference that somebody in this house was suspected."

Lizzie, recognizing this as a weasel answer, had said, "I want to know the truth." The mayor had not responded, and Lizzie had said again, "I want to know the truth." Obviously, what she had wanted to know was whether she was the suspect or whether it was Uncle John.

The mayor then handed Robinson his prime line of defense. He had replied, "Well, Miss Borden, I regret to answer, but I must answer yes. You are suspected."

Lizzie's reply: "I am ready to go now or any time." Emma's parting remark had been, "I want you to do everything you can to find out this murder."

On cross-examination, Robinson questioned the reluctant mayor for all the details. His answers were defensive and evasive, but that did not daunt the ex-governor. He was right at home with witnesses who tried to avoid explicit answers to his questions.

Q. You had said, as I understand it, you did the talking in the parlor?
A. I believe I did.
Q. The marshal did not participate in that?
A. I would not swear he did not.
Q. Do you recall that he did?
A. He may have re-affirmed what I said about the request to remain in the house. I don't recall that he entered into any lengthy conversation.
Q. You had advised them to remain in the house and on the premises?
A. Yes sir, I did.

Q. And thereupon Miss Lizzie said, "Why? Is there anybody in this house suspected?"

A. To the best of my knowledge.

Q. Spoke right up to you earnestly and promptly, did she?

A. She made that statement.

Q. Will you answer my question?

The chief justice: He may answer.

Q. You understand it [the question]?

A. Yes sir.

Q. Will you give me an answer?

A. She spoke up somewhat excitedly, I should say.

Q. She did?

A. Yes sir.

Q. What did you say to her?

A. When she asked me if there was somebody in the house suspected, I replied by stating that Mr. Morse could best answer that question, as the experience of last night would justify him in drawing the inference that there was.

Q. What was the next thing?

A. Lizzie said, "I want to know the truth."

Q. Lizzie said so?

A. Yes sir, and she repeated it if I remember rightly.

Q. Before you answered?

A. Yes sir.

Q. What did you say?

A. I said, "I regret, Miss Borden, but I must answer yes. You are suspected."

Q. And what did she say?

A. She said, as I now recall it, "I am ready to go now."

Q. "Or any time," didn't she?

A. I cannot recall that; she may have said it.

Q. Spoke up earnestly and promptly then, didn't she?

A. It would depend altogether what you mean by "earnestly" and "promptly."

Q. I mean what you know the words mean.

A. She replied in a manner you can call earnestly and promptly. There was no hesitation about it.

Q. That is, promptly; no hesitation, isn't it? You understand that, don't you?

A. I do, yes sir.

Q. Now, did she speak earnestly?

A. Well, I would not say she did not speak earnestly.

Q. What's that?

A. I should say I would not say she did not speak earnestly.

Q. I know you say so. Did she speak earnestly?

A. Well, I should say yes. She spoke earnestly so far as the promptness of the question goes.

Q. Do you know the difference between promptness and earnestness?

A. There is a difference between promptness and earnestness.

Q. Keeping that distinction in mind, you say she answered you, did she, earnestly?

A. She did as far as I am—

Q. What's that?

A. As far as I would be able to determine by her action, she was earnest.

Q. That is what I asked you, prompt and earnest.

So much for pulling teeth.

Historians would wish that Robinson had asked Mayor Coughlin why it was that he, not Marshal Hilliard, had taken charge of this meeting. As mayor, he had no authority in what was, unquestionably, a police matter, most particularly when the town's top law enforcement officer was standing in the shadows of the room. Now we'll never know.

Hannah Reagan was the matron at the Fall River police station where Lizzie had been kept for ten days. She was called to the stand next by the prosecution to tell a story they hoped would cast doubt on Lizzie's innocence.

On August 24, Emma had gone to the station to visit her sister, as she had done many times since Lizzie's arrest. She had been admitted to her cell while Hannah had retired to a toilet room about four feet away. She could hear what she described as "very loud talk" between the sisters, and she had returned to the doorway just in time to hear Lizzie say, "Emma, you have gave me away, haven't you?" Emma had replied, "No, Lizzie,

I have not." "You have," Lizzie said, "and I will let you see I won't give in one inch." Lizzie had turned away, and they had not spoken again during the visit.

Emma, in the days between the murders and that morning, had neither done nor said anything questioning Lizzie's innocence, nor did she at any time before her death more than 30 years later. It is questionable that Lizzie, educated and even lyric in her speech and writing, would have said, "you *have gave* me away." Her supposed retort, "I will let you see I won't give in one inch," is equally a statement with a hazy meaning.

This interaction was leaked within minutes to the press and, with equal speed, denied by Hannah as being untrue. Just to be on the safe side, Attorney Jennings drew up a statement confirming that the story was made up (by *Globe* reporter Edwin Porter), and the Reverend Buck asked the matron to sign it. It read:

"This is to certify that my attention has been called to a report said to have been made by me in regard to a quarrel between Lizzie and her sister, Emma, in which Lizzie said to Emma, "You have *given* me away," etc, and that I expressly and positively deny that any such conversation took place and I further deny that I ever heard anything that could be construed as a quarrel between the two sisters".

She was willing to sign it, but, by then, Marshal Hilliard had got wind of the brouhaha and stepped in. The story had been printed in the *Globe*, and if it was hurtful to Lizzie, then, so be it. He wasn't about to have it retracted. When the Reverend Buck had shown him the statement, he had said to the matron, "You go to your room and I will attend to this business; and you, Reverend Buck, attend to yours."

That put paid to the whole affair. If it had any effect on the jury, no one could tell. It is doubtful that it did, since the quarrel itself was a murky one, and, when coupled with the denial, signed or no, it was impossible to know what had really taken place or what it meant.

The subject of poison was next on the prosecution's agenda. They hoped to establish that Lizzie had, on the day before the murders, attempted to purchase ten cents' worth of prussic acid and to imply this showed she had murderous intentions toward Andrew and Abby.

Druggist Eli Bence was called to the stand to tell what he knew about the incident, and Robinson was on his feet instantly to object. The chief justice retired the jury and Mr. Bence, to hear what he knew would be a protracted argument from both sides. Atttorney Moody went first:

"I perhaps ought first to state what the testimony is that we offer," he said. He stated that Bence had 13 years' experience as a druggist but had never had a request for prussic acid before. (This is hard to believe, since he carried it in stock.) On the third day of August, he said, Lizzie had come to his drugstore and asked for ten cents' worth of it, stating that she planned to use it to clean the sealskin cape she carried.

Bence had informed her that prussic acid could not be bought without a physician's prescription and she had left.

Robinson rose to state his objections to the testimony Bence would give:

"It appears upon the testimony of Professor Wood," he said, "that an examination of the stomachs of the deceased persons showed no traces of any poison whatsoever, or anything but a normal condition. Certainly not any prussic acid. That was directly and fully negatived. So, there is shown no connection, as assailing the lives of these two persons. In fact, this evidence only goes so far as to show, assuming that they may show it for the time being in this discussion, that she asked to buy prussic acid under precisely the circumstances that the offer is now made. She is charged in this indictment with slaying or killing these two people with a sharp instrument; committing the murder with an axe, for instance. Nothing else. Now here, if it has any force at all, suppose it were carried away up to its legitimate result, it is an attempt to charge her with an act causing death by a wholly different means, for which she is not now on trial."

Besides, he continued, it had to be shown that any act on the part of the defendant must have some natural tendency to show she committed the act for which she stood charged. The fact, even if it were proved, that Lizzie had attempted to purchase prussic acid, a legally salable product, did not show that she had committed some other act which might be a crime.

Does it, he asked, have any tendency at all to show that this defendant killed these two persons with an axe? That was what this trial was about.

In rebuttal, Moody began by agreeing with Robinson. If Lizzie had, indeed, attempted to purchase prussic acid, it didn't have any direct linkage to murders by hatchet or axe. It did, however, support the prosecution's charge that the slayings had been done with deliberation and premeditation. It was the Commonwealth's position that the illness that had struck the Borden family on Monday had suggested to Lizzie that poison might be a good way to dispose of Andrew and Abby. She had then, on Wednesday, tried to purchase prussic acid. Failing in that effort, she had resorted to the hatchet.

As in the argument over the admissability of Lizzie's inquest testimony, the prosecution spent the next two hours tediously recalling precedents, all the while admitting that none of them really fit the case at hand. Moody closed his argument, saying:

"I can conceive of no more significant act, nothing which tends to show more the purpose of doing mischief to someone, than the attempt to obtain one of the most deadly poisons that is known to humankind."

Robinson addressed the three justices again, and said there had been nothing placed on the record to indicate murderous intent prior to August 4 on the part of Lizzie other than her comment that Abby was not her mother—which was a fact.

"It is not," he said, "as if she had said, 'I intend to kill somebody before the end of the week,' or, 'I have murder in my heart.'" The Commonwealth admitted there was nothing in the evidence to show Lizzie meditated the malice.

"I grant you," Robinson said, "if a man goes to work upon a criminal act, meaning violence in a particular direction, you may draw the logical inference from that. But, if he does an innocent act—we cannot reach *forward* and say, 'You intended to do that which at that time you had no sort of intention to commit, so far as the proof goes.' Would this court sit here for a moment and listen to a proposition that she undertook on a former day to shoot Dr. Bowen, for instance, to show that she had a murderous intent towards Mr. and Mrs. Borden? No, not if she had done it one hour before. That would be setting up a distinct and separate crime."

The justices withdrew to consider the arguments and returned at 4:30.

"The court are of the opinion," the chief justice said, "provided the preliminary evidence comes up to the proffer, the evidence is competent." In lay terms, the justices would listen to the Commonwealth's presentation and then decide whether or not it was competent for the jury to hear.

On this upbeat note for the prosecution, court adjourned day nine.

It was inevitable, given the setting, that some imaginative reporter would draw a comparison between the condition of the witches of Salem, Massachusetts, and the young woman from Fall River in the dock. The writer for *The Boston Globe* who had replaced the late Trickey, undertook it on day ten:

> It would be interesting to know just what was the usual demeanor of the Puritan maidens when they were on trial before the witch burners, knowing the hopelessness of their plight, feeling the implacable sternness of their judges, stripped of sympathy and companionship, badgered, and having every word and look tortured into evidence against them.
>
> "In time, did they not become stoical and callous and indifferent to all but the worst? Such is the view her critics have taken of the general conduct of Lizzie Borden. For ten months she has been in the grasp of the city marshal of Fall River and his police. If she is not hanged, they will think the ten months wasted and that any law except their own is worse than worthless. The Puritan maiden now on trial has seemed to behave like a girl with nothing to hope for— hardened to unkindness and suspicion.

Charles H. Lawton, Nathaniel Hathaway, and Henry H. Tillson took the stand when court reconvened on June 15 for day ten of the trial. Lawton was a pharmacist, Hathaway an analytic chemist, and Tillson a dealer in ladies furs.

They told of the usage of prussic acid to clean furs and to kill humans, and its properties when used as an insecticide.

When they had finished, there was a conference at the bench between the attorneys and the justices. It was off the record, so no transcript of the whispered conversation exists, but the decision handed down by the three judges made all the headlines the next day.

The Commonwealth had not been able to keep the proof within the limits they had agreed on with defense counsel, and all the poison evidence was therefore excluded.

The Boston Globe reporter continued:

> At the conclusion, she burst into tears—into a convulsion of plea-sure, gratitude, and sudden relief that wracked her body. She had learned to brace herself against adversity and unkindness, but mercy and active friendliness were so new to her that she broke down then.

The third leg of the prosecution's triad had broken, and it is reasonable to assume that Knowlton wished he, like Attorney General Pillsbury, were sunning himself on the beaches of Florida.

Knowlton was on his feet. "The Commonwealth rests," he said.

The announcement took everyone by surprise; only the three justices remained impassive. There was a great stir among the spectators, occasioned partially, one must suppose, by their anticipation that the defense might move immediately for dismissal of charges and their days of vicarious excitement would be over. The jurymen stiffened in their seats, many undoubtedly thinking their own imprisonment might soon come to an end. Lizzie beamed, the evidence of her excitement being the rapid flicking of her fan.

The rumor had been repeatedly passed around that the defense would not present a rebuttal to what the Commonwealth had put forth. Among the spectators at the trial, at least, the feeling was that the government's case had melted away like a cake of ice in the broiling sun. The general feeling among the press corps was that the trial would do one of two things: fail for a lack of proof or become the most complete vindication of the potency of circumstantial evidence ever known.

The reporters bolted the courtroom to flash the news to their papers. The stenographers scurried downstairs to their cramped quarters to type the official transcript.

Henry Ford may have taken his cue from the assembly line of stenographers and typists who set down the record of the Borden trial. The on-duty stenographer, one of a troop of like men, sat at a desk in front of the witnesses, working a five-minute shift. As soon as he approached his limit of time, another man moved in beside him, nudged, and took over like the hand-off runner in an Olympic relay race. At that, the on-duty stenographer sped from the room, raced down the stairs, and delivered his steno pad to one of a battery of young lady typists. In the meantime, a third stenographer was making his way up the stairs. The system was so efficient that one hour after a witness had testified, both counsels and the judges had before them a typed transcript neatly bound and stitched.

By now, Sheriff Wright had restored order, decorum, and silence in the second-floor courtroom, and Andrew Jennings opened for the defense. He was quick, nervous, and resolute, a small, slender, and excitable man with a face full of anxiety. He opened with a personal allusion:

"One of the victims of the murder charged in this indictment," he said, "was for many years my client and my personal friend. I had known him since boyhood. I had known his oldest daughter for the same length of time, and I want to say right here and now, if I manifest more feeling than perhaps you think necessary in making an opening statement for the defense in this case, you will ascribe it to that cause. The counsel, Mr. Foreman and gentlemen, does not cease to be a man when he becomes a lawyer.

"Fact and fiction have furnished many extraordinary examples of crime that have shocked the feelings and staggered the reason of men, but I think no one has ever surpassed in its mystery the case you are now considering."

It was, he said, a crime that had shocked the whole civilized world. The brutality of the wounds, the audacity of the time and place chosen, and the accusation of the victim's youngest daughter, he said, made this the act "of an insane person or fiend."

There is an outcry of human hearts, he continued, to have somebody punished for the crime. "But, Mr. Foreman and gentlemen, no matter how much you want somebody punished for the crime, it is the guilty and not the innocent that you want."

The law of Massachusetts, he continued, "draws about every person accused of this crime or any other, the circle of the presumption of his or her innocence, and allows no juryman or jury to cross it until they have fulfilled the conditions required. Until they show that it has been proved beyond a reasonable doubt that he or she is the guilty party they are not allowed to cross the line and take the life of the party who is accused.

"There is not one particle of direct evidence in this case, from beginning to end, against Lizzie Andrew Borden. There is not a spot of blood—there is not a weapon that they have connected with her in any way, shape or fashion. They have not had her hand touch it or her eye see it or her ear hear of it. There is not, I say, a particle of direct testimony in the case connecting her with this crime. It is wholly and absolutely circumstantial."

Jennings systematically called up the three fabled necessities to prove guilt in circumstantial evidence cases: motive, means, and opportunity.

"There is absolutely no motive whatsoever for the commission of this crime by the defendant," he said, and reminded the jury of Bridget's testimony about the quietness of the house and the politeness of the family.

"Though they furnish you with a motive on her part to kill the stepmother, they have shown you absolutely none to kill the father. Absolutely none; unless they advance what seems to me the ridiculous proposition that she, instead of leaving the house after killing the mother, waits there an hour or an hour and a half for the express purpose of killing her own father, between whom and herself there is shown not the slightest trouble or disagreement whatsoever."

As for means, "The blood that was shown upon the axes, which were guarded so carefully at first in this case, has disappeared like mist in the morning sun. The claw-headed hatchet that Dr. Dolan was so sure committed this deed at the Fall River hearing—so sure that he could even see the print which the claw head of the hatchet made in the head of Mr. Borden, has disappeared from the case. I contend that, as to the weapon, they have either got to produce the weapon which did the deed, and, having produced it, connect it some way directly with the prisoner, or else they have got to account in some reasonable way for its disappearance."

As for opportunity: "I want to call to your attention right here that, in all this search and investigation that has been made about the whereabouts and the doings of Mr. Andrew J. Borden upon that morning, there has not been a living soul put on the stand here to testify that they saw Andrew J. Borden come downstreet from his house. From his house to the Union Savings Bank, he has been absolutely invisible. Was it any easier for him to be unseen than it would be for somebody escaping from this house if they walked quietly away?"

He promised, further, that the defense would prove Lizzie had been in the barn just as she had said she was, and that the burned dress would be put into perspective as their case was presented.

Sarah Hart was their first witness. At about 9:50 on the morning of the murders, she had been passing by the Borden house with her sister-in-law and had observed a young man standing in the gateway, resting his head on his left hand, with his elbow on the gatepost. She had paused and chatted for about five minutes with her nephew, who was passing by, and the stranger was still there when she went away.

Charles Sawyer, who had been pressed into service as a guard by Officer Allen when the alarm was first given, testified that Lizzie had been sitting in a rocking chair being ministered to by Miss Russell, Mrs. Churchill, and Bridget. He had been close to her all the time and had seen no bloodstains on her head, hair, face, hands, or dress.

Mark Chace was called next and told of having seen a strange man in a buggy parked in front of the Borden house at the time of the murder.

Dr. Benjamin Handy confirmed what Mrs. Hart had said. He, too, had seen a young man acting strangely, so strangely that he had stopped his carriage and turned to watch him. He seemed to be mentally agitated; he stopped at times and then walked on. His actions were different, he said, from those of anyone he had ever seen on the street in his life.

Charles N. Gifford was another in the parade of witnesses who testified to seeing strange people around the Borden house. He described a man, weighing from 180 to 190 pounds, sitting on the side steps the night before. He had a straw hat pulled down over his eyes.

When Walter P. Stevens took the stand, it became clear for the first time why Robinson had not panicked when Officer

Medley had testified in detail how he had gone to the loft, sighted along the floor, and found no footprints in the dust. Conclusion: Lizzie had not been up there that morning.

Mr. Stevens was a reporter for the Fall River *News*. He had been at the police station when Officer Allen had rushed back to get reinforcements. Stevens had double-timed it back to the house. In his news-gathering activities, he had gone out to the barn at the same time Officer Medley arrived at the house. He had not gone up to the loft, but while he was on the ground floor, he heard three people go up the steps and walk around the loft . . . *before* Medley made his tour of inspection.

Alfred C. Clarkson, a steam engineer, was called, and he identified himself as being one of the three. He added that he had seen two others go up . . . *before* Medley.

"Me and Brownie" put the icing on the cake.

The testimony of 12-year-old Thomas E. Barlow provided one of the lighter moments of the trial. He was "me," and his buddy, Everett Brown, also 12 years old, was "Brownie."

Tommy, referring every time to "me and Brownie," told how they were playing on the sidewalk and had arrived at the Borden house just as the first cry of alarm had been sounded. Having thoughts of a great adventure, "me and Brownie," refused admission to the house by guard Sawyer, went to the barn with the idea of capturing the murderer hiding in the straw. "Me and Brownie" had gone up to the loft and hunted around and played a while but had found no murderer. That had all taken place before Officer Medley arrived on the scene. In cross-examination, Knowlton tried very hard to shake the youngster as to what time "me and Brownie" had been in the loft, but "me and Brownie" knew when playtime began. It was always at 11:00 A.M. Who could challenge a 12-year-old as to what time his chores were done and he could go out to play?

The defense had made their point. Here were either five or seven people who had been up in the loft before Medley sighted along the floor and saw nothing. Attorney Jennings, in his opening statement, had said Medley's trip to the loft had been a "cakewalk—a figment of his imagination."

It was more than that. It was vital to the prosecution to strip Lizzie of her alibi of being in the barn when Andrew was killed.

It was obvious Medley wasn't merely mistaken; his description had been too detailed and meticulous. He had perjured himself, just as Fleet had done earlier.

Nor was this the first time Medley had fiddled with the evidence. During the investigation, he had reported to Fleet that Charles O. Cook, one of Andrew's property managers, had told him Andrew had said two days before the murders that he needed to get around to making a will. Cook vehemently swore at the preliminary hearing that he had made no such statement.

Thomas F. Hickey, a reporter for *The Boston Globe,* was called by Robinson to add his knowledge of Hannah Reagan's story of a Lizzie-Emma quarrel. He had seen Hannah just after the story had appeared in the Fall River *Globe.* He had chided her, saying "I see you're getting yourself in the paper." "Yes," Hannah had responded, "but they have got to take all that back."

"I asked her about the quarrel and she said there had been no quarrel. I asked her if she had repeated any of the words of the sisters; asked her if there was any truth in the report, and she said, 'Absolutely none.' "

The defense had another bombshell when Hyman Lubinsky was called. He was a Russian immigrant and spoke only the basic words of English. On the fateful Thursday, he had picked up his ice cream wagon and horse just a few minutes after 11:00 A.M. By a complicated formula, he could prove he left the stable between 11:05 and 11:10 and passed the Borden house just minutes later.

"I saw a lady," he said, "come out of the way from the barn right to the stairs at the back of the house. She was wearing a dark-colored dress."

He had delivered ice cream to the Borden house many times before, and the lady he saw was not Bridget; he knew her. His testimony fit to the minute the time Lizzie had said she had returned to the house from the barn. He had told Officer Medley, among others, but apparently the police were not interested in his story. The staff of Lawyer Jennings had sought him out, however, and brought him to the court to testify.

Knowlton, in cross-examination, had no patience with Lubinsky's inability to speak fluently. Several times during the questioning, Lubinsky protested, "You ask me too fast!" A reporter for the New York *Sun* wrote: "Never did a lawyer try harder to confuse a witness than did Mr. Knowlton on this occasion. He walked up and down between the witness and his desk, prodding him with rapid questions. He was nervous, agitated, and scolding in his tone."

But, he added, he made no dent in Lubinsky's testimony.

14

The Defense Rests

*C*OINCIDENTAL WITH THE END of the prosecution's presentation came full abatement of the scorching heat that had numbed spectators and participants alike. Overnight, the temperature dropped 37 degrees, from 92 on Thursday night to a crisp 55 on Friday morning. It was a tonic to all.

The eleventh day of the trial saw a continuation of witnesses denouncing Hannah Reagan's story of a quarrel between Emma and Lizzie.

Mrs. Marianna Holmes, wife of banker Charles Holmes, testified that she had questioned the matron about the story soon after it was published, and Mrs. Reagan had told her it was not true; she had not heard a quarrel between the sisters. She would be willing to sign a statement to that effect if Marshal Hilliard would let her. However, Hilliard had told her she would sign it only against his orders. Obviously fearing for her job if she crossed the marshal, she had not signed the paper drawn up by Jennings and presented by the Reverend Buck.

Her husband, Charles, took the stand and said the same thing; the story was a lie.

So did newspaper reporter John R. Caldwell, and so did Mrs. Mary E. Brigham.

How much of this whole quarrel story was the product of *Globe* reporter Edwin H. Porter's fertile imagination and how much was the machinations of the police can never be known, but, insofar as the jury was concerned, it had been watered down by the testimony of reliable witnesses and was believable now only by the anti-Lizzie faction.

Emma Borden was the star witness of day eleven.

Then 42 years of age, Emma looked it; more than anything like a prim New England maiden schoolteacher. She was dressed with exceeding neatness in plain black with the impress of a Borden in every feature. As she stood in the witness box, there was no swaying of her slender form, no drooping of her straight-out eye, no quivering of her tight-shut mouth. She stood with perfect self-possession, answered every question with deliberation and decision, and met the skillful cross-examination of Knowlton without defiance, but with an evident determination to have the meaning of her well-weighed words thoroughly understood.

Andrew had, of course, been well known to all in Fall River, either respected, feared, or loathed, depending on the relationship. Abby had been little short of a recluse. Her trips to market and sporadic church attendance had been her only outings. She had not been involved in either the social or civic activities of Fall River.

Lizzie was the outgoing member of the family. Little was known about Emma then or now. Significantly, there are dozens of photographs of Lizzie, many of them taken in professional studios, but only two exist of Emma. It is almost as if her goal in life was to be inconspicuous.

But her evidence in support of Lizzie was forceful and positive. She spoke clearly and without hesitation. The trial appearance was, perhaps, her finest hour.

Jennings immediately sought to establish that murder for inheritance was not the motive.

Emma produced records to show that Lizzie had $170 on deposit in the B. M. C. Durfee Bank, $2,000 in the Massasoit Bank, $500 in the Union Savings, and $141 in the Fall River Five Cents Savings. This, in addition to various shares of stock. By 1892 standards, this was a formidable amount of money for a young lady to have.

Jennings then set out to accent the fond relationship that existed between father and daughter:

Q. Did your father wear a ring, Miss Emma, upon his finger?
A. Yes sir.
Q. Was or was not that the only article of jewelry which he wore?
A. The only article.
Q. Do you know from whom he received the ring?
A. My sister, Lizzie.
Q. How long before his death?
A. I should think 10 to 15 years.
Q. Do you know whether previously to his wearing it she had worn it?
A. Yes sir.
Q. Did he constantly wear it after it was given to him?
A. Yes sir.
Q. Do you know whether or not it was upon his finger at the time he was buried?
A. It was.

Next, the elusive dress and the searches that had been made for it. First, how many dresses were in the various closets?

A. Somewhere about 18 or 19.
Q. And whose were those dresses?
A. All of them belonged to my sister and I except one that belonged to Mrs. Borden.
Q. How many of those dresses were blue dresses or dresses in which blue was a marked color?
A. Ten.
Q. To whom did those belong?
A. Two of them to me and eight to my sister.

Q. Were you there on the afternoon of Saturday while the search was going on?

A. Yes sir.

Q. What, if anything, did Dr. Dolan say to you as to the character of the search which had been done?

A. He told me the search had been as thorough as the search could be made unless the paper was torn from the walls and the carpets taken from the floor.

Q. Did you or Miss Lizzie, so far as you know, at any time make any objection to the searching of any part of that house?

A. Not the slightest.

Q. Did you assist them in any way you could?

A. By telling them to come as often as they pleased and search as thorough as they could.

She then described the blue cotton Bedford cord dress Lizzie had burned. It had, she said, a very light blue ground with a dark figure measuring about an inch by three-quarters of an inch. It had been an insignificant dress of cheap material costing 12½ cents a yard or, perhaps, 15 cents.

The dressmaking, as was quite common then, had gone on in the guest room where Abby had been slain. Soon after the dress was made, painters had been at the Borden house, painting the outside and trimming the inside.

Q. Do you know anything about her getting any paint on it at that time?

A. Yes, she did.

Q. Where was the paint upon it?

A. I should say along the front and on one side toward the bottom and some on the wrong side of the skirt.

Q. How soon was that after it was made?

A. Well, I think within 2 weeks; perhaps less time than that.

Q. Now where was that dress, if you know, on Saturday, the day of the search?

A. I saw it hanging in the clothes press over the front entry.

Q. How come you to see it at that time?

A. I went in to hang up the dress that I had been wearing during the day and there was no vacant nail and I searched around to find a nail and I noticed this dress.

Q. Did you say anything to your sister about that dress in consequence of your not finding a nail to hang your dress on?

A. I did.

Q. What did you say to her?

A. I said, "You have not destroyed that old dress yet? Why don't you?"

Q. What was the condition of that dress at that time?

A. It was very dirty, very much soiled and badly faded.

Q. When did you next see that Bedford cord dress?

A. Sunday morning, I think, about nine o'clock.

Q. Now will you tell the court and the jury all that you saw or heard that morning in the kitchen?

A. I was washing dishes and I heard my sister's voice and I turned around and saw she was standing at the foot of the stove, between the foot of the stove and the dining-room door. This dress was hanging on her arm and she says, "I think I shall burn this old dress up." I said, "Why don't you?", or "You had better," or "I would if I were you," or something like that. I can't tell the exact words, but I meant, do it. And I turned back and continued washing dishes and did not see her burn it and did not pay any more attention to her at that time.

Q. What was the condition of the kitchen doors and windows at that time?

A. They were all wide open, screens in and blinds open.

Q. Were the officers all about at that time?

A. They were all about the yard.

Jennings tried to establish that, in the Borden house, they didn't keep a rag bag for such material as the old dress. It is doubtful, however, that he wanted her to tell that the reason they didn't was because Andrew wasn't about to pay to have trash hauled away that could be burned.

Knowlton objected to the question and was sustained.

Alice Russell, a friend of Emma's, had been present at the time of the dress burning. The following day, Monday, she had told Emma that Detective Hanscom had asked her if all the dresses were there that were there on the day of the murder and she had told him "Yes." Emma had asked her why she had told him that.

"The burning of the dress was the worst thing Lizzie could have done," Miss Russell had said.

"Why didn't you tell me before I burned the dress?" Lizzie had asked. "Why did you let me do it?"

Emma had told Miss Russell that she should tell Hanscom about the burned dress and also that she and Lizzie had told her to do so.

Jennings asked her about the so-called quarrel with Lizzie:

Q. Now, Miss Emma, do you recall a story that was told by Mrs. Reagan about a quarrel between yourself and your sister?

A. Yes sir.

Q. Was your attention called to the fact by me?

A. It was.

Q. How soon after it, do you know?

A. The morning following.

Q. Now, Miss Emma, on that morning, did you have any conversation with Miss Lizzie, in which she said, "Emma, you have given me away, haven't you?"

A. I did not.

Q. And did you say in reply, "No, Lizzie, I haven't." "You have," she says, "and I will let you see I won't give in one inch." Was there any such talk as that?

A. There was not.

Q. Anything like that?

A. Nothing.

Q. That morning or any morning?

A. No time. Not any time.

Q. Was there ever any trouble in the matron's room between you and your sister while she was there?

A. There was not.

On cross-examination, Knowlton queried Emma about the transaction that was supposed to have crystallized the animosity between the elder Bordens and the younger, the purchase of a house for Abby's half-sister, Mrs. Whitehead.

Mrs. Whitehead had owned half of the house in which she lived and Abby had owned the other half. Fearing that her half-sister might find herself homeless in her old age, Abby had importuned Andrew to buy Mrs. Whitehead's half and give it to her. The price had been $1500.

Q. Did that make some trouble in the family?
A. Yes.
Q. Between whom?
A. Between my father and Mrs. Borden, and my sister and I.
Q. And also between you and your sister and your step-mother?
A. Yes sir.
Q. Did you find fault with it?
A. Yes sir.
Q. And did Lizzie find fault with it?
A. Yes sir.
Q. And in consequence of your faultfinding, did your father also make a purchase for you or give you some money?
A. Not, I don't think, because of our faultfinding.
Q. Did he, after the faultfinding, give you some money?
A. Yes sir.
Q. How much?
A. Grandfather's house on Ferry Street.
Q. And was there some complaint that that was not an equivalent?
A. No, sir. It was more than an equivalent.

Emma's answer to his next question must have surprised and shaken Knowlton. The prosecution had anchored their case against Lizzie on the bad blood they contended existed between her and her stepmother. Emma's testimony was to the contrary. Lizzie had been the forgiving one. She, on the other hand, had not.

Q. Were the relations between you and Lizzie and your step-mother as cordial after that occurrence of the house that you have spoken of, as they were before?
A. Between my sister and Mrs. Borden, they were.
Q. They were entirely the same?
A. I think so.
Q. Were they so on your part?
A. I think not.

For the next hour, Knowlton grilled Emma on this point, reading back to her the testimony she gave at the inquest and the preliminary investigation. The best he could do was to establish that her answers were subject to interpretation. Right then, her responses were unequivocal. Lizzie's relationship with Abby had been more cordial than hers.

He next sought to show there was hostility between the sisters, illustrated by the fact that Emma, at one time, had occupied the larger of the two bedrooms but had later relinquished it to Lizzie. It was a weak line of questioning, terminated when Emma said she had traded rooms voluntarily and at her own suggestion.

An equally futile effort was made to shake her testimony on points where it conflicted with what Alice Russell had said took place when the dress was burned.

Alice's testimony had been that Emma had asked Lizzie what she was going to do with the dress she was holding. Emma said that was not her remembrance; that hers was of Lizzie speaking first, saying, "I think I am going to burn this old dress up." Pressed, Emma said she had not spoken first, and, "the reason that I say I didn't say it is because I didn't say it."

The cross-examination was now down to haggling and snapping, availing the prosecution nothing.

The dressmaker, Mrs. Mary A. Raymond, took the stand to say that she had made the Bedford cord dress in question during a three-week stay at the Borden's. It had been paint-stained almost immediately; as a matter of fact, while she was still in the house making other dresses. When faded, she said, Bedford cord has a drab appearance.

Mrs. Phoebe Bowen, wife of Dr. Bowen from across the street, told of Lizzie's distraught condition minutes after the murder. She was positive in her identification of the dress Lizzie had given to the police as being the one she was wearing on that morning.

Not surprisingly, little of this defense testimony was contained in Edwin Porter's history of the Borden murders. Many of the witnesses were not even mentioned as testifying. Those that were were covered by a sentence or two containing little that was positive about their evidence.

The final witness for the defense was Mrs. Annie White, court stenographer at the inquest and the preliminary hearing. She read from her notes Bridget's testimony at the inquest that Lizzie had been crying when she first learned of Andrew's murder.

It may have had an impact on the jury; we don't know. But it had none on the enduring legend of Lizzie, the unemotional, Lizzie the callous.

On day twelve, the defense rested its case.

Most of the newspapers covering the murders and the trial formed an opinion about Lizzie's innocence or guilt early on and stuck with it. The sensationalism of the Fall River *Globe* and its penchant for manufactured stories was obvious. *The Boston Globe*, with its air of superiority and with the Trickey fiasco firmly clamped around its neck, vacillated and watered down its coverage. The Fall River *Herald* and the *Evening News* were, in the main, supportive of Lizzie. The coverage of the *Providence Journal*, another of the area's prominent newspapers, was riddled with inaccuracies and apparently in the hands of a journeyman reporter.

The New York Times reported with accuracy and impartiality. Its editorial that day caught the essence of the trial and the predicament of the prosecution:

WILL IT REMAIN A MYSTERY?

It is many a year since a criminal case in this country has excited such universal interest and been the subject of so much discussion as that of the Borden murders. It has all the fascination of a mystery about which there may be a thousand theories and upon which opinions may differ as variously as the idiosyncracies of those who form them. There is so little absolute evidence that everybody can interpret the probabilities and the circumstantial indications to suit himself, and much will depend upon his general view of human nature and its capabilities. There seems to be little prospect that the mystery will be cleared up by the trial that is going on at New Bedford. The verdict, if there shall be a verdict, will make little difference unless there is to be some disclosure of which there is yet no sign.

The whole case is a tangle of probabilities and improbabilities, with little that is certain except that a man and wife were murdered in their own home on a frequented city street in the middle of an

August forenoon, with nobody about the premises, so far as has been shown, but the daughter and a servant girl. It was improbable enough that such a crime should be committed at such a time and place at all. That anyone should enter the house from the outside and commit it and get away without being observed or leaving any trace behind was most improbable. But the officers of the law were unable to find any evidence that the crime was perpetrated by anyone outside of the family, and the testimony brought by the defense to show that it might have happened in that way has proved nothing as to the crime.

The utter absence of any other explanation was the sole support of the suspicion against the daughter. In spite of the circumstances that made it look dark for her, there was as complete a lack of direct evidence against her as of any kind of evidence against anybody else. If circumstantial evidence is a chain only as strong as its weakest link, we have presented here, an attempt to make a chain out of wholly disconnected links, which has no continuity or binding strength at all. Almost as strong a case could be made out against anybody who had the misfortune to be in a house where murder was committed and not on the happiest terms with the victim. The utter absence of proof of anything except the fact of murder, and the lack of real evidence against anybody, is likely to leave this as a baffling mystery, unless a revelation should be made of which there is as yet no premonition.

15

Robinson
for the Defense

*T*HERE ARE THOSE WHO SAY that Robinson's closing argument was a letdown, but they are probably Perry Mason fans or those who hold that, in order to carry the day, the defense (or the prosecution) must, in the antepenultimate minute, wring a confession from the guilty or at least wind up a trial in a blaze of oratory comparable to William Jennings Bryan pressing down a cross of gold on the backs of the populace.

Such theatrics are more often the device of an attorney who has a poor case to argue and must resort to dazzling footwork to hide his predicament.

At this point, ex-Governor Robinson must have known that the prosecution had lost its case, and perhaps he had considered moving for a dismissal of the charges. While it would have demonstrated the complete confidence the defense felt in Lizzie's innocence, it would have been a brash move fraught with great hazard.

The prosecution had offered no practical evidence against Lizzie, no weapon, no hard motive, no bloodstained clothing, only the same opportunity that, conceivably, others shared with her. Robinson's closing was tailored to make these points clear to an already skeptical jury. He took them step by step in an address that consumed the better part of the day. These are the highlights:

"One of the most dastardly and diabolical crimes that was ever committed in Massachusetts," he began, "was perpetrated in August, 1892, in Fall River. The enormity and outrage startled everybody, and set all into the most diligent inquiry as to the perpetrator of such terrible acts. The terrors of those scenes no language can portray. The horrors of that moment we can all fail to describe.

"And so we are challenged at once, at the outset, to find somebody that is equal to that enormity, whose heart is blackened with depravity, whose whole life is a tissue of crime, whose past is a prophecy of that present. A maniac or fiend, we say. Not a man in his senses and with his heart right, but one of those abnormal productions that Deity creates or suffers—a lunatic or a devil."

The import was, of course, that Lizzie was none of these.

As for the inquest, the preliminary hearing, and her indictment, "You have nothing to do with what was done in Fall River any more than you have with what is now proceeding in Australia. The finding of Judge Blaisdell, worthy man as he may be, is of no sort of consequence here. We would not be safe if, in these great crises, our lives hung upon the decision of a single man in a prejudiced and excited community."

Then why was Lizzie Borden here in the dock?

"Policemen are human, made out of men, and nothing else, and when [he] undertakes to investigate a crime, he is possessed and saturated with the thoughts and experiences he has had with bad people. He is drifting and turning in the way of finding a criminal, magnifying this, minimizing that, throwing himself on this side in order to catch somebody, standing before a community that demands the detection and punishment of the criminal, blamed if he does not get somebody in the lockup before morning.

" 'What are the police doing?' say the newspapers. 'Look here, Mr. City Marshal, these murders were committed yesterday. Haven't you the murderer in the lockup? Get somebody in.'

"They make themselves, as a body of men, ridiculous, insisting that the defendant shall know everything that was done on a particular time, shall account for every movement of that time, shall tell it three or four times alike, shall never waver or quiver, shall have tears or not have tears, shall make no mistake."

And here, Robinson summed up what this trial was all about. Certainly, the jurors, just like the public, had a terrible curiosity as to what had happened there on Second Street, but that was not why they were sitting in the jury box. Robinson doubtlessly feared they might be so consumed with the mystery that they would feel an obligation, not unlike the public, to solve the puzzle, to find *someone* guilty. Since Lizzie stood in the dock, it would be her. He reminded them:

"Now, gentlemen, it is not your business to unravel the mystery. You are not here to find out the solution of that problem. You are here not to find out *who* committed the murders. You are here to pursue something else. You are simply and solely here to say, Is *this woman defendant* guilty? That is all. Not, *Who* did it? Not, *How* could it have been done? But, Did *she* do it? That is all.

"Now, there is absolutely no direct evidence against Miss Borden. Nobody saw or heard anything or experienced anything that connects her with the tragedies. No weapon whatever, and no knowledge of the use of one, as to her, has been shown. If you found her with some weapon of that kind in her control, or in her room, or with her belongings, that would be direct evidence. But there is nothing of that kind. It is not claimed. It is not shown that she ever used an implement of the character that must have produced these murders. It is not shown that she ever touched one or knew of one or bought or had one. In fact, the evidence is that she didn't know where in the house the ordinary things of that kind were.

"And the murders did not tell any tales on her, either. There was no blood on her, and blood speaks out, although it is voiceless. It speaks out against the criminal. Not a spot on her, from her hair to her feet, on dress or person anywhere. Think of it! Think of it for an instant!"

He ridiculed the police testimony concerning the missing handle. Had there ever been one? And, if so, where was it? "For heaven's sake," he pleaded, "get the 125 policemen of Fall River and chase it until they can drive it in somewhere and hitch it up to its family belongings!

"What reason is there for saying that this defendant is guilty? What right have they to say anything about it? Well, I want to run it through and tell you why they claim that she did it.

"In the first place, they say she was in the house in the forenoon. Well, that may look to you like a very wrong place for her to be in. But, it is her home! I suspect you have an impression that it would be better for her if she had been out traveling the streets. I don't know where I would want my daughter to be, than to say that she was at home, attending to the ordinary vocations of life, as a dutiful member of the household. So, I don't think there is any criminal look about that.

"Now, a person may say, 'Where is the note?' Well, we would be very glad to see it; very glad. They looked for it and they could not find it. The construction of Miss Russell was that Abby had burned it up. Very likely that was it. The note may have been a part of the scheme in regard to Mrs. Borden. It may have got there through foul means and with a criminal purpose. We don't know anything about that. But that a note came there, you cannot question.

"That Lizzie lied about it is a wrongful aspersion, born out of ignorance of the facts as they were to be developed in this case. It is not true that Lizzie told a lie about it. If she did, Bridget did the same, and I would not say that for a minute.

"Now she told about her visit to the barn, and they undertake to tell you that she did not go out to the barn. They say that is another lie. If she did not go out to the yard or the barn, then she was there at the time when the murder of her father was committed. Did she go to the barn? Well, we find that she *did*—find it by independent, outside witnesses, thanks to somebody who saw her. Possibly this life of hers is saved by the observation of a passer on the street. There comes along a peddler, an ice-cream man, known to everybody in Fall River.

He is not a distinguished lawyer, or a great minister, or a successful doctor. He is only an ice-cream peddler, but he knows what an oath is, and he tells the truth about it, and he says he passed down that street that morning, and as he passed right along, it was at a time when he says he saw a woman—not Bridget Sullivan, whom he knew—coming along, walking slowly around that corner just before she would ascend those side steps. Now there was no other woman alive in that house except Bridget and Lizzie at that time. He knew it was not Bridget because he had sold her ice cream and he knew her.

"Then they tell us about the ill feelings. Well, gentlemen, I am going to consider that in a very few words, because I say to you that the government has made a lamentable failure on that question. They say that it is the motive that so qualifies the different acts that are testified to here, that it puts this defendant in close connection with the murder of Mrs. Borden, and then they say Mrs. Borden being murdered, Lizzie murdered *Mr.* Borden for his property, or, possibly they will say, murdered him to conceal her crime.

"What have they proved? They have proved that from five or six years ago, Lizzie did not call Mrs. Borden 'Mother.'

"Lizzie is now a woman of 32 or 33 years old; 32 when these crimes were committed. Mrs. Borden was her stepmother; she was not her own mother. Mrs. Borden came there when Lizzie was a little child of two or three years and sometimes we see that where a stepmother has come into a family and has brought up a family, the children know no difference and always call her 'Mother' just the same.

" 'Now,' says Mr. Fleet, in his emphatic police manner, Miss Borden said to him, 'She is not my mother; she is my stepmother.' Perhaps she did. We will assume that she said it, but there is nothing criminal about it or nothing that indicates it, or nothing that savors of a murderous purpose.

"Bridget Sullivan lived in that family two years and nine months and was nearer to all of them than anybody else. She told you the condition of the household. She says, though brought in constant contact with them, she never heard anything out of the way. There was no quarreling. Everything seemed cordial among them. And, mark you, that Thursday morning on which they tell you that Lizzie was entertaining that purpose or plan to murder both these people, that Lizzie was talking with Mrs. Borden. Bridget Sullivan says, 'I heard them talking together calmly, without the least trouble; everything all right.' Was that an angry family? Was that a murderous group?

"Emma Borden comes on the stand to tell you the inside condition of the family and she went on to say that they had trouble five or six years ago in regard to property and there was no resentment. As far as Lizzie was concerned, it was all adjusted.

"Here was an old man with two daughters. He was a man that wore nothing in the way of ornament, of jewelry but one ring—and that ring was Lizzie's. It had been put on many years ago when Lizzie was a little girl, and the old man wore it and it lies buried with him in the cemetery. He loved her as his child; and the ring that stands as the pledge of plighted faith and love, that typifies and symbolizes the dearest relation that is ever created in life—that ring was the bond of union between the father and the daughter. No man should be heard to say that she murdered the man that loved her so.

"Then they say she burned a dress. The government stakes its case on that dress. The government says: 'You gave us the blue dress that lies before me. That is not the dress.' The defendant says that *is* the dress. The government says, 'We want that Bedford cord and if we had that Bedford cord, we should know all about it and you burned the Bedford cord.'

"Now, let us look at it. There is a dispute here among the persons who saw what Lizzie wore that morning, some of them saying that she had this very dress, or a dark-blue dress, and Mrs. Churchill speaking of it as a lighter blue than that. Now, between the two there is a difference of recollection. But you will remember that, at that time, there were several ladies in there, and Bridget was there with a lighter colored dress so that those who speak of a lighter colored dress may have had in mind what Bridget had on. It was not a time for examining colors, and afterwards, they recollected as well as they could.

"Well, suppose they had this Bedford cord and Lizzie had it on that morning. The witnesses all say, and every single person who has testified says, that while she was there and about with them—including Mrs. Churchill, Bridget, Dr. Bowen, and Mrs. Bowen, and others—that there was not a particle or spot of blood on it. They say there was no blood on her hands, her face, or her hair. Policemen were coming in all about there. She was lying on the lounge. They tell you that the dress was covered or had blood spots on it—but not a living person saw or suggested it. Suppose she did burn it up? The time that had elapsed for observation would be long enough. They all had it to look at at that time. They had all seen her and everyone says that there was not a spot of blood on it.

"Then, in obedience to Emma's injunction, Lizzie walks down into the kitchen with it that Sunday morning, the windows all open, no blinds shut, policemen in the yard looking right in at everything that was going on and—deliberately, and in the presence of Emma, Emma saying to her, 'Well, I think you had better do it'—put it into the fire and burned it up.

"Had not she time enough from Thursday morning down to that time, to burn it up without anybody's knowing it, if it was covered with blood? Had not she time enough to have got it out of the way? And if she had that purpose to cover up this crime, if she had committed it, would she have burned it in the presence of her sister and Miss Russell—and *say* she was going to do it? That is not humanly probable.

"If Lizzie Borden killed her mother at 9:45 o'clock in that morning, and then was ready to come downstairs and greet her father, having on that blue dress, do you think that it is probable, besmeared and bedaubed as she would have been with the blood of her first victim? Standing astride her and chopping her head into pieces by those murderous blows, blood flying all over the walls and the furniture, on the bed and everywhere, wasn't she touched all over with that testifying blood?

"Then of course they are going to say, 'Oh, but she changed her dress and then, when she killed her father, she either had that back again or she put on another.'

"Did she have it back again? Then, she had to put that on over her clothes again and over her person, exposing herself to have her underclothing soiled. And then, if she put on another dress, then there were *two* dresses to burn and dispose of, instead of one! And the government only wants one. They have all the rest.

"Think of it! That she walked right into that sea of blood and stood there, splashing it over herself in the first murder, and then took off that dress and laid it away until her father came in, and then dressed herself for the second slaughter.

"It is horrible to contemplate. I say it was not morally or physically possible.

"Then they say that she murdered these two people because Mrs. Reagan—I forbear almost to mention her name—came up here and told you that those sisters had a quarrel and that Lizzie said to Emma, 'You have given me away.' Gentlemen, if there is anybody given away in this case, it is Mrs. Hannah Reagan, and nobody gave her away but herself. And she is gone so completely that the government did not think it worth while to call her on the stand again.

"Lizzie did not try to get Bridget out of the house. If she had undertaken to do these deeds, think you not that she would not have sent Bridget downstreet to buy something, to go for the marketing, to go to the store, one thing and another—or send her on some errand—and then have time undisturbed? But, instead of that, everything goes on as usual and Bridget was about her work."

Robinson, sailing along, relaxed, was confident enough to introduce a little whimsy into his remarks. He took up the subject of the murder weapon:

"Now, what was it done with? The government has a theory about it, or at least *seems* to have a theory about it, and then does *not* seem to have a theory about it. You have had all the armory of the Borden house brought here. First, these two axes. I put them down because they have the seal of the Commonwealth; they are declared innocent.

"Then I pick up this one [the plain-head hatchet] and they tell me it is innocent and had nothing to do with it. I put it down in good company. I pick this one up [the claw-hammer hatchet] and they tell me today that this is innocent and I put it down immediately in the same good companionship. Let us see.

"The claw-hammer hatchet is four and one-half inches wide on the edge. Dr. Dolan says in his testimony that that could be an adequate instrument and a sufficient instrument to produce all the wounds.

"Then comes Dr. Draper who says that the cutting edge of the instrument which caused the wounds was $3\frac{1}{2}$ inches, not $4\frac{1}{2}$ inches.

"Dr. Cheever says that he puts the cutting edge at 3¹/₂ inches but it might have been very considerably less. It could be done with one 3 inches wide. Possibly by one 2³/₄ inches wide. These are our *experts* that they are talking about. We do not usually hang people upon the testimony of experts. It is not safe. You see that. The doctors themselves do not agree and they cannot agree and they do not know.

"Well, then comes this little innocent-looking fellow called the handleless hatchet—and that is the one on which you first think the government is going to stand. Now, whether Mr. Mullaly or Mr. Fleet is right about it, there is no handle here now, and we will leave them to explore, and when they find it, I hope they will carry it to the British Museum. And I hope they will be there to deliver a lecture upon it, to tell the astonished multitude which one of them found it and which one did not find it, and which one of them saw the other put it back into the box when he did not put it back into the box.

"Now this hatchet was not referred to at the preliminary examination at all. Their theory, I suppose, is that it was used, and after it was used, washed thoroughly so as to get all the blood off, and then the handle broken off by the person that used it. And their theory is that the blood was all gotten off. But this piece of wood was inside of the eye, and Professor Wood tells you that blood will flow into a narrow place. And he boiled it with iodide of potassium, and says he cannot get the slightest trace of blood. There *was* no blood, as I tell you, and as a last resort they come in here timidly and haltingly at the opening of this case, and say, "We bring you this handleless hatchet, but we do not tell you whether it is the hatchet or not.

"They said they would prove to you that there was exclusive opportunity. They said nobody else could have done it. Emma was gone. Morse was gone. Bridget was outdoors and later in her room. They said that the defendant was really shut up in that house with the two victims and that everybody else was actually and absolutely shut out.

"The cellar door was undoubtedly locked. The front door, in the usual course, was bolted up by Lizzie Wednesday night and unbolted by her Thursday morning. It doesn't make any difference whether it was bolted afterwards or not so far as anybody's coming in is concerned, because if he did, he couldn't have bolted the door behind him when he went out; and it doesn't appear anybody else did, and that is all the significance it has.

"The side screen door was unfastened from about nine o'clock to 10:45 or 11:00. Now, if that door wasn't locked, Lizzie wasn't locked in and everybody else wasn't locked out.

"Suppose the assassin came there and the house was all open on the north side and suppose he came there and passed through. Where could he go? Plenty of places. He could go upstairs into the spare room; he could go into the hall closet; he could go into the sitting room closet; he could go into the pantry. He could go into such places in that house as all these common thieves run into if they can find a door open. It was easy enough for him to go up into that bedchamber and secrete himself, to stay there, until he finds himself confronting Mrs. Borden.

"Now what is going to be done? He is there for murder; not to murder her, but to murder Mr. Borden, and he must strike her down.

"And when he had done his work and Mr. Borden had come in, he made ready then to come down at the first opportunity. Bridget was outdoors, Lizzie was outdoors. And he could do his work quickly and securely and pass out the same door, if you please, that he came in at, the side door.

"We say that nobody saw him go in and nobody saw Mr. Borden go out down the street.

"There was somebody out there. Dr. Handy described to you a man on the sidewalk he saw there just before the murder. And Mrs. Manley and Mrs. Hart came along there at ten minutes before ten and found a man on the outside looking out for things. This was not done by one man alone; there was somebody else in it and there was a man standing there at the gatepost. You can see then how everything in this idea of "exclusive opportunity" falls to the ground, because there is no exclusive opportunity.

"Take the facts as they are. What is there to prove to you absolutely, as sensible men, the guilt of this defendant? Were she a villain and a rascal, she would have done as villains and rascals do. There was her uncle, John Morse, suspected as you have heard, followed up, inquired about, and she is asked and she said, "No. He did not do it." The busy finger was pointed at Bridget Sullivan and Lizzie spoke right out determinedly and promptly, "Why, Bridget did not do it." Then somebody said, "Why, the Portuguese on the farm." "No," says Lizzie, "and my father has not any man that ever worked for him that would do that to him. I cannot believe it of any of them."

"How do you account for that except in one way? She was virtually putting everybody away from suspicion and leaving herself to stand as the only one to whom all would turn their eyes. Gentlemen, as you look upon her, you will pass your judgment that she is not insane.

"To find her guilty you must believe she is a fiend. Does she look it? As she sat here these long weary days and moved in and out before you, have you seen anything that shows the lack of human feeling and womanly bearing?

"With great weariness on your part, but with abundant patience and intelligence and care, you have listened to what I have had to offer. So far as you are concerned, it is the last word of the defendant to you. Take it; take care of her as you have and give us promptly your verdict of 'not guilty,' that she may go home and be Lizzie Andrew Borden of Fall River, in that blood-stained and wrecked home where she has passed her life so many years."

Robinson, weary after four hours of addressing the jury, returned to the defendant's table and sat beside Lizzie, his head in his hands.

She did not speak, but touched him lightly on the arm.

16

Knowlton for the Commonwealth

*H*OSEA MORRILL KNOWLTON, 46, was 13 years the junior of ex-Governor Robinson. He was born in Durham, Maine, in 1847 and graduated from Tufts College 20 years later. Two more years at Harvard Law School and he had passed the bar exam and hung up his shingle.

At age 29, he was elected representative in the lower house of the Massachusetts legislature and, after two years, elevated to senator. Within another two years (he was then 32), he became district attorney for the southern district of Massachusetts, the post he held.

He was a "solid man," a revered term in New England. He had been a superior student, a successful lawyer, and a conscientious legislator. In his 14 years as district attorney, his experience had been varied and notably successful.

But, as he had written Attorney General Pillsbury two months earlier, he had no hope of obtaining a conviction this time. The Fall River police had put together a case so weak it should never have been presented to a grand jury, and they had spent the intervening months trying to knit together what little they had. After reviewing everything before him, Knowlton knew all the prosecution had was little more than what they had started with: "She *must* have done it."

He began his summation much as Robinson had started his, by deploring what had taken place on August 4 last. Then he continued:

"The prisoner at the bar is a woman, and a Christian woman, as the expression is used. We are trying a crime that would been deemed impossible but for the fact that it was, and we are charging with the commission of it, a woman whom we would have believed incapable of doing it but for the evidence that it is my duty, my painful duty, to call to your attention."

But, he argued, no station in life was a guarantee against the commission of crimes. Widows and orphans were routinely swindled by respectable bankers; ministers were known to have been found to be "as foul as hell inside." Sex was no guarantee because women had been murderesses before, as had youths of tender years. As for this particular crime, the murder of Andrew and Abby Borden, it was a crime that challenged their most sober and sacred attention.

"That aged man, that aged woman, had gone by the noonday of their lives. They had borne the burden and heat of the day. They had accumulated a competency which they felt would carry them through the waning years of their lives, and, hand in hand, they expected to go down to the sunset of their days in quiet and happiness. But for that crime, they would be enjoying the air of this day."

He defended the Fall River police department, which had been criticized by the press, the public, and the defense:

"As soon as this crime was discovered, it became the duty of those who are entrusted with the detection of crime to take such measures as they thought were proper for the discovery of the criminal. They made many mistakes. The crime was beyond the experience of any man in this country or in this world. What wonder that they did? They left many things undone that they might have done. What wonder that they did? It was beyond the scope of any man to grasp in its entirety at that time. But honestly, faithfully, as thoroughly as God had given them ability, they pursued the various avenues by which they thought they might find the criminal.

"I have heard many an honest man say he could not believe circumstantial evidence. But, gentlemen, the crime we are trying is a crime of an assassin. It is the work of one who does his foul deeds beyond the sight and hearing of men. When one sees the crime committed or one hears the crime committed, then the testimony of him that sees or hears is the testimony of a witness who saw it or heard it and is direct evidence. All other evidence is circumstantial evidence. Did you ever hear of a murderer getting a witness to his work who could see it or hear it? Murder is the work of stealth and craft in which there are not only no witnesses, but the traces are attempted to be obliterated."

It was a fair, legal, and reasonable explanation of what constitutes circumstantial evidence, but Knowlton was arguing against a prejudice that has plagued prosecutors since the very inception of courts, the hesitance of jurors to convict when faced with a paucity of direct evidence. This was the fact of life Knowlton was alluding to in his letter to Pillsbury when he said he saw no course other than to proceed with a trial. But, with determination, he pressed on:

"Andrew Jackson Borden probably never heard the clock strike 11 as it pealed forth from the tower of city hall. And all the evidence in the case points to the irresistible conviction that when Andrew Borden was down at his accustomed place in the bank of Mr. Abraham Hart, the faithful wife he had left at home was prone in death in the chamber of the house he had left her in. At half-past nine, the assassin met her in that room and put an end to her innocent old life.

"Gentlemen, that is a tremendous fact. It is a *controlling* fact in this case because the murderer of this man was the murderer of Mrs. Borden. It was the malice against *Mrs.* Borden that inspired the assassin.

"There she lay bleeding, dead, prone by the hand of an assassin. In all this universe, there could not be found a person who could have had any motive to do it.

"It is said there is a skeleton in the household of every man, but the Borden skelton—if there was one—was fairly well locked up from view. They were a close-mouthed family. They did not parade their difficulties. Last of all would you expect they would tell the domestic in the kitchen, which is the whole tower of strength of the defense, and yet, there was a skeleton in the closet of that house.

"It is useless to tell you that there was peace and harmony in that family.

"That correction of Mr. Fleet, at the very moment the poor woman who had reared that girl lay dead within ten feet of her voice, was not merely accidental. It went down deep into the springs of human nature.

"This girl owed everything to her. Mrs. Borden was the only mother she had ever known and she had given to this girl her mother's love and had given her this love when a child, when it was not her own and she had not gone through the pains of childbirth, because it was her husband's daughter.

"And then there was a quarrel. A man worth more than a quarter of a million dollars, wants to give his wife, his faithful wife who has served him 30 years for her board and clothes, who has done his work, who has kept his house, who has reared his children, wants to buy and give to her the interest in a little homestead where her sister lives.

"How wicked to have found fault with it.

"She kept her own counsel. Bridget did not know anything about it. She was in the kitchen. This woman never betrayed her feelings except when someone else tried to make her call her "Mother," and then her temper broke forth.

"I heard what Miss Emma said Friday, and I could but admire the loyalty and fidelity of that unfortunate girl to her still more unfortunate sister. I could not find it in my heart to ask her many questions. She was in the most desperate strait that any innocent woman could be in: her next of kin, her only sister, stood in peril and she must come to the rescue. She faintly tells us the relations in the family were peaceful, but we sadly know they were not.

"Lizzie had repudiated the title of mother. She had lived with her in hatred. She had gone on increasing in that hatred until we do not know—we can only guess—how far that sore had festered, how far the blood in that family had been poisoned.

"I come back to that poor woman, lying prone, as has been described, in the parlor. Was anybody in the world to be benefitted by her taking away? There was one. There was one woman in the world who believed that the dead woman stood between her and her father.

"Let us examine the wounds upon that woman. There was nothing in these blows but hatred and a desire to kill. Some struck at an angle, badly aimed; some struck in the neck, badly directed; some pattered on top of the head and didn't go through; some, where the skull was weaker, went through. A great strong man would have taken a blow from that hatchet and made an end of it. The hand that held the weapon was not the hand of masculine strength. It was the hand of a person strong only in hate and desire to kill."

It was an argument virile in passion but weak in forensic proof. It equalled Robinson at his best. Any tutored referee in debate would face a wrenching decision as to which attorney had soared the higher in their flights of rhetoric. A comparison of the two closing arguments, each taking approximately four hours, would surely lead to a deadheat at best, or a slight edge to Knowlton.

Robinson had drawn a sketchy scenario of how an outsider could have entered the house, committed the crimes, and then slunk out the side door. He had not spent much time with the argument, since, as he said, it was not up to him or the jury to explain the mystery. But, in order to convict Lizzie, the outsider theory had to be demolished totally, and Knowlton set about the task:

"Never mind the impossibility of imagining a person who was so familiar with the habits of that family, who was so familiar with the interior of that house, who could foresee the things that the family themselves could not see, who was so lost to all human reason, who was so utterly criminal as to set out without any motive whatsoever, as to have gone to that house that morning, to have penetrated through the cordon of Bridget and Lizzie, and pursued that poor woman up the stairs to her death, and then waited, weapon in hand, until the house should be filled up with people again that he might complete his work. I won't discuss with you the impossibility of that thing for the present.

"The dead body tells us another thing. It is a circumstance, but it is one of those circumstances that cannot be cross-examined nor made fun of nor talked out of court. The poor woman was standing when she was struck, and fell with all the force of that 200 pounds of flesh, flat and prone on the floor. That jar could not have failed to have been heard all over that house.

"No matter how craftily murder is planned, there is always some point where the skill and cunning of the assassin fails him. It failed her. It failed her at a vital point, a point which my distinguished friend has attempted to answer, if I may be permitted to say so, and has utterly failed. She was alone in that house with that murdered woman. She could not have fallen without her knowledge. The assassin could not have come in without her knowledge. She was out of sight and Mrs. Borden was out of sight, and by and by, there was coming into the house a stern and just man who knew all the bitterness there was between them. He came in; he sat down; she came to him, and she said to him, 'Mrs. Borden has had a note and gone out.'

"No note came; no note was written; nobody brought a note; nobody was sick. Mrs. Borden had not had a note.

"Little did it occur to Lizzie Borden when she told that lie to her father that there would be manifold witnesses to the fatality of it. They have advertised for the writer of the note which was never written and which never came. Ah, but my distinguished friend is pleased to suggest that it was part of the scheme of assassination. How? To write a note to get a woman away when he was going there to assassinate her? What earthly use was there in writing a note to get rid of Mrs. Borden, when there would still be left Lizzie and Bridget in the house? Oh, no, that is too wild and absurd.

"God forbid that anybody should have committed this murder, but somebody did, and when I have found that she was killed, not by the strong hand of a man, but by the weak and ineffectual blows of woman, when I find that those are the blows of hatred rather than strength, when I find that she is left alone at the very moment of the murder, shut up in that house where every sound went from one end to the other, with the only person in God's universe who could say she was not her friend, with the only person in the universe who could be benefitted by her taking away, and when I find, as I found, and as you must find, if you answer your consciences in this case, that the story told about a note coming is as false as the crime itself, I am not responsible, Mr. Foreman, *you* are not responsible for the conclusion to which you are driven.

"There may be that in this case which saves us from the idea that Lizzie Borden planned to kill her father. I hope she did not. But Lizzie Andrew Borden, the daughter of Andrew Jackson Borden, never came down those stairs, but a murderess. She was coming downstairs to face Nemesis.

"There wouldn't be any question of what he would know of the reason why that woman lay in death. He knew who disliked her. He knew who could not tolerate her presence under the roof. He knew the discussion which had led up to the pitch of frenzy which resulted in her death, and she didn't dare let him live, father though he was, and bound to her by every tie of affection."

This was the high point of Knowlton's address to the jury. His summation, like Robinson's, took more than four hours and, like Robinson's, is condensed here. In the half-dozen preceding paragraphs, Knowlton did all anyone could do to persuade the jury of Lizzie's guilt. Most of his assumptions, while rooted in logic, were not backed by hard evidence, but then, nothing about the entire case was. He was laboring with what the police of Fall River had given him.

He went on to face the alibi that Lizzie had been up in the barn loft when Andrew was murdered, but he had no ammunition to disprove it. The Medley "cakewalk" hung heavily in the air. The certainty that others had been up in the loft before Medley had made his sighting along the floor for footprints in the dust a fabrication that could not be defended. Of the Lizzie-in-the-loft defense, Knowlton could only say, "I assert that that story is simply absurd. I assert that that story is not within the bounds of reasonable possibilities." But there was no force in the denial.

Of the lack of bloodstains on her person or her clothing, his rebuttal was even weaker:

"How could she have avoided the spattering of her dress with blood if she was the author of these crimes? As to the first crime, it is scarcely necessary to attempt to answer the question. In the solitude of that house, with ample fire in the stove, with ample wit of woman, nobody has suggested that, as to the first crime, there was not an ample opportunity, ample means, and that nothing could be suggested as a reason why all the evidence of that crime could not have been amply and successfully concealed."

This suggested a new theory, that either the dress, petticoat, stockings, and shoes worn by Lizzie had been burned in the kitchen stove or had been hidden somewhere in the house. Burning abundant garments like a dress and petticoat as worn in that time could not have been done without the notice of Bridget or without a substantial residue of ashes not seen by the police when the stove was emptied and sifted.

To posit hiding two bloodstained outfits from the *three* intensive searches by the police was little short of desperation.

"As to the second murder," he admitted, "the question is one of more difficulty. I cannot answer it. You cannot answer it. You are neither murderers nor women. You have neither the craft of the assassin nor the cunning and deftness of the sex."

Obviously, sexist thinking did not originate in the twentieth century; it was extant in the 1890s. Regardless, the explanation that bundles of bloodstained clothing could, somehow, be made to disappear by the wiles, cunning, and deftness of women, but not men, was drivel, nonsense, a humbug.

Throughout the trial and, most especially, during his summation, Knowlton referred to the dress Lizzie had worn on the morning of the murders as a "silk" dress:

"This dress has been described to you as a silk dress—a dress which is not cheap, a dress which would not be worn in ironing by any prudent woman. Of course not. It is an afternoon dress. Do your wives dress in silk when they go down in the kitchen to work, and in their household duties in the morning before dinner?"

The dress was not a silk dress; it was a cotton dress. The material, then costing about 20 cents a yard, was a blend of 90 percent cotton and 10 percent silk and a very common material for cheap day dresses. It was called "bengaline silk" for the same reason glass beads were called "faux" pearls, a seller's gimmick to make a product sound as if it is better than it is.

Nor did Knowlton's deception take into account Lizzie's explanation that she had dressed for going shopping when she got up that morning.

"What is the defense, Mr. Foreman?" Knowlton concluded. "What is the answer to this array of impregnable facts? Nothing; nothing. I stop and think and I say again, nothing.

"The distinguished counsel, with all his eloquence which I can't hope to match or approach, has attempted nothing but to say, 'Not Proven.'

"Are you satisfied that it was done by her? I have attempted— how imperfectly, none but myself can say—to discharge the sad duty which has devolved upon me. I submit these facts to you with the confidence that you are men of courage and truth.

"Rise, gentlemen, rise to the attitude of your duty. Act as you would act when you stand before the great throne at the last day. What shall be your reward? The ineffable consciousness of duty well done."

It was nearing the noon hour when Knowlton sat down and Justice Dewey declared the court in adjournment until 1:45, when he would charge the jury. The ordeal was almost over.

17

Justice Dewey
for the Court

A S CALLED FOR BY MASSACHUSETTS LAW, three justices of
the superior court—the chief justice and two associate
justices—had sat for the twelve-day trial of Lizzie Borden. It
was Chief Justice Albert Mason who gavelled for order on the
afternoon of Tuesday, June 20, 1893.

"Lizzie Andrew Borden," he said, "although you have now
been fully heard by counsel, it is your privilege to add any word
which you may desire to say in person to the jury. You now
have that opportunity."

Throughout Knowlton's long summation, Lizzie had listened
with intensity, her eyes fixed on his every move. Surely she
had been comforted by Robinson, Jennings, and the Reverend
Buck; assured that the jury would not find against her. But,
still, there was no look of complacency on her face as she had

heard herself repeatedly damned and accused by Knowlton's passionate summation. The small bouquet of flowers lying on the table before her went untouched. The fan that she had carried every day and that she had furled and unfurled, laid down, and picked up a hundred times, was beside the bouquet.

She rose without assistance but seemed for just a moment to find it hard to speak. But then, quietly:

"I am innocent," she said. "I leave it to my counsel to speak for me."

Associate Justice Justin Dewey, III, born in Alford, Massachusetts, was 57 years old and small of stature. He had graduated from Williams College and practiced law for 26 years before being appointed to the court by Governor Robinson.

After the trial, the anti-Lizzie brigade was savagely critical of his charge to the jury. It was a second summation for the defense, they said, but this was a grossly unfair accusation. At no time did he question the *facts* of either presentation, only urging clear reasoning in interpreting them, well within the purview of what a judge is expected to advise a jury unlettered in law. He reinforced that point in his opening remarks. These are the highlights:

"Mr. Foreman and gentlemen of the jury, you have listened with attention to the evidence in this case and to the arguments of the defendant's counsel and of the district attorney. It now remains for me, acting in behalf of the court, to give you such aid toward a proper performance of your duty as I may be able to give within the limits for judicial action prescribed by law. And, to prevent any erroneous impression, it may be well for me to bring to your attention, at the outset, that it is provided by a statute of this state that the court shall not charge juries with respect to matters of fact, *but may state the testimony and the law.*

"I understand the government to concede that defendant's character has been good; that it has not been merely a negative and natural one that nobody heard anything against, but one of positive, of active benevolence in religious and charitable work.

"Judging of this subject as reasonable men, you have the right to take into consideration her character such as is admitted or apparent. In some cases it may not be esteemed of much importance. In other cases it may raise a reasonable doubt of a defendant's guilt even in the face of strongly criminating circumstances."

In short, Lizzie's moral past could be taken into consideration, but whether or not it had any bearing on the charges was up to the individual juror.

During the trial, seamstress Hannah Gifford had testified that, during one of the dressmaking sessions at the Bordens, when Abby's name had come up in conversation, Lizzie had said, "Don't call her mother; she is my stepmother and she is a mean, hateful old thing." Judge Dewey tried to put the value of that comment into context.

"I understand the counsel for the government to claim that defendant had towards her stepmother a strong feeling of ill-will, nearly if not quite, amounting to hatred. And Mrs. Gifford's testimony as to a conversation with defendant in the early spring of 1892 is relied upon largely as a basis for that claim.

"In judging wisely of a case, you need to keep all parts of it in their natural and proper proportion and not put on any particular piece of evidence a greater weight than it will reasonably bear, and not to magnify or intensify or depreciate or belittle any piece of evidence to meet an emergency. But take Mrs. Gifford's just as she gave it and consider whether or not it will fairly amount to the significance attached to it.

"What you wish, of course, is a true conception of the state of the mind of the defendant towards her stepmother, not years ago, but later and nearer the time of the homicide. To get such a true conception, you must not separate Mrs. Gifford's testimony from all the rest, but consider also the evidence as to how they lived in the family, whether, as Mrs. Raymond, I believe, said, they sewed together, whether they went to church together, sat together, returned together—in a word, the general tenor of their life. You will particularly recall the testimony of Bridget Sullivan and of the defendant's sister Emma bearing on the same subject. Weigh carefully all the testimony on the subject and then judge whether or not there is clearly proved such a permanent state of mind on the part of the defendant toward her stepmother as to justify you in drawing against her upon that ground inferences unfavorable to her innocence."

This was one of the comments the anti-Lizzie brigade dispar-
aged most. "Uncalled for," they cried. "Foul!" Yet, this caution
is clearly within the guidelines the judge had cited. An unbiased
reading of it shows a fine impartiality. It says only, "Keep Mrs.
Gifford's statement in perspective. Give it its due weight, but
do not be inflamed by this single comment. Remember also the
testimony of Bridget and Emma, all of which told of politeness
and courtesy between the daughter and the stepmother."

"Now you observe, gentlemen, that the government submits
this case to you upon circumstantial evidence. This is a legal
and not unusual way of proving a criminal case, and it is clearly
competent for a jury to find a person guilty of murder upon
circumstantial evidence alone.

"However, failure to prove a fact *essential* to the conclusion of
guilt, and without which that conclusion would not be reached,
is fatal to the government's case.

"All would admit that the necessity of establishing the presence of the defendant in the house when, for instance, her
father was killed, is a *necessary* fact.

"The question of the relation of this handleless hatchet to the
murder. It may have an *important* bearing upon the case—
whether the crime was done by that particular hatchet or not—
but it cannot be said that it bears the same *essential* and necessary relation to the case that the matter of her presence in the
house does. It is not claimed by the government but what that
killing might have been done with some other instrument.

"I understand the government to claim substantially that the
alleged fact that the defendant made a false statement in regard
to her stepmother's having received a note or letter that morning bears an essential relation to the case.

"Now what are the grounds on which the government claims
that that statement is false, knowingly false?

"First, that the one who wrote it has not been found. Second,
that the party who brought it has not been found. Third, that no
letter has been found.

"What motive had she to invent a story like this? What
motive? Would it not have answered every purpose to have her
say—and would it not have been more natural for her to say—
that her stepmother had gone out on an errand or to make a
call? What motive had she to take upon herself the responsibil-

ity of giving utterance to this distinct and independent fact of a letter or note received, with which she might be confronted and which she might afterwards find it difficult to explain, if she knew that no such thing was true.

"But, it is said, no letter was found.

"Might it not be a part of the plan or scheme of such a person by such a document or paper to withdraw Mrs. Borden from the house? If he afterward came in there, came upon her, killed her, might he not have found the letter or note with her? Might he not have a reasonable and natural wish to remove that as one possible link in tracing himself? Taking the suggestions as the one side and the other, judging the matter fairly, not assuming beforehand that the defendant is guilty, does the evidence satisfy you as reasonable men, beyond any reasonable doubt, that these statements of the defendant in regard to that note must necessarily be false?"

Again, a carefully balanced assessment of whether there had been a note and, if so, what had happened to it. It was not sufficient for the government to say, simply, there had been no note and Lizzie had lied. They either had to prove it, which they had not, or inevitably, leave open the possibility that there had been a note, but that no one knew what happened to it. This, of course, was exactly what the situation was.

"Something has been said to you by counsel as to defendant's not testifying. I must speak to you on this subject. The Constitution of our state, in its bill of rights, provides that no subject shall be compelled to secure or furnish evidence against himself.

"The superior court, speaking of a defendant's right and protection under the Constitution and statutes, uses these words: 'Nor can any inference be drawn against him from his failure to testify.' Therefore I say to you, and I mean all that my words express, any argument, any implication, any suggestion, any consideration in your minds unfavorable to defendant, based on her failure to testify, is unwarranted in law. Nor is defendant called upon to offer any explanation of her neglect to testify. If she were required to explain, others might think the explanation insufficient. Then she would lose the protection of the statute.

"If you are convinced beyond reasonable doubt of the defendant's guilt, it will be your plain duty to declare that

conviction by your verdict. If the evidence falls short of produc-
ing such conviction in your mind, although it may raise a suspicion of guilt, or even a strong probability of guilt, it would be
your plain duty to return a verdict of not guilty. If not legally
proved to be guilty, the defendant is entitled to a verdict of not
guilty.

"Gentlemen, I know not what views you may take of the
case, but it is the gravest importance that it should be decided.
If decided at all, it must be decided by a jury.

"The law requires that the jury shall be unanimous in their
verdict, and it is their duty to agree if they can conscientiously
do so.

"And now, gentlemen, the case is committed to your hands,
the tragedy which has given to this investigation such wide-
spread interest and deeply excited public attention and feeling.
The press has ministered to this excitement by publishing,
without moderation, rumors and reports of all kinds. You must
guard, as far as possible, against all impressions derived from
having read in the newspapers accounts relating to the question
you have now to decide.

"And entering on your deliberations with no pride of opinion, with impartial and thoughtful minds, seeking only for the
truth, you will lift the case above the range of passion and
prejudice and excited feeling, into the clear atmosphere of reason and law."

The jury filed from the room, their faces solemn and in no
way communicative as to what their private thoughts might be.
Certainly the trial had been an experience none would ever for-
get. As the years passed, each of them would always be known
as "one of the jurors in the Lizzie Borden trial," and when each
died, his obituary would recall that highlight of their lives.

As it had done throughout the investigation and the trial, *The
New York Times* gave unstinted praise in an editorial that day to
the court and the trial participants:

CONDUCT OF THE BORDEN TRIAL

Whatever may be the result of the Borden trial there can hardly be
two opinions as to the superiority of the manner in which it has been
conducted over that which is apt to characterize "sensational" murder cases in this state. It is, in fact, a credit alike to the bench and the

bar of Massachusetts. It has been prompt and orderly, without any sign of the laxness or the scandalous incidents with which we are too familiar here. This appeared conspicuously on the first day in the selection of a jury. The examination of the talesmen was conducted wholly from the bench, and was confined almost entirely to certain statutory questions touching the qualifications of jurors. It is doubtful if there could have been found in Bristol county 12 men of mature age and sound mind who had not read about the case, discussed it more or less, and formed some kind of opinion about it, but the crucial question was whether they were in a state of mind to render a verdict upon the legal evidence to be submitted. If it was shown that they had no personal interest or prejudice in the case, that is considered by Massachusetts law as being sufficient, and with the statutory right of challenge, affords an ample guarantee of fairness. The result was that a jury was obtained in a single day in a community in which the case had been a matter of discussion for months.

The court and counsel have alike been disposed to observe the legitimate limits of evidence and of argument, and there have been no unseemly wrangles or unnecessary delays. Important questions as to the admission of evidence have come up and have been argued pertinently and incisively and decided promptly. There has been expert medical and chemical testimony, but it has not been biased or conflicting. It so happens that it was submitted by the prosecution, but proved to be wholly favorable to the defense. There was no attempt to twist or distort it or to make it prove anything but what might appear as the result of an expert examination of the facts.

Whatever there may be that is discreditable in this case must appear in the efforts of the police authorities of Fall River to unravel a mystery which baffled their moderate skill and in the preliminary examination, which seems to have been directed to fixing the crime upon the only person whom those authorities could subject to suspicion. The trial itself has been conducted ably and expeditiously and kept within the limits of the proper dignity of a judicial proceeding. There has been a dearth of evidence for the prosecution and, consequently, little for the defense to do in meeting it, but in such a case under lax methods there is apt to be all the more straining for sensational effect and greater efforts to overstep the bounds of regulated procedure. The Borden trial, considering the sensational aspects of the case, has been a model proceeding from the opening day and can now only be marred by the conduct of the jury.

The New York Times would have additional comments to make the next day, but, right then, it was 3:30, everyone was wrung out, and it is probable that the bars and coffee houses

near the courthouse enjoyed a rush of customers as the jury
retired to the cramped jury room to begin their deliberations.

Exactly one hour later, they informed the justices they had
reached a verdict. Actually they had come to their verdict ten
minutes after reaching the jury room, but out of respect for the
prosecution had waited an additional 50 minutes before passing
the word.

The news spread instantly in the corridors and the rush was
on. All seats filled immediately, and the overpowered bailiffs
could not hold back the crowd until the aisles were filled with
spectators. The three judges threaded their way to the bench
behind Sheriff Wright.

The clerk called the roll and each juror intoned his presence.

"Lizzie Andrew Borden, stand up."

Lizzie rose uncertainly and faced the jury.

"Gentlemen of the jury," the clerk asked, "have you reached
a verdict?"

"We have," said the foreman.

"Please return the papers to the court. Lizzie Andrew Borden, hold up your right hand. Mr. foreman, look upon the
prisoner. Prisoner, look upon the foreman. What say you, Mr.
Foreman?"

"Not guilty!"

The courtroom erupted in a cheer that might, it was reported,
have been heard half a mile away.

Lizzie's shoulders sagged and she sank into her seat with
tears and sobs wracking her body. Although the transcript of
the trial says the demonstration was instantly stopped, newspaper reports say that it continued for minutes, and Sheriff
Wright made no effort to stop it. His eyes, they wrote, were
filled with tears. Whether they were tears of joy or frustration
was not said.

Columnist Joe Howard:

> Jennings, overcome as few men are ever seen to be, and trembling
> like an aspen leaf, cried, "Oh, thank God!" and pushed his way to
> the rail of the dock. Lizzie held out her hand to him; he grasped it
> and made it red with squeezing. Robinson dodged under the rail of
> the bar and pushed by the now useless deputy who had guarded the
> prisoner. He stooped down and put his face against hers and his left
> arm slipped around her waist as he lifted her up.

All her old friends crowded around her. Mr. Holmes was the first to press her hand and Reverend Buck who was weeping, was next. She reached out a hand to her counsel, Melvin Adams and in turn, he took both of hers. Emma, meanwhile, was surrounded by a separate crowd and cut off from Lizzie.

The jurors, in Indian file marched by to shake hands with the woman for whom they had done so much, and she gave each of them warm smiles and grateful remarks of thanks.

The Reverend Jubb and Attorneys Robinson and Jennings surrounded Lizzie and eased her into the corridor and to refuge in the judges' chambers. It was another hour before a once more composed Lizzie left the court building a free woman. The waiting crowd burst into song, cheers, and applause, and a long retinue of carriages followed hers to the station and the train back home to Fall River.

18

Should Old Acquaintance Be Forgot

*T*HE BOSTON *HERALD* led the newspaper comments the day after the trial:

> The verdict of the jury in the Lizzie Borden case is simply a confirmation of the opinions entertained by those who followed the evidence submitted by the prosecution and witnessed the effect upon it of a vigorous cross-examination. The government was obliged to prove guilt beyond a reasonable doubt and this it failed to do. The verdict has been given and the accused is forever free from all possibility of further legal judgment. The tragedy remains quite as much a mystery as it was before. Nothing has been proved except that no evidence was brought out at the trial that would justify the conviction of Lizzie Borden as the one guilty of the act.

The New York Times echoed this opinion, but in a sharper criticism of what had transpired:

It will be a certain relief to every right-minded man or woman who has followed the case to learn that the jury at New Bedford has not only acquitted Miss Lizzie Borden of the atrocious crime with which she was charged, but has done so with a promptness that was very significant.

The acquittal of the most unfortunate and cruelly persecuted woman was, by its promptness, in effect, a condemnation of the police authorities of Fall River and of the legal officers who secured the indictment and have conducted the trial.

It was a declaration, not only that the prisoner was guiltless, but that there never was any serious reason to suppose that she was guilty.

She has escaped the awful fate with which she was threatened, but the long imprisonment she has undergone, the intolerable suspense and anguish inflicted upon her, the outrageous injury to her feelings as a woman and as a daughter are chargeable directly to the police and legal authorities. That she should have been subjected to these is a shame to Massachusetts which the good sense of the jury in acquitting her only in part removes.

The theory of the prosecution seems to have been that, if it were possible that Miss Borden murdered her father and his wife, it must be inferred that she did murder them. It was held, practically, that if she could not be proved innocent, she must be taken to be guilty. We do not remember a case in a long time in which prosecution has so completely broken down, or in which the evidence has shown so clearly, not merely that the prisoner should not be convicted, but that there never should have been an indictment.

We are not surprised that the Fall River police should have fastened their suspicions upon Miss Borden. The town is not a large one. The police are of the usual inept and stupid and muddle-headed sort that such towns manage to get for themselves. There is nothing more merciless than the vanity of ignorant and untrained men charged with the detection of crime, in the face of a mystery that they cannot solve, and for the solution of which they feel responsible. The Fall River police needed a victim whose sacrifice should purge their force of the contempt that they felt they would incur if the murderer of the Bordens was not discovered, and the daughter was the nearest and most helpless. They pounced upon her.

But the responsibility of the law officers was very different. They were trained in the law, accustomed to analyzing and weighing evidence. They knew what justice required in the way of proof of the crime of murder.

> It is not easy to believe they did not know that no such proof,
> and nothing like it, was in their possession. Indeed, they seemed to
> have entered upon a trial without it, and groped along afterward in
> clumsy efforts to develop it.
> We cannot resist the feeling that their conduct in this matter was
> outrageous; that they were guilty of a barbarous wrong to an inno-
> cent woman and a gross injury to the community. And we hold it to
> be a misfortune that their victim has no legal recourse against them
> and no means of bringing them to account. Her acquittal is only a
> partial atonement for the wrong she has suffered.

In 500 words, *The New York Times* editorial had encapsulated
the entire Borden case. From 11:30 A.M. on August 4, 1892, until
4:00 P.M. on June 20, 1893, the investigation, indictment, and
trial had all been travesties.

Happening in a small city, the grotesque daylight murder of
two prominent, elderly citizens in their home on a busy street
had naturally been a sensation. It would have been one regardless of who had committed it. The fact that the police concen-
trated their investigation on, and later indicted, the daughter
only added to the wonder of it all.

The total irresponsibility of the Fall River *Globe* reporting and
editorializing contributed more fuel to an already excitable situation. The police force of Fall River was not the conglomeration
of stupid and muddle-headed boobs *The New York Times* accused
them of being, though certainly it was not a force experienced
in detection or forensic science. The lack of the force was not
dedication, it was leadership.

Marshal Hilliard was titular head of the department, but
Assistant Marshal Fleet was responsible for the day-to-day
investigation, and he was as hotheaded as he was determined.
The force had been hazed by the newspapers and the citizenry,
and they had panicked. They had to arrest someone or face the
contempt of the public.

Fleet was convinced the moment Lizzie failed to show him
proper respect and had snapped that Abby was not her mother.
From that time, the efforts of the police were bent toward proving her guilt. True, other leads had been followed up routinely
and rumors had been run to ground, but the essence of the
investigation had been to build up the proposition that Lizzie
was the miscreant.

Perhaps that procedure at first cannot be totally faulted, because it accurately portrayed the prevailing sentiment, but, when it became apparent that practical evidence substantiating her guilt could not be found, three options existed: first, indict and try her with the flawed circumstantial evidence they had; second, direct the search toward other suspects; or, third, put the arrest and indictment on hold until conclusive evidence could be gathered.

Giving in to the taunts of the press and the pressure from the people, they took the wrong option. As *The New York Times* said, the harrassed police department might be forgiven for succumbing, but the district attorney and the officers of the court could not.

Knowlton, having no confidence in her guilt, should have stamped the file *Nolle Prosequi* when it came to his desk. Better yet, he should have told Fleet and Hilliard they had no case and not to forward a file until they did.

The report from Harvard showing no bloodstains on the handleless hatchet, dress, shoes, and hose should have been in hand before any arrest was made or any "inquest" held. To have proceeded without it was, at least, foolish; at worst, derelict.

For motive, the police had a story or two of dissent or even hatred in the family; stories that may well have been true, but they could not be effectively substantiated. Even their own witness, Bridget, testified strongly to the contrary, and few would doubt she knew more about it than any casual acquaintance who only dropped by now and then.

Nor was Fleet able to break down Lizzie's alibi of being in the barn at the time Andrew was murdered, not even with the help of Medley's manufactured testimony about the absence of footprints in the dust.

Without a plausible motive (or, with a decidedly weak one, even if proved), without a weapon or the surely bloodstained clothing, and without that prime requisite, exclusive opportunity, the case against Lizzie was simply not a case at all. They had obtained an indictment but held a busted flush for a hand. They could prove nothing.

The author and the reader are in just about the same position Knowlton and Hilliard were when they felt the pressure to go to court. We, however, are not besieged by newspapers and the voters. We are able to assay calmly the meager proceeds of the investigation and we can choose to say:

"Bring us more evidence than this. If you can't find a blood-stained dress, then *prove* Lizzie burned it or otherwise disposed of it. You haven't done either. If you can't show us the instrument used to kill Abby and Andrew, then give us a substantive reason why not or tell us where it went. Don't give us sleight of hand. Somehow, connect it with the accused. Tell us if there was or was not a handle. Satisfy us that the Borden household was a cauldron of hatred so intense that it triggered this inhuman slaughter. Lizzie says she was in the barn loft at the time of the murder and even has a witness to sustain her. Your rebuttal is obviously perjured testimony by one of your officers. No! This is not enough to take this woman's life."

Why did most of Fall River, at the time and for several generations afterward, accept so readily that a woman of Lizzie's Christian upbringing and impeccable social history could have murdered with the savagery so evident in the event? Certainly those who had believed her guilty from the beginning were bolstered by the immediate announcement by Marshal Hilliard that there would be no further investigation; the case was closed. The inference was unavoidable. As far as the police were concerned, they had caught the killer; the jury had turned her loose.

At this distance in time, we cannot conjure up a picture of Lizzie, hatchet in hand, crouching over the prostrate form of Abby, crashing down blow after blow after blow on the head of the old woman and repeating the performance downstairs, this time on the benign form of her father, for whom she undeniably had a great sense of companionship and love in spite of his penurious ways. But we are not residents of Fall River in 1893. The scene has the mythical force of Medea slaughtering her children, or of Oedipus slaying his father at the crossroads, and it seems clear that Fall River—perhaps most of America—needed such a myth at the time, just as the ancient Greeks needed their myths. I will leave further investigation of the question in the hands of historians, psychologists, and anthropologists—even, perhaps, philosophers and theologians—much more qualified to answer it than I.

The murders had been the work of a maniac unleashed, and that description simply did not fit the calm, Christian young lady in the box, nor the facts as they were presented at the trial.

The news of Lizzie's acquittal flashed over the telegraph wires just minutes after the decision was announced, and word spread through Fall River with the same speed the news of the murders had ten months earlier. Prevailing opinion had been that the jury would deadlock over the verdict; the majority would find her guilty, but it would not be unanimous. That was Knowlton and Pillsbury's opinion as well and a consummation they devoutly wished. If the jury failed to reach a verdict, they could drop the case with impunity and get on with their lives.

Once again, Lizzie became the sole subject of every street-corner conversation. Money changed hands as bets were paid off or collected, and the mob began assembling in front of the house on Second Street as it had done before. Word was that Lizzie would be arriving from New Bedford in a carriage. Fall River's most famous resident was triumphantly coming home!

A squad of 12 officers was dispatched to keep the streets cleared and the mob in control. Lights were seen burning in the kitchen. Bridget was back at her old job and preparing a snack for the return of her mistress, the gossip ran. But, as usual, it was wrong; Bridget never returned to 92 Second Street.

By 8:00 P.M., the crowd of more than 2,000 was restless and disappointed, as it had been so often before. A runner came with word that Lizzie had arrived by train and was going to the home of Charles Holmes on Pine Street. A groan went up from the crowd, but half of them, determined this time to catch a glimpse of the town's celebrity, took off for Pine Street.

They were too late to see the carriage pull up in front of the Holmes residence. Lizzie was first out and first up the steps. She was followed quickly by Mr. Holmes, Emma, and Miss Annie Holmes. Several reporters had met the train and tagged after the Holmes carriage, but only one was invited inside where Dr. Bowen and the Reverend and Mrs. Jubb made up the welcoming party.

Lizzie proclaimed herself "the happiest woman in the world," but refused to discuss the trial or, of course, the murders that had brought it on. It was a vow of silence she would keep for the rest of her life.

Meanwhile, on Second Street, the crowd continued to grow, on the assumption that, sooner or later, Lizzie would return home to spend the night. About 11:00, a band appeared from nowhere to join the celebration, and the strains of "Auld Lang Syne" could be heard.

19

Epilogue

*N*OW THAT THE TRIAL WAS OVER, Lizzie had a choice. She could return to Fall River, the town of her birth, or she could begin life anew somewhere else. She told a reporter, "A good many persons have talked to me as if they thought I would go and live somewhere else when my trial was over. I don't know what possesses them. I am going home and I am going to stay there. I have never thought of doing anything else."

Lizzie returned to "that bloodstained and wrecked home" Robinson described in his summation, but it was only for a short time. She and Emma wore joint heirs to the money and property of Andrew and Abby, to the value of about $400,000, a princely sum in 1893.

One of their first purchases after the estate was settled was a home on 7 French Street, up on The Hill, where Fall River society lived. She had the name "Maplecroft" set in concrete on the top step. It was an elegant three-story Queen Anne-style "mansion" that still stands, now shabby with peeling paint and a placard on the door, "R. Dube, Public Fire Adjustor - Notary." A Grecian bust peers apprehensively out the front window as if to see if crowds are gathering again a century later.

When the two sisters moved in, it was a gracious and warm contrast to that cold and narrow railroad house on Second Street. The French Street house was Lizzie's choice, and it was her taste that decorated it. In some of the 14 rooms, the wallpaper she selected is still visible. The designs are uniformly the quaint and innocent patterns of the Victorian era—small flowers, delicate, entwined vines and, here and there, fluttering butterflies.

The entry hall was richly paneled in mahogany, and on the right, a broad stairway with rosewood banisters curved up to the second floor. In a niche on a handsome circular table was a life-size bust in Grecian style, perhaps the one that now stares out from the glassed-in front porch.

To the left was the spacious living or receiving room, with a broad fireplace of marble dominating the inner wall and six windows the opposite. The rug was a soft lilac, supposedly Lizzie's favorite color.

The dining room was formal in decor, wallpapered with a floral motif and with heavy drapes of rose silk.

The kitchen and breakfast room were a far cry from the cubbies Bridget had cooked and served in. The kitchen was equipped with all the newfangled conveniences of the day, and the dinette was bright and airy.

Lizzie had twin bedrooms on the second floor, one spanning the front width of the house that she used in winter, and a like room at the rear that she occupied in summer. Over the fireplace, a poem was carved in the wooden frontispiece:

And old true friends, and twilight plays
And starry nights, and sunny days
Come trouping up the misty ways
When my fire burns low.

The poem is vintage Lizzie, lover of romantic poetry and music, whose library filled her bedrooms and two adjoining rooms and whose tenderness with the squirrels and birds that flocked to the spacious lawn of Maplecroft was legendary. It was this Lizzie that confounded and infuriated those who *knew* beyond a reasonable doubt that she really was a soulless, satanic murderer. She just wouldn't behave like one.

The third floor of Maplecroft quartered the servants, a maid and a housekeeper rumored to be the best paid servants in Fall River at $10 per week. Later, a chauffeur was added to drive a handsome black Packard phaeton. Nowhere did Lizzie skimp on the decoration or furnishings. The servants' quarters and the garage were paneled with the same quality materials used in the rest of the home.

For the first time, there was a telephone in the Borden house (Ring 378), listed in the name "Lizbeth A. Borden," as she referred to herself for the rest of her life.

Before she bought her sleek Packard and acquired a chauffeur, Lizzie went shopping and to her social engagements in her pony cart. Whenever it was spotted on the streets or when she was seen entering or leaving an emporium, groups would gather, whisper, and point her out to any newcomers to town. She feigned not to notice her notoriety and, as she went about her daily affairs, her clear, ice-blue eyes were invariably fixed straight ahead. But the trips downtown soon became rarities. More and more, her shopping, save for food and household supplies, which were bought by the servants, was done in Boston, Washington, or New York.

It was folly, of course, for her to have assumed that, just because a jury had taken only ten minutes to find her not guilty, she was now a free woman, made whole again. The stigma of the indictment alone, which the Reverend Jubb and Attorney Jennings had prayed not be brought against her, was sufficient to condemn her in the eyes of many in Victorian Fall River. Indictment and trial were tantamount to guilt, never mind this presumption of innocence business.

The Fall River *Globe* resumed its campaign of vilification. It left no doubt that it was their opinion there had been a great miscarriage of justice. Lizzie had wisely refused all newspaper interviews and would make no comments on press stories in the belief (hope?) that if she did not help keep the story alive, it would ultimately fade away. But that is not the way of the press; they print every day.

Every rumor about her—and there were new ones every week—was gleefully reported as solid fact. If none was currently making the rounds, the *Globe* would make one up. One alleged that, when Lizzie moved into Maplecroft, she had asked a neighbor to take down the fence that separated their properties. The indignant, unnamed man was said to have replied, "If you are moving next door, I will build it even higher!" The truth was that no such fence and no such neighbor existed, but that didn't matter to the *Globe*.

Soon after she returned to Fall River, Lizzie made a trip back to Taunton, to thank Sheriff and Mrs. Wright for their care of her during the ten months she was imprisoned. Learning of the trip, the *Globe* ran a corker of a scoop:

IN JAIL!
LIZZIE BORDEN GIVES HERSELF UP
VOLUNTARILY SURRENDERS TO SHERIFF WRIGHT
BIGGEST SENSATION OF SENSATIONAL CASE

The *Globe* fed the story to the Associated Press and it went out on the wire service to all their subscribers. The AP ran an apology the following day, but the *Globe* didn't carry it or print a retraction. It was all in a day's work for Edwin H. Porter.

As far as Fall River society was concerned, Lizzie Borden was a social pariah; she could well be the daughter of Abraham and Hagar, sister of the outcast Ishmael. Her name, when it was necessary to speak it, was uttered with contempt. Many of her friends, even those who had supported her during her imprisonment and trial, ultimately drifted away. Peer pressure prevented many from continuing their acquaintance, and they passed her without a nod or sign of recognition.

She returned to the Congregational church where she had sung in the choir, headed the Christian Endeavor Society, and taught a Sunday school class, but, the story was, the congregation had turned away from her. She never returned: an Episcopalian rector presided over her funeral.

She lived, shut off from the world almost as if she were behind prison bars, condemned to solitude by barriers stronger than bars—the silent, inexorable censure of those around her.

There was no tangible finger of scorn—no open declaration of hostility—just that insistent, maddening, universal aloofness.

Her every going in and coming out was debated, and all manner and kind of construction placed upon every unimportant detail of her mode of living and acting. Some would say she drove her pony cart too recklessly down the street. Some would repeat the legend that she had shown no emotion at the funeral. Others would say she had made a too-ostentatious display of her new wealth when she had moved to The Hill. If she appeared in a sober, subdued frame of mind, that could mean only one thing: she was depressed over her guilt. If she had occasion to smile, well, that proved it, didn't it—she was a heartless soul. She could do nothing right.

But, true to that nature no one had bothered to fathom, she never asked for mercy; never pleaded to be understood; never by any word or sign expressed indignation over her treatment.

Her closest friend was Helen Leighton, founder of the Fall River Animal Rescue League. She would say in later years that Lizzie was bitterly unhappy; that tragedy and sorrow overshadowed her.

"In later years," she said, "she questioned the wisdom of having remained in Fall River. She did so on the advice of friends who told her it would appear as if she were running away if she went elsewhere to live. This seemed wise to her at first, but in after years she wondered if it would not have been better had she settled in another place.

"She was not as friendless as she has been described. She had at least a dozen devoted friends who did all they could to cheer and brighten her life. Miss Borden was most appreciative of the solicitude shown her and she bestowed many, many kindnesses upon her friends. She disliked to accept gifts but could never do enough for her friends.

"Many, many individuals were aided by Miss Borden. She delighted to help people and gave most generously of her means. She helped several young people to obtain a college education. Fond of good reading herself, she saw to it that many persons who enjoyed good books but could not afford to buy them were well supplied with reading matter. Very few people knew of the extent of her charities."

Though she was shunned by many, the exception seemed to be the children. Though it was they who gleefully chanted the doggerel of the 40 whacks when they jumped rope, she is said to have had a smile or a touch on the head for all those who approached her. She could be seen almost daily, accompanied by her favorite cat and dogs, tending the squirrel and bird houses that filled the large side yard. On these occasions, there would often be cookies for the neighborhood children and permission for them to pick up the fallen fruit.

Two things combined to keep the murder story alive. The first was that no investigation into other possibilities was undertaken. The second was the *Globe's* anniversary story, which occupied the center of their front page every August 4th. Well into the twentieth century, it ran these "editorials," pandering to the suspicion, resentment, and hostility of those who continued to believe that justice had, indeed, been blind in Lizzie's case. They were undisguised declarations that she was a murderess.

Following are portions of the one appearing on the twelfth anniversary. If there is a more flamboyant example of purple prose extant in journalism, the author has not seen it.

A DOZEN YEARS
SINCE THE BORDENS WERE BRUTALLY BUTCHERED
AND YET THE HORRIBLE CRIME IS UNPUNISHED
PERHAPS MURDERER, OR MURDERESS, MAY BE IN THE CITY
WHO CAN TELL?

Twelve years ago this morning, when God's radiant sunshine was dispelling its August warmth and casting its brilliant reflection over all in this peaceful community, the just and the unjust, the rich and the poor, the contented and the envious, the pharisee and the publican, there sallied forth from the midsummer peace, on outrage bent, a demon in human form, whose quickly accomplished hellishness, was destined to make Fall River occupy a place in the center of the stage under the entire country's observation, such as has been the misfortune of few civilized communities to stand in.

On that fateful fourth of August 1892, there was enacted a scene of carnage and red-handed slaughter that, never in all the years that have passed since the butchery was perpetrated, has been approached for horror, vileness and unnatural and degenerate greed for gore and gain, by man or woman on murder bent. . . .

An old man, fast nearing the brink of that fateful precipice which marks the dividing line between the present and the hereafter, was brutally and wickedly hastened to that end, which in the natural sequence of earthly things, he could have escaped but a few days more. And why? Was it because he had lingered longer in the control and possession of those worldly stores he set so much value upon . . . ? Who can tell.

Perhaps that incarnate fiend in human form [who] rained cruel, vengeful, bloody blow after blow upon Andrew J. Borden's venerable head can answer.

There was more work for that willing, wicked arm on the upper floor, where . . . one more unfortunate awaited the bloody coming of the destroyer. . . .

Although one blow ended all connection with life for poor and inoffensive Abby Borden, it was not enough to satiate the hate, the venom and the vengeance of that daylight assassin, for he—or she—continued to rain crash after crash . . . upon the quivering and unconscious form of the victim, furnishing the best evidence . . . that long pent-up hatred, malice and murder were linked together as inspiring motives . . . in the base, sordid and selfish mind of the butcher. . . .

But why enumerate and why discuss the whole unhappy incident at this late day, may be asked.

Simply to establish and re-establish and confirm and emphasize that . . . there occurred one dozen years ago today, one of the most shocking, unnatural, base, and mercenary crimes that ever befouled the pages of civilized history and the demon that swung the axe which sent two souls into eternity at that time, has never yet been punished for his—or her—foul crime.

Perhaps the good people of Fall River may be daily meeting him—or her—in hall or store or railroad train. . . .

Perhaps before another year rolls around, self-accusing conscience may have taken up the task laid down by the criminal law authorities of the state and the man—or woman—who shocked the people of two continents with one of the most ghastly, cruel, selfish, and brutal double murders 12 years ago, may deliver himself—or herself—into the hands of the avenging law, as an escaped criminal. Who can tell?

Unless, in the event of some unexpected and improbable sequence as this, the butchery of the Bordens—legally speaking— is likely to remain as big a mystery as it was 12 years ago . . . although "legally speaking" is the only sense in which the murderer—or murderess—have anything left of "mystery" for the men with memories that can stand a 12-year strain.

Of course, these annual "recollections" of the Borden tragedy were not the kind of legitimate anniversary stories so beloved by newspapers even today. They were simply excuses for the *Globe* to vent its galling frustration over Lizzie's exoneration. They were close to libelous, but, as in *The Boston Globe*-Trickey affair, Lizzie neither commented nor filed suit. There can be no doubt that these diatribes kept alive and exacerbated the feelings of hostility against her, and had she put an end to them, perhaps, as she had hoped, the memory of the tragedy might have begun to fade.

When Lizzie's acquittal was announced, there was no person or group in Fall River more thwarted than the *Globe* and its crime reporter, Edwin H. Porter. After all, they had told their subscribers the day after the murders who the killer was. They had printed scores of stories and editorials urging her indictment, trial, and conviction. How could that muddle-headed jury and that "sanctimonious old jurist," as they called Judge Dewey, have failed to agree with them?

After nearly 20 years, and as the "editorials" grew more and more vicious in tone, a group of ministers and merchants approached the editor and urged him in the name of humanity to discontinue them.

Not long after, the *Globe*, suffering from a loss of advertising and subscribers, was bought up by a competitor, the name was changed, and the paper shut down.

John Vinnicum Morse, that *eminence grise* of the Borden affair, was never again seen in Fall River after the trial. He died in Hastings, Iowa, on March 1, 1912. In an interview shortly before, he told of having visited a fortune teller prior to his trip to Fall River the day before the murders. The gypsy had taken one look at his palm and told him no amount of money would tempt her to tell his fortune. "You don't want it told," is all she would say.

Andrew's vengeful brother-in-law, Hiram Harrington, was never invited across the threshold on French Street, because he, Lizzie always maintained, was actually the murderer.

George Dexter Robinson sent a bill for $25,000. He died in 1896. Associate Justice Blodgett retired from the bench in 1900 and died the following year. Associate Justice Dewey died in

1900, never forgiven for what the anti-Lizzie brigade called his "second summation" for the defense. Chief Justice Mason passed away in 1905.

Hosea Knowlton took Attorney General Pillsbury's place when he retired the year after the trial. He served until 1901 and died in 1902. Attorney Jennings succeeded Knowlton as district attorney and remained in that office until he retired in 1898. He died in 1923.

Attorney Moody went on to serve in the executive, legislative, and judicial branches of the U.S. government. He was elected to the House of Representatives and was later appointed secretary of the Navy, attorney general, and, finally, in 1906, associate justice of the Supreme Court.

Bridget left Fall River, date unknown, and supposedly returned to Ireland. Naturally, the story was soon making the rounds that she had been given "a fortune" by Lizzie and sent away. Nothing supported the rumor, and it is all the more to be doubted since she was, after all, a witness for the prosecution, not the defense, and the story she told the police immediately after the murders was the same story she told at the trial.

At some point, again date unknown, Bridget returned to the United States, where she is said to have married a man with the same last name and settled down in Butte, Montana. She died in a hospital there on March 26, 1948, at the age of 82.

Neither Lizzie nor Emma ever married, but romance may have come to Lizzie a few years after the trial.

A brief notice appeared in the Fall River *News*, a scrupulously accurate paper, that an announcement would be soon forthcoming of her engagement to a school teacher who taught at Swansea, where one of the Borden farms was located.

Once more, reporters poured into Fall River seeking interviews with Lizzie (refused) and the young man (who promptly went into hiding). Lizzie wrote him:

My dear friend:
   I am more sorry than I can tell you that you have had any trouble over the false and silly story that has been about the last week or so. How or when it started, I have not the least idea. But never for a moment did I think you or your girls started it. Of course I am

feeling very badly about it but I must just bear it as I have in the past. I do hope you will not be annoyed again. Take care of yourself, so you can get well.

No engagement announcement was made, and there was no wedding.

Lizzie's name was in all the papers again in 1897. In February, the *Providence Journal* headlined a story:

LIZZIE BORDEN AGAIN
A WARRANT FOR HER ARREST ISSUED FROM A LOCAL COURT
TWO PAINTINGS MISSED FROM TILDEN-THURBER CO'S STORE

The story was that two small enamel paintings had disappeared from their Providence jewelry store, and one had been brought back to be mended by a customer who said Lizzie had given it to her. A warrant had been signed for her arrest but not issued. (Shades of her first arrest!) Lizzie hurried to Providence to protest that she was not a petty thief. The matter was apparently settled to the shop owner's satisfaction, since the charges were dropped and the warrant never served.

But a new Lizzie legend had been created.

Unnamed sources were quoted who could give minute details of the meeting that supposedly took place at Tilden-Thurber's, including how Lizzie's face was flushed and her voice a shriek; how she paced the floor and glowered at her accusers. She was told that if she would sign a confession that she had, indeed, murdered the Bordens, the shoplifting charge would be dropped. The tale was that at the dramatic stroke of midnight, she signed a 16-word "confession":

"Unfair means force my signature here admitting the act of August 4, 1892 as mine alone."

Lizbeth A. Borden

The absurdity that anyone would confess to double murder to avoid arrest for shoplifting was lost on those who wanted to believe anything about Lizzie as long as it was bad.

It was not until 1960—63 years later—that the president of the American Society of Questioned Document Examiners and also past president of the American Academy of Forensic Sciences had a chance to examine the document and pronounce it a rank forgery. The signature had been very poorly traced from the one on her will published 29 years later and would have fooled no one.

The years passed at 7 French Street (now number 306) where the sisters lived. Because of the stir caused by her every appearance in town and, too, because the latest fashions could hardly be found in the small shops of Fall River, Lizzie made frequent trips to Boston, Providence, Washington, D.C., and New York. Invariably, the story was, there would be gourmet meals in expensive restaurants, luxurious hotel suites, and tickets for the theatre.

The last may well have been true, because Lizzie was a devotee of the stage, attracted, no doubt, by the glamour and gaiety so missing in her life. She was a particular fan of Nance O'Neil, the resident ingenue of a Providence troupe. Whenever any theatrical performance was scheduled in Fall River, though she would not attend, she bought blocks of tickets, distributed them among her friends and, quite often, hosted a party for the cast at her home after the show.

The lights, music, and laughing and cavorting of the actors and actresses long into the night were all too much for Emma. She believed that, after the tragedy that had blighted their lives, it was their duty, like Queen Victoria, to live out their days in somber, melancholy ways, dressed always in black and with never a smile in public.

They were in no way alike. While Lizzie had attempted to play the ancient piano Andrew had installed in the parlor on Second Street, Emma had not. Lizzie was a doer at church; Emma sat quietly in pew 21. Lizzie yearned to travel; Emma never left the boundaries of New England. Insofar as anyone knew it, Emma had never had a beau or a gentleman caller; Lizzie, on the other hand, was quick of wit and tongue and possessed of a presence that charmed both men and women.

A million descriptive words have been written about Lizzie, but Emma remains still in the shadows. What little is known or

remembered suggests that she was without distinguishing features, a quiet, prim being who wanted nothing more out of life
than anonymity.

And so, in 1905, Emma moved out of the home on French
Street and lived for a while with the Reverend Buck and his
family. She later moved from Fall River, first to Fairhaven,
then to Providence, and, finally, to Newmarket, New Hampshire, where she found at last the obscurity she wanted. It
is said that the two sisters were estranged and never communi-
cated again. Twenty years after the murders, Emma broke her
silence and granted the only interview she ever gave. These are
the highlights.

> The tragedy seems but yesterday, and many times I catch myself
> wondering whether it is not some frightful nightmare, after all.
> Often it has occurred to me how strange is the fact that no one save
> Lizzie was ever brought to trial for the killing of our father and
> stepmother.
>
> Some persons have stated they considered Lizzie's actions decid-
> edly queer. But what if she did act queerly? Don't we all do some-
> thing peculiar at some time or other? But as for her being guilty, I say
> "No" and decidedly "No."
>
> When veiled accusations began to be made, she came to me
> and said, "Emma, it is awful for them to say I killed poor father and
> our stepmother. You know that I would not dream of such an awful
> thing."
>
> Later, after her arrest and during the trial, Lizzie many times
> reiterated her protest of innocence to me. And after her acquittal,
> she declared her guiltlessness during conversations we had at the
> French Street mansion.
>
> The strongest thing that has convinced me of Lizzie's innocence
> is that the authorities never found the axe or whatever implement
> it was that figured in the killing. Lizzie, if she had done the deed,
> could never have hidden the instrument of death so that the
> police could not find it. There was no hiding place in the old
> house that would serve for effectual concealment. Neither did she
> have the time.
>
> Another thing to be remembered is Lizzie's affection for dumb
> animals. She fairly dotes on the dogs, cats and squirrels that
> are at the French Street mansion. She was always fond of pets.
> Now, any person with a heart like that could never have commit-
> ted the awful act for which Lizzie was tried and of which she was
> acquitted.

She concluded, "A jury declared Lizzie to be innocent, but an unkind world has unrelentingly persecuted her. I am still the little mother, and though we must live as strangers, I will defend 'Baby Lizzie' against merciless tongues."

In 1926, at age 66 and suffering from gall bladder trouble, Lizzie checked into a Providence hospital under the name Mary Smith Borden, a final attempt to shelter everyone from an inevitable onslaught of reporters.

On June 1, 1927, she died at her home.

For the first and only time, the Fall River *Globe* wrote about Lizzie without rancor. It took her obituary to bring it about.

Lisbeth* Borden Dies After Short Illness, Age 68[†]

Miss Lisbeth A. Borden died this morning[†] at 306 French Street, where she had made her home for about 30 years. She had been ill with pneumonia for about a week, although for some time she had been in failing health.

A member of one of the old Fall River families, having been the daughter of Andrew J. and Sarah Anthony[‡] Borden, she had lived here all of her life. With her two maids, she lived a quiet retired life, paying occasional visits to out-of-town friends and receiving a few callers whose staunch friendship she valued highly.

Taking an intense pride in the surroundings in which she lived, she did much to improve the locality, purchasing adjoining property, that the same refined atmosphere might be maintained. Greatly interested in nature, she was daily seen providing for the hundreds of birds that frequented the trees in her yard, taking care that the shallow box where they gathered was filled with crumbs, seeds and other foods that they favored. She had miniature houses erected in her trees and, in these, frivolous squirrels made their homes. Her figure as she visited with her wild callers, many of whom became so friendly that they never seemed to mind her approach, was a familiar one in that section.

Another pastime in which she greatly delighted was riding through the country roads and lanes. She made frequent trips about

---

*Although she never legally changed her name, after the trial she used "Lizbeth," not "Lisbeth."
†She was 67.
‡She died the day before.
‡Sarah's maiden name was Morse.

the town in her motor car, but was never so pleased as when winding through the shady country by-ways.

The death of Miss Borden recalls to many one of the most famous murder trials in the history of the state. On the fourth of August, 1892, Andrew J. Borden and his wife, Abby D. Borden, were found murdered in their Second Street home. After a preliminary investigation, Lisbeth Borden was arrested and formally charged with the murder of her father. After a hearing in Fall River she was indicted by the grand jury and in November 1892,* was tried and acquitted in New Bedford.

The trial attracted statewide interest. No further arrests were ever made and the murder has remained an unsolved mystery since. Following her acquittal, Miss Borden lived a rather retired life and devoted much of her time to private charities of which the public knew but little.

In her will, written a year before her death, Lizzie remembered those who had befriended her and remained loyal. The servants received sums from $1,000 to $5,000, the city of Fall River, $500, the income from which was to be spent for the perpetual care of the Borden plot in Oak Grove Cemetery.

The largest bequest by far, $30,000 in cash and all her stock in the Stevens Manufacturing Company, went to the Fall River Animal Rescue League. An additional $2,000 was bequeathed to the Animal Rescue League of Washington, D.C.

"I have been fond of animals," her will said, "and their need is great and there are so few who care for them."

The anti-Lizzie brigade, of course, scoffed when the will was read. To those who had remained her friends, it was just another evidence of her true character. Those in the neutral zone could only ponder this anachronism.

In the later years of her life, Lizzie's cousin, Mrs. Grace Howe, grew to be one of her closest friends. She was the wife of Louis Howe, who later became Franklin D. Roosevelt's aide, and she herself was appointed postmistress of Fall River during the 1940s. It was to her and Mrs. Helen Leighton, head of the Animal Rescue League, that Lizzie bequeathed her jewelry, books, furniture, china, and her one-half ownership of the A. J. Borden Building. There were 29 other bequests to old friends and for the education of children.

---

*June 1893.

She did not include Emma in her will but explained that, since she had inherited half of their father's estate, she already had enough to make herself comfortable.

Her faithful friends gathered at the French Street home for a private funeral service. A brief prayer and benediction was said and a choir member sang "My Ain Countree."

Emma was not present for Lizzie's funeral. The day Lizzie died, Emma fell in her New Hampshire home and suffered a broken hip. She died ten days later.

It was her deathbed wish that she, too, be buried without ceremony in the Oak Grove plot.

Even as Lizzie was lowered into her grave, a new legend was being created. As a typical example of the inventiveness of those who have written about her, this account is by Victoria Lincoln in her book, *A Private Disgrace*. "After brief, unattended services at the undertaker's her black-draped coffin had been carried by night to Oak Grove, where it was laid in the grave by black-clad men, Negroes chosen so that not even the pale gleam of a face or a hand might betray the secrecy."

The truth was that no service had been held at the undertaker's and her undraped coffin had been lowered into her grave at 2:30 on Saturday afternoon, in broad daylight by four white men, Fred Coggeshall, Ernest Perry, Norman Hall, and Edson Robinson.

The fame—the notoriety—that Lizzie Borden brought to the gaunt old town of Fall River will not go away, not even after a hundred years. Those who knew her are all gone now. The generations remember only the legends.

The detail that Lizzie was *acquitted* of giving her "mother" 40 whacks and her father 41, is forgotten. Ask the youth at the filling station and his answer will likely be, "Oh, that old woman who killed her parents? Don't know nothing about it. Happened a long time ago."

Patently, Fall River wishes the ghost of Lizzie Borden would go away; they are tired of being asked about her. They dread the hundredth anniversary of the murders in 1992 and the renewed interest it will bring.

"I wish she had never been born," one hears from the elderly, who have spent their lives answering questions. But they seem to know that, despite its worthy history and its present attractions, it will always be known, foremost, as the home of Lizzie Borden and the scene of the Borden murders.

In Oak Grove Cemetery, the Borden plot is identified by a weathered, native stone marker on one corner, listing those that lie there and with Lizzie's middle name misspelled "Andrews."

No one was left in the family to have it corrected.

Andrew lies between his two wives, Sarah and Abby. Beside Sarah is their daughter Alice Esther, who died as a child. At Andrew's feet are his two other daughters, Lizzie and Emma, and on his little finger he wears a golden ring.

What is the truth of what took place at 92 Second Street? It is the eternal enigma. The story will forever remain unfinished. Perhaps Lizzie was the only person who knew the truth.

Perhaps not.

The Cast
of Characters

Adams, Col. Melvin O.   One of Lizzie's trial lawyers.

Adams, Dr. Thomas   First Congregational Church minister who read the service at the interment of Andrew and Abby.

Allen, George A.   First patrolman to arrive at the scene.

Almy, Frank   Early business partner of Andrew.

Almy, Mrs. William   Responded to "sanity survey."

Auriel, Antonio   Portuguese arrested and released.

Barlow, Thomas C.   Youth who played in the barn with "Brownie."

Batchelder, Moulton   Conducted the "sanity survey."

Bence, Eli   Druggist who said Lizzie attempted to purchase prussic acid.

Blaisdell, Judge Josiah C.   Judge, Second District Court of Bristol County. Presided over "inquest and preliminary hearing."

Blodgett, Judge Caleb   Associate justice at trial.

Borden, Abby Durfee Gray   Victim. Wife of Andrew Jackson Borden.

Borden, Abraham B.   Father of Andrew.

Borden, Alice Esther   Middle daughter of Andrew. Died at age 2.

Borden, Andrew Jackson   Victim. Husband of Abby and father of Lizzie and Emma.

Borden, Emma Lenora   Sister of Lizzie.

Borden, Lizzie Andrew   The Accused.

Borden, Sarah Morse   First wife of Andrew. Mother of Lizzie and Emma.

Borden, Simeon   Trial clerk. Not related.

Bowen, Mrs. Phoebe   Wife of Dr. Seabury Bowen. Testified.

Bowen, Dr. Seabury W.   Borden family physician and member of the autopsy team.

Brayton, John S.   Responded to "sanity survey."

Brigham, David Sewall   Responded to "sanity survey."

Brigham, Mrs. Mary E.   Friend of Lizzie. Testified.

Brown, Everett   "Brownie," who played in the barn.

Brownell, Jennie   Friend visited by Emma in Fairhaven.

Buck, the Reverend Edwin A.   City missionary and friend to Lizzie.

Burrill, John P.   Cashier, National Union Bank. Testified.

Caldwell, John R.   Newspaper reporter.

Case, Rescome   Responded to "sanity survey."

Chace, Mark   Testified.

Chagnon, Dr. J.B.   Neighbor to rear of Borden house.

Chagnon, Marienne   Wife of Dr. J.B.Chagnon. Testified.

Chaves, Joseph   Provided alibi for Antonio Auriel.

Cheever, Dr. David W.   Harvard medical expert. Testified.

Churchill, Adelaide B.   Neighbor called over by Lizzie. Testified.

Clarkson, Alfred   Was in the barn loft before Officer Medley.

Clegg, Jonathan   Testified.

Cole, Frank G.   Trial Juror.

Connors, Patrick   Fall River policeman.

Cook, Everett M.   Cashier, First National Bank. Testified.

Coughlin, Dr. John W.   Mayor of Fall River.

Cowles, Dr. Edward   Responded to "sanity survey."

Cunningham, A. John   Reported the murders to the police.

Dean, William F.   Trial Juror.

Dedrick, Dr. Albert C.   One of the autopsy team. Testified.

Desmond, Dennis   Fall River policeman.

Devine, John   Fall River policeman.

Dewey, Judge Justin   One of the three trial judges.

Doherty, Patrick   Fall River policeman.
Dolan, Dr. William A.   Fall River medical examiner. Testified.
Donnelly, John   Fall River policeman.
Draper, Dr. Frank W.   Professor, Harvard Medical School. Testified.
Dutra, Dr. Emmanuel C.   Member of autopsy team.
Dyson, James   Fall River policeman.
Eddy, William   Manager of Andrew's lower Swansea farm.
Edson, Francis L.   Fall River policeman.
Emery, Mrs. Daniel   Niece who was visited by John Morse.
Ferguson, George   Fall River policeman.
Finn, John C.   Trial Juror.
Fleet, John   Assistant city marshal in charge of investigation.
Gifford, Charles H.   Manager of one of Andrew's Swansea farms.
Gifford, Charles N.   Testified.
Gifford, Hannah H.   Seamstress for Lizzie. Testified.
Gray, Oliver   Father of Abby.
Griffiths, Edward L.   Saw strange man on morning of murder.
Griffiths, Robert P.   Brother of Edward who also saw strange man.
Gunning, Dr. Thomas   Member of the autopsy team.
Hammond, Judge J. W.   Superior Court judge.
Handy, Dr. Benjamin   Testified.
Hanscom, O. M.   Boston Pinkerton agent hired by Lizzie.
Harrington, Hiram C.   Brother-in-law of Andrew.
Harrington, Laurana   Sister of Andrew; wife of Hiram.
Harrington, Philip   Fall River policeman.
Hart, Abraham G.   Treasurer, Union Savings Bank.
Hart, Sarah   Testified.
Hathaway, Nathaniel   Analytic chemist.
Hickey, Thomas F.   Reporter, *The Boston Globe*. Testified.
Hilliard, Rufus B.   City marshal of Fall River.
Hodges, Louis B.   Trial juror.
Holmes, Charles J.   Testified.
Holmes, Marianna   Acquaintance of Lizzie and Emma.
Howard, Joe   Newspaper columnist.
Howe, Mrs. Grace H.   Cousin of Lizzie; beneficiary in her will.
Hyde, Joseph   Fall River policeman.
Jelly, George F.   Boston psychiatrist consulted by Pillsbury.
Jennings, Andrew J.   Borden family attorney and trial attorney.
Johnson, Alfred   In charge of Andrew's upper Swansea farm.
Jubb, The Reverend William Walker   Pastor of Central Congregational Church.

Kieran, Thomas   Civil engineer. Testified.

Knowlton, Hosea Morrill   District attorney, Southern District of Massachusetts.

Lawton, Charles H.   Pharmacist.

Leary, Dr. John H.   Member of autopsy team.

Leduc, Peter   Andrew's barber.

Leighton, Miss Helen   President of Animal Rescue League.

Leonard, Augustus B.   Clerk, Second District Court.

Lubinsky, Hyman   Ice cream peddler. Testified.

McCarthy, John   Fall River policeman.

McHenry, Edwin D.   Created the *The Boston Globe* hoax story.

Maher, John D.   Drunk who was suspected.

Mahoney, Samuel F.   Fall River policeman.

Manley, Delia S.   Testified.

Mason, Judge Albert   Chief justice at the trial.

Mather, James   Testified.

Mayall, Joseph   Fall River policeman.

Medley, William O.   Fall River policeman.

Miller, Southard H.   Friend of Andrew.

Minnehan, John   Fall River policeman.

Moody, William H.   District attorney, Western District of Massachusetts.

Morse, John Vinnicum   Brother-in-law of Andrew.

Mullaly, Michael   Fall River policeman.

O'Neal, Nance   Actress; friend of Lizzie.

Peckham, Anson C.   Member of the autopsy team.

Pillsbury, Albert E.   Attorney general of Massachusetts.

Porter, Edwin H.   Author of *The Fall River Tragedy;* Fall River *Globe* reporter.

Potter, George   Trial juror.

Raymond, Mrs. Mary A.   Seamstress for Lizzie.

Reagan, Michael   Fall River policeman.

Reagan, Hannah   Matron at the Fall River police station.

Richards, Charles I.   Foreman of the trial jury.

Robinson, George Dexter   Principal defense attorney.

Russell, Miss Alice M.   Acquaintance of Lizzie and Emma. Testified.

Sawyer, Charles S.   Stood guard at side door.

Seaver, George F.   Massachusetts state policeman.

Shortsleeves, Joseph   Testified.

Smith, Alfred A.   Crank who "confessed."

Smith, D. R.   Drugstore owner.

Stafford, Capt. James C.   Responded to "sanity survey."

Stevens, Walter P.   Reporter, Fall River *News.* Testified.
Sullivan, Bridget   Borden household servant. Testified.
Swift, Augustus   Trial juror.
Tillson, Henry H.   Fur dealer.
Tourtellot, Dr. J. Q. A.   Member of the autopsy team.
Trickey, Henry G.   Involved in *The Boston Globe* hoax story.
Walsh, James A.   Official photographer.
Westcott, William   Trial juror.
White, Annie M.   Court stenographer.
Whitehead, George   Husband of Sarah Whitehead.
Whitehead, Sarah   Abby Borden's half-sister.
Wilbar, Frederick C.   Trial juror.
Wilber, Lemuel K.   Trial juror.
Wilbur, John   Trial juror.
Wilson, Charles H.   Fall River policeman.
Winward, James E.   Fall River undertaker.
Wixon, Frank   Deputy sheriff.
Wood, Dr. Edward S.   Harvard chemist. Testified.
Wordell, Allen H.   Trial juror.
Wright, Andrew   Sheriff of Bristol County and trial bailiff.
Wright, Mrs. Andrew   Matron of Bristol County jail.

Bibliography

FULL LENGTH BOOKS

Brown, Arnold R. *Lizzie Borden: The Legend, The Truth, The Final Chapter*. Nashville, TN: Rutledge Hill Press, 1991.

de Mille, Agnes. *Lizzie Borden: A Dance of Death*. Boston: Atlantic, Little Brown, 1968.

Dougal, Lily. *The Summit House Mystery*. London: 1905. The first novel written incorporating the Borden mystery.

Engstrom, Elizabeth. *Lizzie Borden*. New York: TOR, St. Martin's Press, 1991.

Flynn, Robert A. *The Borden Murders An Annotated Bibliography*. Portland, ME: King Philip Publishing Co., 1992.

Hunter, Evan. *Lizzie*. New York: Arbor House, 1984.

Lincoln, Victoria. *A Private Disgrace: Lizzie Borden by Daylight*. New York: G. P. Putnam's Sons, 1967.

Lunday, Todd. *The Mystery Unveiled: The Truth About the Borden Tragedy*. Providence, RI: J.A. & R.A. Reid, 1893
———— *Facsimile Edition*. Portand, ME: King Philip Publishing Co., 1990.

Marshall, John David. *Lizzie Borden and the Library Connection*. Tallahassee, FL: School of Library & Information Studies, Florida State University. 1990.

Pearson, Edmund. *The Trial of Lizzie Borden*. New York: Doubleday Doran & Co., 1937.

Phillips, Arthur S. *The Borden Murder Mystery: In Defence of Lizzie Borden*. Portland, ME: King Philip Publishing Co., 1986. (First full length book on story by Phillips published in his 3 volume *History of Fall River*.)

—— *Phillips' History of Fall River* Fall River, MA: Dover Press, 3 Vols. Published separately. 1944 & 1946.

Porter, Edwin H. *The Fall River Tragedy: A History of the Borden Murders.* Fall River, MA: George R. H. Buffinton; Press of J. D. Munroe, 1893.

—— *(Facsimile edition).* Portland, ME. King Philip Publishing Co. 1985. (Limited edition of 1,000 copies; Foreword by Robert A. Flynn).

Radin, Edward D. *Lizzie Borden: The Untold Story.* New York: Simon & Schuster, 1961.

Spiering, Frank. *Lizzie.* New York: Random House, 1984.

Sullivan, Robert. *Goodbye Lizzie Borden.* Brattleboro, VT: Stephen Greene Press, 1974.

Williams, Joyce G; Smithburn, J. Eric, & Peterson, M. Jeanne. *Lizzie Borden: A Case Book of Family and Crime in the 1890's.* Bloomington, IN: T.I.S. Publications Division/Indiana University, 1980.

SHORT STORIES

Adams, Barbara Johnston. "The Fall River Murders. In *Crime Mysteries.* New York: Franklin Watts, 1988.

Ayotte, John U. "The Unfathomable Borden Riddle." *Yankee Magazine,* Dublin, NH: 1966.

Brophy, John. "Heat Wave at Fall River" in *The Meaning of Murder* New York: Thomas Y. Crowell Co., 1967.

Carter, Angela. "The Fall River Axe Murders." in *Saints and Strangers.* New York, 1986.

Davis, Judge Charles G. "Conduct of the Law in the Borden Case." Boston, MA. *The Daily Advertiser.* 1894. 47 pages. Compiled from 5 letters to the editor in 1893.

Early, Eleanor. "Did Lizzie Do It?" in *A New England Sampler.* Boston, MA: Waverly House, 1940.

Freeman, Mary E. Wilkins. "The Long Arm" In *American Detective Stories.* Chosen by Carolyn Wells. New York: Oxford, 1927. (Based on the Borden murders. First appeared in *The Pocket Magazine,* New York, 1895.)

Gustafson, Anita. "Guilty or Innocent: Could A Woman Do That?" New York: Holt, Rinehart, Winston, 1985.

Gibson, Walter B. "The Last of the Borden Case" in *The Fine Art of Murder.* New York: Grosset & Dunlap. 1965.

Gross, Gerald. "The Pearson-Radin Controversy Over the Guilt of Lizzie Borden." in *Masterpieces of Murder.* Boston: Little, Brown & Co., 1963.

Henson, Robert. "Lizzie Borden," *PM Quarterly Review of Literature.* Vol. XVIII 3–4. 1973. pp.314–344.

Jacob, Kathryn A. "She Couldn't Have Done it, Even if She Did: Why Lizzie Went Free" New York: American Heritage Pub., Co., 1978. Vol. 29, No. 2.

Jones, Ann. "Women Who Kill." New York: Holt, Rinehart and Winston, 1980.

Jones, Elwyn. "On Trial; Seven Intriguing Cases." London: McDonald & Jane, 1978.

Kunstler, William Moses. "First Degree." New York: Oceana, 1980.

Lester, Henry. "Lizzie Borden." In *Unsolved Murders and Mysteries.* Seacaucus, NJ: Chartwell Books, Inc.

Logan, Guy B. H. "Verdict and Sentence." London: Eldon, 1935.

Lustgarten, Edgar. "Verdict in Dispute." New York: Charles Scribner' Sons, 1950.

—— "The Murder and the Trial." New York: Charles Scribner's Sons, 1958.

—— "The Lizzie Borden Axe Murder Case." In *Great Courtroom Battles*. Chicago, I.L.: Playboy Press, 1973.

Manning, Lisa & Abergaria, Afonso, Jr. "People and Culture of Southeastern Massachusetts." in *Lizzie Hot, Lizzie Cold, Lizzie Warmed Over. A Panel Discussion of the Lizzie Borden Case*. New Bedford, MA: Spinner Publications, 1982.

—— "People and Culture of Southeastern Massachusetts." in *The Price of Maplecroft: Memoirs of Lizzie Borden*. New Bedford, MA: Spinner Publications, 1982. pp 81–96. Vol II.

Patrick, Q. "The Case for Lizzie." *Pocket Book of True Crime Stories*. New York: Pocket Books, Inc. 1943.

Pearson, Edmund L. "The Borden Case." in *Studies in Murder*. New York: Macmillan Co., 1924.

—— "The Bordens: A Postscript." in *Murder at Smutty Nose: And Other Murders*. New York & London: Doubleday, Page & Co., also Heinemann Ltd., 1927.

—— "Five Murders." Crime Club. New York: Doubleday, Doran & Co., 1928.

—— "Legends of Lizzie." in *More Studies in Murder*. New York.: Harrison Smith & Robert Haas, 1936.

Powers, Richard. "The Death of a Massachusetts Trojan." Washington, D.C. *The Chief of Police*. Vol. IV–No. 4, July-August 1989. Official publication of Nat'l Assn. of Chiefs of Police. pp. 34–45.

Rubenstein, Richard E. "Great Courtroom Battles." Chicago: Playboy Press, 1953.

Search, Pamela. "Women." in *Great True Crime Stories*. London: Arco Publications, Ltd., 1957.

Snow, Edward Rowe. "The Lizzie Borden Murder Case." in *Piracy, Mutiny and Murder*. New York: Dodd, Mead & Co., 1959.

—— "Lizzie Borden," in *Boston Bay Mysteries and Other Tales*. New York: Dodd, Mead, 1977.

Solomon, Louis. "The Ma and Pa Murders and Other Perfect Crimes." New York: Lippincott, 1976.

Sutherland, Sidney. "The Mystery of the Puritan Girl," in *Ten Real Murder Mysteries-Never Solved!* New York; London: G. P. Putnam's Sons, 1929.

Usher, Frank Hugh. "World Famous Acquittals." By Charles Franklin (Pseud.). Feltham: Oldhams, 1970.

—— "The World's Worst Murderers; Exciting and Authentic Accounts of the Great Classics of Murder." By Charles Franklin (Pseud). Feltham: Oldhams, 1970.

Watters, Barbara. "Was Lizzie Borden Guilty?" in *The Astrologer Looks at Murder*. Washington, D.C.: Valhalla Paperbacks, Ltd., 1969.

PLAYS

Bast, William. *The Legend of Lizzie Borden*. A television production, George LeMaire Productions in association with Paramount Pictures. Hollywood, 1974.

Colton, John & Miles, Carlton. *Nine Pine Street*. New York. Samuel French, 1934.

De La Torre, Lillian. *Goodbye Miss Lizzie Borden*. Boston, Walter Baker Co., 1947.

Denham, Reginald & Percy, Edward. *Suspect*. Chicago, Dramatist's Play Service, 1940.

Henderson, Donald. *The Trial of Lizzie Borden*. Radio play. Published by Hurst & Blackett, London. 1946. Broadcast on BBC, July 16, 1945.

Kelly, Tim. *Lizzie Borden of Fall River*. Denver, CO. 1976.

Kent, David. *Slaughter on Second Street.* Shreveport, LA, 1991.

Lawrence, Reginald. *The Legend of Lizzie.* Chicago, Dramatic Publishing Co., 1959.

Pollock, Sharon. *Blood Relations.* Playwright's Union of Canada, Toronto, Canada. 1981.

Reach, James. *Murder Takes the Stage.* New York, Samuel French, 1957.

Norfolk, William. *The Lights Are Warm and Coloured.* London, Samuel French.

OPERA

Beeson, Jack. *Lizzie Borden.* "A Family Portrait In Three Acts." Composed by Beeson; Libretto by Kenward Elmslie; Scenario by Richard Plant. Boosey & Hawkes, Inc. New York, 1966, 1967.

BALLET

de Mille, Agnes. *Fall River Legend—A Ballet.* New York. Music by Morton Gould. Premiere by Metropolitan Opera House, New York, April 22, 1948.

TRANSCRIPTS

Burt, Philip H. *Borden, Lizzie A.—Trial of.* Official transcript of the trial in the Massachusetts Superior Court. Two vols. 1893. Microtext at Boston Public Library.

ARTICLES AND ESSAYS

Aymar, Brandt & Sagarin, Edward. *A Pictorial History of the World's Great Trials.* New York: Bonanza. 1967. pp. 172–191.

Barzun, Jacques & Taylor, W. H. *A Catalogue of Crime.* New York: Harper & Row, 1989.

Beeson, Jack. "The Autobiography of Lizzie Borden." *Opera Quarterly,* Vol.4, 1, Spring 1986.

Berger, Meyer. "The Lizzie Borden Case." New York Times *Sunday Magazine*, Aug. 9, 1942. pp. 10, 26–27.

Bierstadt, Edward Hale. *What Do You Know About Crime?* New York: F.A. Stokes Co., 1935. Questions and answers on famous crimes. Illustration.

Boss, Judith A. *Fall River, A Pictorial History.* Norfolk, VA: Donning Co., 1985. Illustrations pp. 102–104.

BPC Publishing, Ltd. "Crimes and Punishment." *The Symphonette Press.*, Vol. 7. pp.116–126. 1974.

Bristow, Prof. A.T. "Medico-Legal Inspections and Post-Mortem Examinations." New York. Published in Vol. I of *A System of Legal Medicine,* edited by Allen McLane Hamilton. E.B. Treat. 1894. Concerns errors by Medical Examiner in Borden case.

Cohen, Daniel. *The Encyclopedia of Unsolved Crimes.* New York: Dodd Mead, 1988. pp. 135–141.

Frank Leslie's Weekly. *The Borden Case.* Full-page illustration. Pg 417, June 29, 1893.

Franklin, Charles. *World Famous Acquittals.* Feltham, Middlesex, UK: Oldhams Books; The Hamlyn Pub. Group, Ltd. 1970. pp. 255–267.

House, Brant & Boucher, Anthony. *Crimes That Shocked America.* New York: Ace Books, Inc., 1961. Contains "The Borden Case" by Edmund Pearson. pp. 39–105.

Jones, Richard Glyn. *Unsolved! Classic True Murder Cases.* New York: Peter Bedrick Books, 1987. Contains "Edmund Pearson, The Borden Case" pp 185–270. "Afterword" essay by Jones, p. 271.

Jordan, Elizabeth. *Three Rousing Cheers.* New York: D. Appleton-Century Co., 1938. pp. 116–123.

Lyons, Louis M. *Newspaper Story—One Hundred Years of the Boston Globe.* Cambridge, MA: Harvard University Press, 1971. pp. 86–96.

Martinez, Lionel. *Great Unsolved Mysteries of North America.* New Jersey: Chartwell Books, 1988. pp. 83–88.

Nash, Robert Jay. *Almanac of World Crime.* New York: Anchor Press/Doubleday, 1981. pp. 118, 122, 185, 191–194.

Pearson, Edmund L. *Instigation of the Devil.* New York: Charles Scribner Sons, 1930. pp. xi–xiii, 156–157, 329–331.

Pic Magazine. *The Pic Album of Notorious American Murders.* New York: No. XXV in series. Dec. 13, 1938. Contains 4 pages of illustrations.

Review of Reviews. *Vindication of Lizzie Borden.* New York: Vol. VIII. Aug. 8, 1893. Page 138.

Roughead, William. *The Murderer's Companion.* New York: Reader's Club, 1941.

Sandoe, James. *Murder: Plain and Fanciful.* New York: Sheridan House Pub., 1948.

Silvia, Jr., Philip T. *Victorian Vistas: Fall River 1886–1900.* Fall River, MA: R.E. Smith Co., 1988. pp. 333–355.

Tanikawa, S. M. Wada, M. & Hirano, K. *Mother Goose Rhymes—Vol. 2.* Tokyo, Japan: Kodansha Pub. Co. 1981. (In Japanese w/translation) Erroneously attributes "40 whacks" jingle to Mother Goose.

Treasure Press. *Infamous Murders.* London: Verdict Press, MacDonald & Co., Ltd., 1975. pp. 134–142.

Welschler, Shoshana. "The Lizzie Borden Case—1892." Garden City, NY: Doubleday, 1975. In *The People's Almanac* by David Wallechinsky and Irving Wallace. 1975.

Wigmore, John H. "The Borden Case" 27 American Law Review. 1893.

Winn, Dilys. *Murder, Ink: The Mystery Reader's Companion.* New York: Workman Publishing Co., Inc., 1977. pp. 205–6, 457, 476.

Wilson, Colin & Pitman, Pat. *A Casebook of Murder.* New York: Cowles Book Co., 1969. pp. 90, 189–194.

Woolcott, Alexander. "The Theory of Lizzie Borden." *Vanity Fair.* Sept. 29, 1927. Reprinted in Vanity Fair *Selections From America's Most Memorable Magazine,* edited by Cleveland Amory & Frederick Bradlee. New York: Viking, 1960.

NEWSPAPER SCRAPBOOKS

Emery, William M. Bound vol. of extensive clippings from many newspapers compiled contemporaneously by Emery while reporting Lizzie's trial for the New-Bedford *Journal.* Owned by Robert A. Flynn, Portland, ME.

Harvard University. *"Case and Trial of Lizzie A. Borden."* Law Library. Bound vols. of clippings from *Boston Herald* and *Boston Record.*

MISCELLANEOUS

Gould, Morton. *Fall River Legend.* Orchestral suite from the deMille ballet. 1948. Recorded on Mercury Label.

James, Edward T. *Notable American Women 1607–1950. A Biographical Dictionary.* Cambridge, MA: Harvard University Press, 1971.

Keylin, Arleen & DeMarjan, Arto, Jr. *Crime as Reported by The New York Times.* New York: Arno Press, 1976.

Ross, John. *Trials in Collections: Index to Famous Trials Throughout the World.* Metuchen N.J. & London: 1983.

Watkins, John Elfreth. *Famous Mysteries.* Philadelphia. PA: 1919.